emotional branding

the new paradigm for
connecting brands to people

by
marc gobé

ALLWORTH PRESS
NEW YORK

© 2001 Marc Gobé

07   06   05   04   03   12   11   10   9   8

Published by Allworth Press
An imprint of Allworth Communications
10 East 23rd Street, New York, NY 10010

Cover design by d/g* worldwide, New York, NY
411 Lafayette Street, 2nd Floor, New York, NY 10003
tel 212/979-8900; fax 212/979-1401

Cover photo credit: Nathan Blake
Page design by Phyllis Aragaki
Page composition/typography by Sharp Des!gns, Lansing, MI

ISBN: 1-58115-078-4

LIBRARY OF CONGRESS CATALOGING-IN-PUBLICATION DATA
Gobé, Marc
Emotional branding; the new paradigm for connecting brands to people / Marc Gobé.
p. cm.
Includes index.
ISBN 1-58115-078-4
1. Brand name products. 2. Brand name products—Marketing. 3. Consumers' preferences.
4. Motivation research (Marketing). I. Title.
HD69.B7 .G62 2001
658.8'27—dc21
00-053428

Printed in Canada

table of contents

foreword

In the spring of 1993, Roberto Goizueta asked me to come back to The Coca-Cola Company as the first-ever Chief Marketing Officer.

I would be in charge of a worldwide budget that exceeded $5 billion, and the very first question that crossed my mind was "How am I going to be able to talk to consumers in an efficient way, while growing the business?"

There were a lot of things that contributed to the success we ultimately experienced. Or should I say to the success of the team that I assembled. I was able to hire the best marketing people in the world and also get the best partners in the world. The only way that we were going to grow the business from nine billion cases to fifteen billion in only three short years was to bring together the very best in every area of the business.

Packaging, as a key component of brand design, had always attracted me. I believe that it is the most efficient way to talk to consumers–and I also believe that it has been misused and mismanaged over the years.

In 1985, during my first tenure at The Coca-Cola Company, on the heels of the introduction of New Coke and at the beginning of the 100 year anniversary of The Coca-Cola Company, I got a phone call from the corporate department of the company asking me to develop a new graphic design so we would have something to show the bottlers at the 1986 celebration of the 100th anniversary. I was shocked at first because I believed that packaging should not be show-and-tell, but an expression of identity that should really be put to work for the brand. But I lost the argument and the packaging got redone. All of the brands of The Coca-Cola Company got reduced to a single design. It was a political design created for the wrong reasons, not for the right causes.

When I came back to the company that August 1993, after a seven year hiatus, I immediately started looking for people who "got it." In the design arena, I was introduced that fall to Marc Gobé in Paris, and the very first two questions I asked Marc were, do you get it and can you help me?

- Do you understand the importance of graphic design as a selling tool?
- Can you help me take the incredible power of the design and the iconography of the logos of The Coca-Cola Company to help us sell more product?

Marc impressed me with his emotionalized approach to brand design, a concept ahead of its time. Over the next three years, the aid that Marc gave me was instrumental in helping us take the volume of The Coca-Cola Company from nine billion to fifteen billion cases a year. It was not only in the design of the graphics of the bottle or the can, which is what all graphic designers do, but more in Marc's great understanding of the role of the hidden assets like the trucks and the uniforms and all of the visual expressions of a brand.

Millions and millions of Coca-Cola impressions are in the streets everyday, as trucks, for example, travel up and down in front of consumers . . . and we had never spent any time really designing them to sell.

When I went to Paris, Marc and his people showed me the design they had done for the Olympics in Albertville, and the design they had done for Boucheron perfume. It was remarkable right away how they had used color–not only the traditional colors–and how they had used design–not the traditional designs–to really communicate the essence of product to connect emotionally with the consumers.

I have always believed that brand design in packaging is a critical part of marketing. It should translate the meaning of the brand for the consumers. Marc and his partner, Joël Desgrippes, understood very clearly that packaging could actually serve to translate the meaning of the brand to the consumers everyday, on every shelf, in every aisle, on every truck, and in every vending machine all over the world. I could probably write a book about my experiences with Marc, about how much I learned from the color blue that Marc had used in creating a corporate identity for the Albertville Winter Olympics, for the Boucheron perfume bottle and store design, and later on in the redesign of Gillette's packaging. It was eventually a color that changed the refreshment appeal of Sprite.

I understood so much about the culture of The Coca-Cola Company and the brand's connection to the color red (that piece of equity and iconography that was critical to the development of our sales). So it wasn't only what the word Coke or Sprite or Fanta would do, it was about using all of the elements of the brand–aggressively and with kick-ass creative.

I went with Marc to the fashion shows in Paris, and together we learned from the great designers of the world about how to use color, shape, and form to connect with consumers. At the time I was probably one of the very few marketing executives from a consumer goods company who had bothered to go to a fashion show. Marc had assured me it would be time well spent; he was right.

In this book Marc mentions briefly the 1996 Olympics effort in Atlanta for Coca-Cola. It's mentioned in a modest way, but for us it was a significant change in managing something that traditionally had been done in a passive way, or rather, something that was done to sell the *Olympics* as opposed to selling Coca-Cola. Our brand presence at the Olympics ranged all the way from the Coca-Cola Olympic City design, to the package graphics themselves, to the uniforms, to what we put in the stadiums and what we put in the airport and train stations. As I write this, I have just returned from the Olympics in Sydney, and I appreciate even more how a proactive, purposeful design works to accent a marketing effort. In Sydney it was obvious that many of the sponsors got lazy. It was a display of disconnected design that ignored an opportunity. Every day in stores I see what I saw in Sydney: lazy design without vision.

What I learned from my work with Marc and Coca-Cola, more than anything else, was that imagination gives dimension to a brand; that its not about where your company is right now, but about where you eventually want to be. Every day, through my Z Group Strategy Consulting company, I preach that an integrated brand strategy is the key to reaching your destination. And, an integrated brand strategy is at the heart of emotional branding.

Emotional branding is about building relationships; it is about giving a brand and a product long-term value. It is about sensorial experiences, designs that make you feel the product; designs that make you taste the product; designs that make you buy the product.

I believe that kick-ass creative is critical to the success of a brand, and no designer is better qualified to explain creative, integrated design identity than Marc Gobé. *Emotional Branding* will help you understand how great brands—from Stew Leonard's in rural Connecticutt, to multinational Coca-Cola—grow their businesses and attract loyal customers.

SERGIO ZYMAN

preface

I wrote this book to share some of my experiences in branding, a business that I love. My company, d/g* worldwide, has had great success in the brand design business for the past thirty years, my partner Joël Desgrippes and I always sharing the same passionate aim to create the most innovative, "sensory driven" and emotionally compelling brand identities on the market. Our goal is to give birth to brand designs that will make hearts beat faster–designs that are based on sensory experiences and an understanding of people's deepest emotional desires.

In 1980, driven by the aspiration to connect better with people, Joël Desgrippes, Patrice Beauchant (a former partner of ours), and I created SENSE®, a proprietary visual process that defines a brand's emotional persona. SENSE® elevates the notion of branding as an awareness and price-driven marketing tool to a sensory and emotionally charged platform for developing brand-design solutions. We first used our SENSE® process to create "stories" around brands to add emotional dimension to some of the work we were doing for major fragrance and cosmetics projects. We then coined the term "Emotional Branding" as a description of the philosophy that underscores all of our brand strategy activities.

Today, I feel, an Emotional Branding approach is quite simply the crucial defining element that separates success from indifference in the marketplace. But only a few companies understand the art of accessing, with intelligence and sensitivity, the true power behind human emotions. Emotional Branding brings a new layer of credibility and personality to a brand by connecting powerfully with people on a personal and holistic level. Emotional Branding is based on that unique trust that is established with an audience. It elevates purchases based on need to the realm of desire. The commitment to a product or an institution, the pride we feel upon receiving a wonderful gift of a brand we love or having a positive shopping experience in an inspiring environment where someone knows our name or brings an unexpected cup of coffee–these feelings are at the core of Emotional Branding.

Tiffany is an emotional brand because of what it means as a quality, prestige brand; and Wal-Mart is an emotional brand because of the extra steps it takes in knowing and serving well the communities in which it operates. Both businesses are strong brands, because they have a culture of unforgettable emotions associated with their character.

Above all this book emphasizes the human connections between corporations and consumers. Emotional Branding is more than a process or research technique; it is based on the connections between people that transcend charts and graphs. It is a culture and a way of living; a fundamental belief that people are the real force in commerce and that business and the street cannot survive separately.

As a designer, I have always felt connected to the markets around the world because of my love of travel and curiosity for understanding world cultures. Designers are part aesthete, part visionary, and part anthropologist. They are driven by a dedication to exploring new concepts and conveying a heightened aesthetic sense that will bring added meaning to our world and enhance our quality of life. It is surprisingly easy to forget at times, but my travels constantly remind me of the basic fact that people are the most important inspiration for everything we do in design! Ultimately, a design will have an immediate, direct contact with the market; it will be on a wall, on a shelf, on a computer screen, or in a mall–reaching out to people, trying to convince them of its value. Designers therefore have to immerse themselves in the everyday world, monitor cultural changes, values, and marketplace trends, and use both their brain and their guts to create responsible, courageous, and beautiful designs. Our job is to be the ambassadors between corporations and the marketplace, the link that creates the language of beauty and emotions. Designers are often known solely for their designs–the expression of their imagination–but they are also an incredible driving force as "conceptual provocateurs." Heartfelt design is passionate and it encompasses our desire to make the world a better place.

In this book, we will discuss and analyze demographic changes and the emergence of strong, compelling new cultures in a revolutionized market. We will look at the winners in today's "emotional economy" whose vision makes our environment more pleasant, more exciting, and more rewarding for all. Finally, I will reveal some of our proprietary research techniques and studies.

acknowledgments

Some people have influenced my life and my career in ways that I would never have thought possible. In this business I have had many fantastic opportunities to learn from some of the brightest minds in commerce. My partner Joël Desgrippes is one of the most talented conceptual product designers I have ever known; a true magician at creating products and images that capture people's dreams. He has designed some of the most beautiful fragrance bottles on the market for brands such as Boucheron, Hermès, Guerlain, and Kenzo. I have learned a great deal from him, and have been a direct beneficiary of his enormous talent in shaping communications programs that have pushed the limits for both our clients and ourselves. Les Wexner, Chairman and CEO of The Limited gave me my first chance in the United States and taught me how to use my design knowledge in creating brand-identity concepts for some of the greatest brands in the United States. As Coca-Cola's chief marketing officer, Sergio Zyman allowed me to work with Coca-Cola and see through his vision how to help build and manage the most powerful brand in the world. Bernd Schmitt, a brilliant professor at Columbia University and author of two great marketing books—*Marketing Aesthetics* and *Experiential Marketing*[1]—allowed me to speak to his classes of very challenging, bright students on numerous occasions and share my thoughts on branding, a topic that we both passionately love. Corporations such as Coca-Cola, Nestlé, Gillette, Dannon, Sears, Godiva, Unilever, Estée Lauder, Lancôme, Boucheron, Reebok, Guess?, Ann Taylor, Victoria's Secret, Bath & Body Works, Abercrombie & Fitch, and IBM trusted us with the thrilling mission of helping them with their visions, an opportunity I could not have thought possible twenty-five years ago. Their courage, passion, and commitment to the development of building strong emotional connections with consumers worldwide have allowed us to build extraordinarily successful partnerships.

The idea of "Emotional Branding" and *Emotional Branding* the book could not have been possible without the support and input of my partners and friends around the world: Peter Levine, Phyllis Aragaki in New York, and Joël Desgrippes, François Caratgé, and Sophie Farhi in Paris. I also want to thank Alisa Clark, my project manager and writing consultant for this book, as well as Bernie Geoghegan, our full-time intern and research arm.

In our organization, where talent is encouraged and breakthrough ideas are the norm, I want to thank all my associates. They are the reason I enjoy every day at the office and receive such pleasure from my work; they help sustain my passion for my job. Last but not least, I want to give the most credit to my wife, who unceasingly supported this project even though it meant I had to work every weekend for eight months.

Emotional Branding: Fuel for Success in the Twenty-first Century

Branding is not only about ubiquity, visibility, and functions; it is about bonding emotionally with people in their daily life. Only when a product or a service kindles an emotional dialogue with the consumer, can this product or service qualify to be a brand.
–Joël Desgrippes, d/g* worldwide

Over the past decade, it has become resoundingly clear that the world is moving from an industrially driven economy where machines are the heroes toward a people-driven economy that puts the consumer in the seat of power. A recent *New York Times* article says that, "Over the last fifty years the economic base has shifted from production to consumption. It has gravitated from the sphere of rationality to the realm of desire: from the objective to the subjective; to the realm of psychology."[1]

Simple ideas, such as computers, have morphed from "technology equipment" into larger, consumer-focused concepts such as "lifestyle entertainment." Airplanes are less about transportation vehicles today, and more about "travel organizations" that can enhance our lives in many ways through their elaborate bonus-point programs. Food is no longer about cooking or chores but about home/lifestyle design and "sensory experiences." And the universities of tomorrow will be branded and will function as modular "knowledge banks," focusing on a new kind of flexible "lifelong, global learning" that caters to students from around the world, both on campus and far away, with differing backgrounds and agendas rather than the traditional, youth-driven highly structured undergraduate and graduate programs. In order to be relevant and survive, it is crucial that brands understand the vast changes afoot and compete differently. We are clearly operating with a completely different set of values today than five years ago. Speed has replaced stability; intangible assets

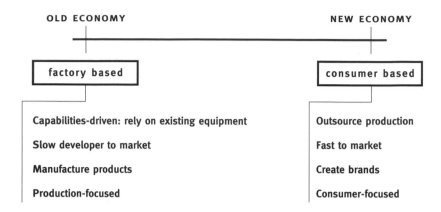

OLD ECONOMY	NEW ECONOMY
factory based	**consumer based**
Capabilities-driven: rely on existing equipment	Outsource production
Slow developer to market	Fast to market
Manufacture products	Create brands
Production-focused	Consumer-focused

have become more valuable than tangible assets. The traditional supply/demand economic models are being completely reevaluated. Corporations have realized that the new market opportunities are not based on squeezing costs and increasing profits around a set business model but are above all in *growing entirely new lines of revenue with innovative ideas.*

In a *Wall Street Journal* article entitled "So Long, Supply and Demand" the conclusion reached is: "The bottom line. Creativity is overtaking capital as the principal elixir of growth. And creativity, although precious, shares few of the constraints that limit the range and availability of capital and physical goods."[2] In this new business atmosphere, ideas are money. Ideas, in fact, are a new kind of currency altogether—more powerful than money. *One single idea—especially if it involves a great brand concept—can change a company's entire future.*

But what exactly constitutes a great brand concept today? In this hypercompetitive marketplace where goods or services alone are no longer enough to attract a new market or even to maintain existing markets or clients, I believe that it is the *emotional* aspect of products and their distribution systems that will be the key difference between consumers' ultimate choice and the price that they will pay. By emotional I mean how a brand engages consumers on the level of the senses and emotions; how a brand comes to life for people and forges a deeper, lasting connection.

This means that understanding people's emotional needs and desires is really, now more than ever, the key to success. Corporations must take definite steps toward building stronger *connections* and *relationships* which recognize their customers as partners. Industry today needs to bring people the products they

The Nescafé creator of emotions campaign presents five new "coffee emotions" instead of flavors, going beyond the product into a sensorial experience.

desire, exactly when they want them, through venues that are both inspiring and intimately responsive to their needs. Welcome to the world of Emotional Branding, a dynamic cocktail of *anthropology, imagination, sensory experiences,* and *visionary approach to change!*

Emotional Branding provides the means and methodology for connecting products to the consumer in an emotionally profound way. It focuses on the most compelling aspect of the human char-

By emotional I mean how a brand engages consumers on the level of the senses and emotions.

acter; the desire to transcend material satisfaction, and experience emotional fulfillment. A brand is uniquely situated to achieve this because it can tap into the aspirational drives which underlie human motivation.

Brand Identity Starts at Home

A brand is brought to life for consumers first and foremost by the personality of the company behind it and that company's commitment to reaching people on an emotional level. Bernard Arnault of LVMH, the hugely successful luxury group that owns Dior, Vuitton, and many other prestige brands, lives by this credo and has built his company around these ideas. He says, "What I like is to feel emotion . . . and I agree even more when I see the sales results."[3]

Given this new emotionally driven paradigm, is it fair to say that consumers are thinking more with their heart or gut than with their head when choosing a product? Or that the public wants to be assured of a corporation's unequivocal commitment to them? I would answer yes to both of these suppositions. The largely uncharted territory of emotions—including how people feel about corporations or the corporate world at large—is an increasingly important part of the buying routine at a time when most products offer the same quality and are in danger of becoming mere commodities in an overcrowded marketplace. And today, with the advent of the Internet and its far-reaching effect on the business world at large, a distinct "win-win" opportunity exists to create a partnership between people and businesses that can lead to increased benefits for both. This win-win partnership model is fast becoming the new standard in business.

WIN-WIN MEANS PLAYING ON THE SAME TEAM!

This has been a painful lesson to learn for some companies. Coca-Cola made unfortunate missteps in Europe in 1999 when it was perceived as being slow and unfeeling in responding to the Belgian public when a batch of spoiled Coke products made people sick. Douglas N. Daft, the new Coca-Cola CEO, has now smartly switched more of the marketing responsibilities previously centralized in Atlanta to the different regions of the world where Coca-Cola has major market presence. The goal of this shift is to foster a better understanding of the consumers in those markets and create a more direct dialogue. Coca-Cola has realized the importance of approaching different markets with sensitivity to individual market demands and cultural differences. The aim is no longer to simply push the ubiquitous Coke brand everywhere. This makes a lot of sense when you consider that, for example in Japan, the biggest Coca-Cola brand is a canned coffee drink!

MTV also learned this lesson after some initial blunders abroad. They now rely primarily on local music and local administration for their programming in Europe, Asia, and South America. By promoting local artists in new markets and training and hiring individuals from the communities they serve, MTV has shed its American-centric stigma and earned the trust of these markets which are wary of cultural imperialism. Now, MTV Asia constitutes the largest of the MTV markets, having surpassed the American market in size!

Nike is another brand that has not taken the right kind of culturally and consumer-sensitive global view in the past. They underestimated the ferocity of the resentment people would feel about their labor practices, a resentment that resulted in many of their customers turning their backs on the brand. They scored low in a nationwide corporate reputation poll using a cross section of average citizens conducted for the *Wall Street Journal* in 1999 because of a tainted image of "exploiting youth overseas and marketing expensive shoes to poor inner-city youth."[4] When Nike realized that the protests on college campuses and elsewhere were not going to stop, it began to temper its arrogance and has begun to make changes in its labor practices. It has begun to understand that success in today's economy is only bestowed upon corporations by people as long as those corporations earn their trust. Nike originally had a rebellious attitude that was very appealing for young people, but it went too far. Nike forgot to listen, and sometimes just listening is the most important thing a corporation can do. No brand, no matter how great, is above it. Coca-Cola is beginning to do this now.

Consumer democracy is becoming more and more of an issue.

Carl Ware, Coca-Cola's executive vice president of communications and corporate affairs, is insightful in saying recently in the *New York Times* that "Consumer democracy is becoming more and more of an issue."[5] Indeed, brands do not belong to corporations anymore, but to people!

CREATIVITY RULES

So, now that we have reached this time when corporations clearly need to fine tune their focus on the consumer psyche and understand the importance of the constantly evolving trends in their consumers' lifestyles, how exactly do we do this? In order to accomplish this feat of emotional connectivity, corporations have to "start at home" by developing a more humanistic and imaginative culture both in terms of how they conduct business and how they manage their employees. Daniel Goleman's enlightening book, *Working with Emotional Intelligence*, exemplifies this "open conduit" approach by discussing the role business people need to play in our world today. Mr. Goleman effectively proves that, as he puts it, "The rules for work are changing. We're being judged by a new yardstick: not just by how smart we are, or by our training and expertise, but also by how well we handle ourselves and each other."[6] Sam Walton of Wal-Mart put it another way when he said that, "It takes a week to two weeks for employees to start treating customers the same way the employer is treating the employee."[7] The most important thing a company can do today is begin to foster a creative, caring business atmosphere internally.

Courage, daring, and energy are contagious forces that can spread through a corporation at breakneck speed if allowed!

St. Luke's advertising agency is a great example of an exciting creative business culture that works. The highly successful 1995 British start-up is based on democratic principles. The company has a nonhierarchical system where everyone in the agency is a stockholder; meaning that the receptionist who has been there for six years may wield more power in corporate decisions than a creative director, for example. Everything in their offices is shared, there is no personal space, and schedules are built around optimizing employee abilities. St. Luke's spontaneously rewards its hardworking staff with benefits such as declaring one summer to be the "Summer of Love," when no new business would be pitched or accepted (they had to turn down an account worth fifty million pounds!), planning instead parties and special events to celebrate. CEO Andy Law says, "Human beings are creative, fun, and inquiring: yet work for so many is monotonous, complex, and dreary. Humans are individual and versatile; yet at work we discover we are all expendable and carefully placed in a well-manicured organogram."[8] St. Luke's is changing that.

The successful companies of this century are successful because they develop an innovative culture that serves as a basis for a real connection and open conduit to clients and consumers. In short, they help people. A great example of this is the success of Ben & Jerry's ice cream company, which ranked extremely high in the *Wall Street Journal* poll because of their offbeat products and ongoing commitment to progressive social causes.[9]

A Visionary Approach to Change (Connecting the Dots)

We are embarking on a new millennium with great eagerness and apprehension, convincing ourselves that the first century will be about humanity and spirituality. In the last hundred years, the speed of globalization led by industrialization and commerce was supported by faster transportation, cable communications, and now an instant connection to each other. The Internet has brought to our homes with vivid immediacy the contrast between innovative and retrograde ideas–social justice and injustice and the explosion of solutions and mixed opportunities of a global community.

The reengineering business practices of the old economy that focused mainly on cost saving for increased profits for corporations completely destroyed what was left of the emotional contract that once existed between employees and corporations. And this lack of trust toward the established authority has also resulted in increased cynicism toward leveraging brands. Gone are the days of lifetime employment and lifetime brand fidelity–say hello to the age of individuality where a new "me first" generation has understood the "art of the deal."

The dot-com entrepreneurs are at the forefront of this change, bringing with them the foundation of a new economy in which every aspect of our lives is changing in the most profound way. This new generation of entrepreneurs is reforming through innovation the nature of the old-world corporations. Dot-com entrepreneurs know well what happened to the lifetime commitment their parents gave to companies. They are in to cash out before it's too late and move on to the next big idea. The Web is allowing innovative entrepreneurs to be heard and giving them the support to achieve their dreams. What this means is that traditional, highly structured, old-world corporations that have been built upon values such as "please the boss, keep my job, don't rock the boat, risk is dangerous," will relinquish the creative power to lean and mean businesses set up for fighting for a dream. Leaders in this economy understand that, unlike in the past, access to greater resources, size, and stability are not nearly as crucial as flexibility, speed, and agility. In dot-com businesses cultures are dynamic, fresh, entrepreneurial, and, most importantly, connected. No ivory towers here.

The model works because a partnership is created between the buyer and seller. On the Web the customers themselves reap the benefit of their contribution if a company succeeds. Web-driven financial institutions or travel sites are using consumer information to bring better rates to their clients with great success. This does not mean that traditional corporations will disappear. It does mean that we will see the corporate world redefined around the concepts of innovation, flexibility, and cultural relevance. The cutbacks at huge conglomerates such as Unilever are prime examples of larger companies striving to shed some of their traditional "dead weight" in order to be able to better compete in the new world order. Image-wise companies such as Procter & Gamble, seen as a "faceless giant" by most consumers,[10] will have to find a new voice with the public as well.

As an entrepreneur and creative consultant, I have witnessed firsthand throughout my career how lethargy within some corporations has caused brilliant ideas to be turned away because *the right to fail in traditional corporations was not acceptable*. Promotions were often not given based on innovation as an important criterion. I have met brilliant and innovative people who were not recognized for their talent; people who could have turned around an industry.

Nortel, recognizing that some of their "idea people" would leave if they were not heard and understanding that it takes money and support to "dot-com" yourself, has developed a program called Nortel Business Venture Group, a review board that identifies the best internal ideas and then allocates the finances for development. Channelware, the result of one of these initiatives, is based on the idea that people would be interested in testing software on the Internet before making a purchase commitment. This concept, which has been called an "intrapreneurship," by *Fast Company*, financially rewards the creators with 15 to 30 percent of the virtual start-up company if it goes public.[11] The right to fail is the most important element of innovation. Dot-com companies have this right given to them by investors. The next idea will make up largely for one that does not work. When a company gives this kind of opportunity internally to people, it can be a big draw for talented and motivated employees.

Consulting as we know it is being redefined to help bring these new ideas to corporations and is no longer performing primarily as cost-cutting "magic." McKinsey & Company has formed a special task-force team called Corporations of the Future to study how big corporations can foster innovative, entrepreneurial environments. In order to better be able to work with Internet companies, the consulting firm KPMG is giving all of its employees intensive crash courses in Internet studies. Ford Motor Company has given free personal computers, printers, and Internet access to its 350,000 employees worldwide as a way of training employees and immersing them in this culture so that the company can get an edge on the new economy. Ford eventually hopes to use the Web extensively to turn itself into a consumer-focused powerhouse.

Universities will have to reinvent themselves to train students to be entrepreneurs, not only managers or consultants. Many universities are scrambling to incorporate the real, e-world into their programs, offering certificates and new programs. I have heard that Boston University is currently creating a new diploma to specifically reflect a new way to look at management training for the future economy. This diploma will include a major in technology so that the graduate students can immediately immerse themselves in the new business world. In a *Wired* magazine article written by a Harvard undergrad with a burgeoning e-business who critiques the disparity between the cultures of entrepreneurship and academia, the young man says about his degree, "I want the diploma as long as it doesn't interfere with my Net start-up."[12] He goes on to point out that in a 1999 study commissioned by the Kauffman Center for Entrepreneurial Leadership, seven out of ten teenagers nationwide want to become entrepreneurs.[13] What will be the value and relevance of the Harvard "brand" if it does not adapt to the future? And where will these bright young entrepreneurs want to work? Companies like Yahoo! (which in a 1999 Forrester survey was rated the number two–ranked brand by teens and young adults),[14] Intel, Apple, Microsoft, and IBM are now topping the list as some of the most successful and admired brands, giving old economy brands a run for their money.

This is the dominance of a people culture over a bureaucratic culture . . .

In this new economy AOL orchestrated a purchase of Time Warner, the revered old-world U.S. company founded in the twenties, based almost purely on a stock valuation of twice that of the old economy icon! The writing is on the wall. This is the dominance of a people culture over a bureaucratic culture, the advent of emotions, creativity, and community over past business formulas.

The Concept of Cool and the Power of Imagination

Most companies are planning their futures today, without the benefit of historical precedent. Not everyone is on the same page, and where technology rules, chaos and unpredictability are a way of life. In light of the fact that some older business models are now being rendered meaningless, it would seem that conventional wisdom is a riskier strategy today than implementing change. The skills required for this change are innovation, risk management, and interdependence. The new "tech industries" are providing what younger generations want . . . to be a part of the future. The best and brightest are deserting traditional corporations and Wall Street. They are looking for cool places to work; making cool products with cool stock opportunities. Imagination is the bloodline of these companies and an enticement to people who want to make the business environment into a new kind of work "zone" that fosters and welcomes thought-provoking and innovative ideas. This group will bring with them their own culture and values. Magazines such as *Fast Company, Red Herring,* and *Wired* are replacing for this generation magazines such as *Forbes* and *Fortune* (who are nevertheless rising to the occasion and trying to reinvent themselves in a less stogy format)! New work titles are also making their way into our culture. We see titles now such as chief learning officer and customer evangelist at Saba, a consulting group; permission marketing manager at Yahoo!; and worldwide change manager at Hewlett-Packard.

The days of silos are gone. The true asset has become knowledge, which is rendered so much more valuable when shared. All this means that it's a great time to be an idea person. We are also living in a global world where the competitive difference between economies is vastly reduced. Innovation can come from even the smallest nations and we see megamerged companies competing with smaller, upstart companies operating in a smart, fast way. Everybody is thinking today, so a new idea or a new product has a shorter window opening of "uniqueness" before a new, further improved idea comes along. The life expectancy of brand images is also shorter, and product development has been streamlined. In the fragrance industry it used to take two years to develop and produce a fragrance. That has now been reduced to less than one year. And it's the same story in the car industry; cars are now designed and produced at lightening speed with a myriad of individualized design features to boot. We are learning together in a time of "unsurpassed connectivity" that will contribute to greater ideas and concepts—the Web melting pot. Marketers will have to respond to these new fundamental sociological changes and expectations with imaginative products, services, and messages that tap into this "cool" factor.

The "cool" factor is ultimately about cultivating the kind of connectivity and intimacy with your market that can serve as a medium to anticipate changes and guide the creative process for new product ideas. The more you know about the real world and real people, the more you can predict people's desires and expectations. Imagination can really come to life in exciting and profitable ways when one is in sync with the expectations of the marketplace.

"You" Is Really "IT"! The Ascendance of the Individual

In their last issue of the twentieth century, the French magazine *L'Express* elected "you" as the person of the year 2000. On the cover of their magazine was a 3×5 mirror, which reflected the face of all their readers of different nationalities, races, religions, and creeds. The statement behind this cover is that people, individually, are the force that needs to be reckoned with in the century to come from a political, cultural, artistic, and business point of view. "You" is really "IT"!

Emotional Branding is a means of creating a *personal dialogue* with con-

sumers. Consumers today expect their brands to know them—intimately and individually—with a solid understanding of their needs and cultural orientation. This is a greater challenge than ever before in today's increasingly complex marketplace where we find global consumers with very different values, origins, and aspirations that reflect the ever-evolving mix of the current three most influential generations: Baby Boomers and Generations X and Y. Add to this picture the dramatic increase in numbers, spending power and expanding social identities of women, ethnic (particularly Hispanic and African-American) and gay and lesbian populations in America, and you realize the challenge and opportunity existing today. In addition, the fact that we now live in a truly global market and are influenced daily by cultures from around the world has made our lives more exciting with an enlarged scope of opportunities and increasing expectations. The age-old human need for variety has new meaning in the rich mosaic of today's marketplace!

How do brands begin to meet this new, more refined and complex need for diversity? Emotional Branding navigates these choppy waters by enabling brands to carry on a personal dialogue with consumers on the issues which are most meaningful to them. The new model will be one of brands connecting with innovative products that are culturally relevant, socially sensitive, and have presence at all points of contact in people's lives.

Most importantly, the biggest misconception in branding strategies is the belief that branding is about market share when it is really always about "mind and emotions share."

SERVING THE WHOLE "YOU"

Since consumers are in the driver's seat, they will experience brands in a different way. People today feel empowered; they are more connected to each other and global events, and feel capable of influencing the world with their beliefs and shaping part of their own future. We will see people seek and redefine for themselves the quality level of their life. They will fulfill their desires for themselves and for everyone around them by bringing on an unprecedented personal and emotional dimension in their choices and decisions. The increasingly important "quality of life" concepts of hassle-free shopping, time management, stress reduction, connectivity, and heightened pleasure will profoundly affect consumers' overall receptivity to new product or marketing ideas. There is a new mandate of tailoring every aspect of business toward *serving the whole person*. Those who don't understand this will miss a big opportunity.

The biggest misconception in branding strategies is the belief that branding is about market share when it is really always about "mind and emotions share."

The future of branding is listening carefully to people in order to be able to connect powerfully with them by bringing pleasurable, life-enhancing solutions to their world. In the future, traditional companies will not be able to rely on their brand history or dominance in classical distribution systems, they will have to focus on providing brands with a powerful emotional content.

Products today are services . . . and services are products. Buyers are sellers. Homes are offices. Workers are capitalists. There is a supermarket in the United Kingdom that does not just provide a bank kiosk in their store, but has now also become a bank brand itself. Martha Stewart is a publisher, designer, TV personality, and role model as entrepreneur and homemaker.

As Bernd Schmitt, the brilliant Columbia University director of the marketing management program, puts it in his book *Experiential Marketing*, "The ultimate goal of Experiential Marketing is to create holistic experiences for customers."[15] Oprah Winfrey has built her phenomenal success by smartly tapping into this consumer need to be viewed and addressed in a holistic manner. Her new multifaceted lifestyle magazine *O*, which is rich in material for "body, mind, and soul" and seeks to help readers become more of "who they are," is a testament to this philosophy. Oprah says in her first issue, "My hope is that this magazine will help you lead a more productive life"–quite a grand endeavor for a magazine (which is, by the way, flying off the shelves in record numbers)!

This holistic, very personal experience one can have with a product is, quite simply, the future of branding and it will affect product distribution. As we can all see, modes of distribution are certainly changing at a rapid rate to help this transition—and this trend is only bound to continue. Many malls are currently victims of a retail glut phenomenon where too many similar brands at highly competitive price points are sold. However, the mall is in the process of being reinvented as a form of exciting and diverse community entertainment and cultural center, such as Easton Town Center mall in Columbus, Ohio, The Mall of America in Bloomington, Minnesota, or the Bluewater Mall in London. These are highly creative, imaginative entertainment complexes with theme parks, restaurants, aquariums, "learning centers," shows and concerts, and so on—you name it! They are places where people can relax and have fun with their families while they shop. The mall of the future will most likely be less about purchasing products than exploring them in a physical setting, while the Internet model, is fast becoming, among other things, the ultimate "one-to-one" distribution machine. This means that retail environments will have to become places to build brand images, rather than just places to sell products. Stores will need to emotionally bond with consumers through retail design and merchandising strategies that incorporate imaginative features, offering the kind of entertainment and sensory appeal that cannot be found on the Web.

Sensory experiences are immediate, powerful, and capable of changing our lives profoundly, but they are not used to their full extent in branding, particularly at the retail level. This is where a dramatic, color-lit waterfall in the middle of a retail space, or sound, music, and scent zones that are activated when the shopper strolls into different sections of the store, or basketball courts for trying out shoes and equipment, or exciting entertainment events can come into play. In the stores of tomorrow, "buying" will be outmoded as a sterile activity and in its place will stand "the art of shopping" which is less about purchasing and more about experiencing a brand.

The trend forecaster maven Faith Popcorn said recently that she believes supermarkets will soon become obsolete; a distribution channel of the past![16] As people lose interest in old modes of distribution that traditional manufacturers are relying upon, it will be crucial to reinvent the way products will be defined and sold in the future. *In navigating these or any other changes, the emotional contact with the consumer will again be the only strategy for success.*

From Branding to Emotional Branding

In order to avoid the dramatic price wars, which affect all commodity products suffering from the lack of a strong image, corporations need to deliver messages about their products, which are tighter and more potent. Over three thousand new brands are introduced each year, not including e-brands! What is the difference between Ralph Lauren's new fragrance Romance and Estée Lauder's Pleasure? . . . between one cola and another cola? . . . a particular sneaker and its competitor? . . . or many different kinds of jeans, coffees, or gas stations? Or between one beauty Web site and another? In this ocean of offerings, all fighting for the same consumer dollar, the emotional connection is what makes that all-important, essential difference. The emotional element is what gives a brand both the foundation and fuel for future business strategies—consumer-driven strategies.

Starbucks coffee shops, as we know, not only sell coffee but are all about coffee places where people can find an environment that is emotionally pleasant and friendly. It's a "people place" that fosters a sense of community, apart from the rat race. Howard Shultz in his book *Pour Your Heart into It* says that "the best way to build a brand is one person at a time!"[17] Instead of building his business in the traditional way—which is to create products that are then mass-distributed and supported with mass advertising, with the goal of grabbing market share from competitors—Starbucks elected to go the emotional route. This value-driven, uniquely managed company first created a people-driven product as a true brand and then set out to educate the customers about coffee and enchant them with the romance of coffee drinking. The product here is, of course, not the coffee or even the place itself—it is the total experience. Part of going to Starbucks has to do with the imaginative, fun, Seattle-inspired atmosphere that is fostered. Servers often joke with customers who then feel very comfortable to explore the place and the products. When Mark McGwire walked into his local Starbucks wanting to buy a baseball cap with the Starbucks logo, the employee preparing his coffee drink, or "barista," as they are called in Italy (and at Starbucks), told him the hats weren't for sale, but the young man promptly gave him his own! And guess what? He wore it in the World Series. And based on his firsthand experience with the brand in the store, he decided to partner with Starbucks in their charitable endeavors and has been involved with Starbucks' children's literacy programs for the past several years.

Have you been to a Godiva store lately? Are you willing to admit how many times you have bought those handmade, delectable fruits dipped in chocolate right before your very eyes? When we created the new store design for this wonderful brand, we emotionalized their retail brand image, which was elegant but slightly intimidating and austere, by using the Art Nouveau style to communicate their heritage of sophisticated European pleasure in a more warm and sensuous manner that heightens the irresistible allure of chocolate. Everything about the Godiva store experience, down to the careful details of the packaging itself, conveys the delicious experience of chocolate. The result? A marked increase in sales worldwide!

JetBlue, a new airline in the Northeast which has been called a "laboratory experiment in contemporary branding,"[18] is not your typical airline. JetBlue is not about "how to get there from here"; it is about a very particular chic, well-orchestrated experience. They offer very inexpensive fares throughout the Northeast, but everything from their stylish urbane plane interiors with cushy leather seats and twenty-four DIRECTV channels for every passenger to their flight attendants' blue Pradaesque uniforms and the ultra-hip design of the terminal gates will wear the brand's particular badge of "coolness."

As a further illustration, just take a look at the Evian water-drop shape millennium bottle. It is not just about water or luxury in the traditional sense. It is about seeing water in a whole new way through groundbreaking design, taste, home decoration, and the evocation of the sensory experience of a water drop.

PHOTO BY PAUL TILLINGHAST.

Emotional Branding is the conduit by which people connect subliminally with companies and their products in an emotionally profound way. *Sony's innovation, France's romance, Gucci's sensual elegance,* Vogue*'s insatiable glamour, and Tiger Wood's amazing drive and spirit reach us emotionally by striking our* *imagination and offering promise of new realms.* This strategy works because we all respond emotionally to our life experiences and we naturally project emotional values onto the objects around us.

Powerful Emotional Branding comes from partnership and communication. *Branding bridges the gap between the provider and the receiver; between authority and freedom. It is about trust and dialogue.* Powerful Emotional Branding comes from partnership and communication. Building the right emotion is the most important investment you can make in a brand. It is the promise you make to consumers, giving them permission to enjoy the world of the brand.

The Ten Commandments of Emotional Branding
Between the old concept of brand awareness and the new concept of Emotional Branding, a dialogue must take place that involves this changing of consumer reality in the decision process and brings a dimension of personalized relationship into the equation.

The following "Ten Commandments of Emotional Branding" illustrate the difference between traditional concepts of brand awareness and the emotional dimension a brand needs to express to become preferred.

1. FROM CONSUMERS → TO PEOPLE
Consumers buy, people live. In communication circles the consumer is often approached as the "enemy" whom we must attack. It's us (meaning manufacturers, retailers, and their communications agencies) against them. Terminology like "breaking down their defenses, decoding their language, and strategizing to win the battle" is, in my day-to-day experience, still commonly used. But why employ this tactic when there is a better way to create desire in customers in a positive manner without harassing or talking down to them? This can be achieved by using a win-win, partnership approach based on a relationship of mutual respect. After all, the consumer is your best source of information.

2. FROM PRODUCT → TO EXPERIENCE
Products fulfill needs, experiences fulfill desires. Buying just for need is driven by price and convenience. A product or shopping experience, such as REI stores' rock climbing walls or the Discovery Channel stores' myriad of "sound

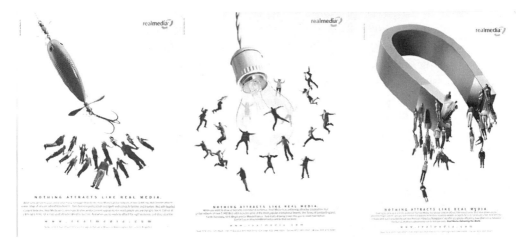

In depicting consumers as moths, fish, and metal shavings in situations of helpless attraction, these ads for a media firm aptly illustrate the mentality Commandment #1 seeks to counteract!

zones" has added value and will remain in the consumer's emotional memory as a connection made on a level far beyond need. For established products to attract and retain consumer interest, it is critical that innovative retailing, advertising, and new product launches capture their imagination. The lines are drawn every day between newness and tradition, between what is expected and the excitement of change. Our curiosity and sense of adventure often wins out over the known. However, a product can be old and new at the same time, if it continues to have emotional relevance for consumers.

3. FROM HONESTY → TO TRUST

Honesty is expected. Trust is engaging and intimate. It needs to be earned.
Honesty is required to be in business today. The federal authorities, consumer groups, and the people in general have an increasingly rigorous standard for products and will rate very quickly what needs to be on the shelf and what doesn't. Trust is something else altogether. It is one of the most important values of a brand and it requires real effort from corporations. It is what you would expect from a friend. One of the most powerful moves toward building consumer trust was retailers' implementation of the "no questions asked" return policy some years ago. This strategy brings total comfort to customers and gives them the upper hand in their choices. A very smart decision indeed. Sincere efforts to know and contribute to the brand's community like those of Wal-Mart and FUBU are also great examples of building trust.

4. FROM QUALITY → TO PREFERENCE

Quality for the right price is a given today. Preference creates the sale. Quality is a necessary offering if you want to stay in business; it is expected and had better be delivered. Preference toward a brand is the real connection to success. Levi's is a quality brand, but it has currently lost its preferential status. Victoria's Secret, a brand that has achieved an enviable and highly charged emotional connection with consumers today, is revolutionizing a new category and redefining the hosiery and beauty businesses—there is no stopping a brand when it is preferred.

5. FROM NOTORIETY → TO ASPIRATION

Being known does not mean that you are also loved! Notoriety is what gets you known. But if you want to be desired, you must convey something that is in keeping with the customer's aspirations. Awareness is obviously not the only criterion to successful branding. Beyond awareness, what does AT&T really mean on an emotional level to consumers? And is there really a difference for people between the well-known (and some would say infamous!) brands ExxonMobil and Texaco? Nike is still a very notorious brand with great visibility, but is it as inspirational as it used to be?

6. FROM IDENTITY → TO PERSONALITY

Identity is recognition. Personality is about character and charisma! Identity is descriptive. It is recognition. Personality is about character and charisma. Brand identities are unique and express a point of difference vis-à-vis the competitive landscape. But this is only the first step. Brand personalities, on the other hand, are special. They have a charismatic character that provokes an emotional response. American Airlines has a strong identity, but Virgin Airlines has personality.

7. FROM FUNCTION → TO FEEL

The functionality of a product is about practical or superficial qualities only. Sensorial design is about experiences. Functionality can become trite if its appearance and usage are not also designed for the senses. Many marketers design for maximum function or visibility and not for the real experience of the consumer. Design is about human solutions, based on innovation that presents a new set of sensory experiences. Creating product identification by stressing product benefits is only relevant if product innovations are memorable and exciting to consumers. Absolut Vodka, the Apple iMac, and Gillette razors are brands that are focused on presenting fresh shapes and sensory experiences consumers appreciate.

8. FROM UBIQUITY → TO PRESENCE

Ubiquity is seen. Emotional presence is felt. Brand presence can have quite an impact on the consumer. It can forge a sound and permanent connection with people, especially if it is strategized as a lifestyle program. There is hardly a stadium, a player uniform, a concert hall, or an urban space of size (billboards, bus stops, walls, and even the inside of bathroom doors) around the world that has not been used to promote a brand. And then, of course, there are the T-shirts, caps, mugs, and so on. But how effective is all this clutter, really? Most brand-presence strategies are based on the concept of quantity, not quality. The fear that a competitor might occupy the physical territory becomes the motivator, instead of a focus on inventive ways of making a real, lasting connection. Joe Boxer's wacky underwear vending machines which call out to passersby "Hey, do you need some new underwear?" and tell jokes is an invetive way of standing out and making a connection!

9. FROM COMMUNICATION → TO DIALOGUE

Communication is telling. Dialogue is sharing. Communication, as conducted by many companies, is primarily about information–and information is generally a one-way proposition. Take it and like it–hopefully. The bulk of most budgets is still spent on advertising efforts that approach consumers with the B1 bomber approach: a massive, all-encompassing blanket advance at the target audience. Not only can advertising deliver more personal, targeted messages, but other media, such as digital communications, PR, brand presence, and promotions can also stretch much further to really speak to consumers where they "live." Real dialogue implies a two-way street, a conversation with the consumer. Progress in digital media is now allowing this evolution to take place, and finally will help foster a rewarding partnership between people and corporations.

10. FROM SERVICE → TO RELATIONSHIP

Service is selling. Relationship is acknowledgment. Who does not feel special when someone in a store or restaurant welcomes you by your own name! Service involves a basic level of efficiency in a commercial exchange. It is what allows or prevents a sale from taking place. But relationship means that the brand representatives really seek to understand and appreciate who their customers are. It is what you feel when you walk into a Quicksilver store and find that the music, the décor, and the salespeople all speak the same language– the customer's! It is the new expectation. Howard Shultz, CEO of Starbucks, speaks about romancing the consumer: "If we greet customers, exchange a few extra words with them and then custom-make a drink exactly to their taste, they will be eager to come back."

The Four Pillars of Emotional Branding: Overview of Four Sections of the Book
The underlying concept of the Emotional Branding process is based on four
essential pillars: RELATIONSHIP, SENSORIAL EXPERIENCES, IMAGINATION, and
VISION. These pillars provide the blueprint of a successful Emotional Branding
strategy and serve as the overall organization of the book:

RELATIONSHIP . . . is about being profoundly in touch with and showing respect
for who your consumers really are and giving them the emotional experience
they really want. Many companies are alarmingly disconnected from the current
changes in consumer populations, such as the rapid expansion of ethnic markets, generational evolutions, and the enormous influence of women in our society today. There are also many crucial corresponding shifts in consumer trends,
attitudes, and behaviors that profoundly affect consumers' brand expectations.

SENSORIAL EXPERIENCES . . . are a hugely underexplored area and a potential
gold mine for brands in the twenty-first century. Research shows us that offering a multisensorial brand experience can be an incredibly effective branding
tool. Providing consumers with a sensorial experience of a brand is key to
achieving the kind of memorable emotional brand contact that will establish
brand preference and create loyalty.

IMAGINATION . . . in brand design executions is the stroke that makes the
Emotional Branding process real. Imaginative approaches to the design of
products, packaging, retail stores, advertisements, and Web sites allow a brand
to break the ceiling of the expected and reach the hearts of consumers in a
fresh, new way. The challenge for tomorrow's brands will be to find both outrageous and subtle ways to continually surprise and delight consumers.

VISION . . . is the ultimate factor of a brand's long-term success. Brands evolve
through a natural life cycle within the marketplace and in order to create and
maintain an edge in today's marketplace, brands must be poised to reinvent
themselves constantly. This requires a strong brand vision. My company's
tools help align a company behind one cohesive brand direction and focus
with emotional resonance for today's consumers.

section I:
relationship

customer, customer, customer!

It's the Twenty-first Century: Do You Know Who Your Customers Are?

I believe that the importance of remembering and reinventing the old-fashioned golden rules of commerce, such as "the customer is always right" will be all the more crucial to success in business as we move more and more into a society influenced profoundly by incredible and rapid technological innovation. This core idea of connecting with and serving consumers as real, living, breathing, complex people will always win out over short-term marketing hype and it will always be the key to creating the kind of brands that have a long-term emotionalized presence in peoples lives.

Of course before meeting anyone's personal needs and making a deep emotional connection you have to really know who they are, and this is an increasingly complex task in our fluid society today. I want to give you now a look at the changing consumer landscape of the twenty-first century, focusing primarily on the dynamic explosion of the three, currently most influential generations—Baby Boomer, Generation X, and Generation Y—and on the growing influence of women and major ethnic groups, as well as on the importance of gay and lesbian populations in the marketplace.

1

A Generational Explosion: Targeting New Emotional Criteria

Three major consuming populations inhabit the retail landscape today: the Baby Boomers (thirty-seven to fifty-five years old), the Gen Xers (twenty-five to thirty-six years old), and Gen Yers (six to twenty-four years old). These three population segments simply don't speak the same language. Baby Boomers respond to cues of achievement, status, and performance, while Gen Xers value imagination, creativity, and relationships, and Gen Y responds to fun, interactivity, and experiences.

Aging Baby Boomers: Not Your Typical Grandma and Grandpa

Born 1946–64, Baby Boomers are used to challenging America's assumptions and used to fighting for what they want. This generation's sheer size has empowered it like no other American generation. In the sixties and seventies *their* mores, *their* music, *their* clothes, *their* politics were the forces that restructured America. As they fought for women's rights and civil rights, Jimi Hendrix composed their new American vision via a psychedelic rendition of the National Anthem they could call all *their* own. Then–exit bell-bottoms and bra-less babes, enter white-picket fences. Haight-Ashbury and the loose joints gave way to Wall Street and martinis. As Boomers marched into the boardrooms and backrooms of the eighties, suddenly they were fighting for success and affluence, redefining success, materialism, and the "American Dream" in the process. Now, this generation finds itself presented with a new obstacle, unlike anything it has ever encountered before: LAF–Life After Forty. But Boomers are LAFing all the way to the bank. As in their previous exploits, Boomers will confront this change with vigor and finesse, co-opting the meaning of maturity and retirement and fitting it to their generation's idiosyncrasies. Well into the first quarter of the new millennium, Boomers will comprise a dynamic and challenging demographic, and the brands that can provide an identity as versatile as the Boomers themselves stand to reap great success.

Boomers bring tremendous influence and merit marketers' careful attention like no generation that preceded them. Born between 1946 and 1964, Baby Boomers comprise eighty-one million people, 30 percent of the population, and command 55 percent of the United States' discretionary income. In the past, marketers disproportionately devoted their promotions to young consumers, based on the assumption that consumers captured early in life would remain loyal for years to come. This could be a costly mistake if applied to Gens X and Y.

Boomers bring tremendous influence and merit marketers' careful attention like no generation that preceded them.

America's love affair with the brand has, well, fallen on hard times. Consumers want attention and affection. Take consumers for granted and they will walk out the door. Hence, aiming for the young consumer *does not* guarantee a long-term bountiful bottom line. Instead, brands should court a lifelong love affair, characterized by a perpetual dialogue surrounding the issues affecting consumers. The specific affluence and concerns of the Baby Boomers require a particular sensitivity and awareness on the part of brands. This generation will not bend to the strains of age. Instead they will revitalize and reshape what it means to be "mature." To the marketers of the twenty-first century, they have one thing to say: "You ain't seen nuthin' yet."

Forever Young

Before we go any further, one thing must be made clear: Boomers are not getting older; they are reaching a youthful maturity. At this peak in their life (one of many—whatever age a Boomer is, is always the best age) they can look forward to indulging in the three big benefits of maturity: wisdom, health, and status. Meanwhile, thanks to Viagra, Renova, and investment portfolios, they can buy their way out of most of the drawbacks of "maturity." At least, that's the plan. In their forties and fifties, Boomers are anxiously indulging in treats with connotations of youth and adventure that reaffirm their youthfulness and energy. If fifty-year-old Boomers are exceptionally convinced of their youth, they may be right. As a group, they are healthier and more active than any previous generation of fifty-year-olds. Competitive careers, demanding families, and a slew of medical advances have kept this group remarkably fit. Furthermore, it is their youthful state of mind that enables some of the

Boomers' highest achievements. By denying their age they are more apt to undertake ambitious projects such as starting a new company or vacationing in rugged terrain (think Billy Crystal in *City Slickers*). Hence, their Peter Pan "never grow up" mentality constitutes an empowering attitude. Brands must keep this in mind and with the goal of further empowering this generation, devote themselves to providing personalized products and care which supplement their youthful maturity.

A glance through any Boomer-oriented magazine, whether it be *Martha Stewart Living, Smithsonian, Newsweek,* or *Forbes,* will quickly illustrate the broad array of advertisers appealing to Boomers. One ad from the MasterCard "Priceless" campaign features the text "Dinner for eight, Chez Marella, $475. One Happy Birthday card, $1.95. One leopard-print, peekaboo nightie, $45. Still being able to make her blush, priceless." The "still being able to make her blush" punch line implies that over the years the couple has retained their vital qualities, including sexuality. Of course such an ad would never have been directed at Boomers ten years ago when some were still in their thirties and there was no reason to defend their sexuality or vigor. Other appeals to the Boomers' desire to preserve youth include Charter Club's "Live the way you feel," or Tropicana's ad for grapefruit juice which depicts a woman in her early forties drinking juice atop a Harley, while her sexy older gentleman companion straddles another Harley in the background.

Among the most striking status symbols in America, vehicles provide an interesting example of Baby Boomers' evolving tastes. I ask you to consider three vehicles: the hot rod, the minivan, and the sports utility vehicle. I know a lot of Boomers who would love to race around town in a hot rod, discarding midlife baggage as they cruise the streets. This appeals to Boomers' desirous Id. The minivan, meanwhile, comes out of the Boomer's responsible Ego. It's safe and practical. And finally, we have the sports utility vehicle, which I deem to be a synthesis of the two—the embodiment of the Boomer's Superego. It shuns both the midlife-crisis ostentation of a sports car, as well as the sedate, responsible (and adult) family motif surrounding the soccer-mom minivan. The SUV is a four-wheel-drive door to adventure *and* wintertime safety. It boasts the capacious interior of a minivan *and* the adventure of a hot rod. The SUV carries the premium of empowerment and excitement as well as sensibility, which Baby Boomers have responded to in droves. Surely, wealthy Boomers will account for significant sales in all three categories, but I think there is a particular logic behind the prosperous SUV industry.

dinner for 8, chez marcella: $475

one happy birthday card: $1.95

one leopard-print, peekaboo nightie: $45

still being able to make her blush: priceless

there are some things money can't buy.
for everything else there's MasterCard.

© 2000 MasterCard International Incorporated   www.mastercard.com

However, for the purposes of the future, brands must remember to pay special attention to the Boomer Id. Boomers have been told they're responsible, Boomers know they're responsible, and that said, they're ready to indulge in pricey pleasure purchases. For example, in 1980, the average age of the registered motorcyclist was twenty-six. Today, 60 percent of riders are between the ages of thirty-five and sixty-four. But are they buying the same vehicles they did twenty years ago? Not at all. Harley-Davidson, for example, has equipped

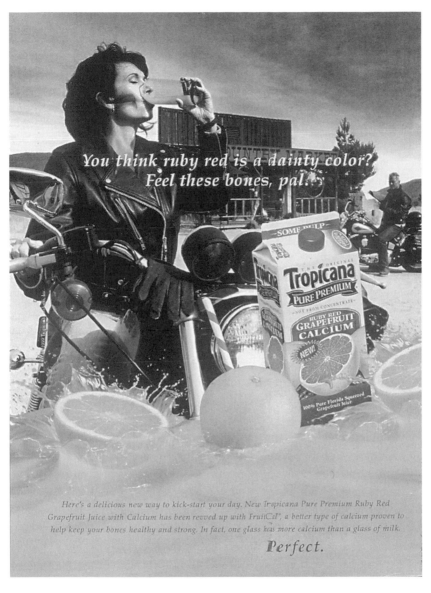

You think ruby red is a dainty color?
Feel these bones, pal.

Here's a delicious new way to kick-start your day. New Tropicana Pure Premium Ruby Red Grapefruit Juice with Calcium has been revved up with FruitCal®, a better type of calcium proven to help keep your bones healthy and strong. In fact, one glass has more calcium than a glass of milk.

Perfect.

many of its upper-end vehicles with wider seats and increased safety features to attract this more mature audience. Meanwhile, Harley's marketers organize events with family appeal and distribute ad brochures depicting middle-class couples. This intelligent redesign, both of the product and the image, accounts for a large part of the Harley-Davidson success, and provides a compelling model for Boomer branding.

In the rush to meet the demands of aging Boomers, intelligent product and marketing design is key to attracting them, without making them feel old or infirm. Products that present themselves as panic purchases, catering to Boomers fleeing the fates, will flop. However, products that take into account universal design principles will meet with success. *Universal design principles take into account the needs of all consumers, whether*

Emotional Branding is about comfort, reassurance, and solutions for this group.

they're seventeen or seventy. Based on the principles of ergonomics, innovations such as pens equipped with soft, rubber encasing, door levers instead of door-knobs, and large, easily read dashboard displays are accommodating and pleasing to all consumers. Rather than marketing these innovations as "Aids for the Elderly," they are presented as "Intelligent Innovations for All." This is essential. For example, savvy hotel chains have begun refurbishing select rooms with features such as larger buttons on remote controls, bedside control panels for lighting and drapes, and carefully disguised bathroom railings. These rooms are marketed as the luxurious counterpart to traditional rooms, rather than "over the hill–friendly." Vehicles again illustrate this point. Today's sports cars, such as BMW Z3 or the Ford Thunderbird, which are aimed at Boomers, feature stiffer bodies, larger door cuts, heated seats, more leg room, and other features that accommodate Boomers who may not have the same bodies they did in the racing days of their teendom.

In addition to appealing to the playful, adventurous Id, Emotional Branding is about comfort, reassurance, and solutions for this group. Many of yesterday's brands attempted to scare consumers into buying their products. Today's brands romance the consumers and demonstrate understanding. The fashion industry's evolving affair with the Boomers provides another illustration. Women in their forties, fifties, and beyond have been making appearances throughout ads and runway shows recently. Brooks Brothers, Jean-Paul Gaultier, and Bloomingdale's, to name a few, have tapped into the talents of beautiful mature women to showcase their products and deliver a subtle message to older audiences saying "These are for you." Since Estée Lauder brought back Karen Graham, one of its most prominent models in the seventies and eighties, it has received a constant stream of letters from older customers who appreciate seeing their elder cohorts in fashion print. Similarly, in 1999, *Vanity Fair* determined that the magazine's main clientele is women between thirty-five and fifty-four. This, despite a magazine full of eighteen- and twenty-year-old models. Since then *Vanity Fair* has made a point of incorporating beautiful

So many women say that it bothers them to see young wrinkleless women in ads for antiaging products!

older models, with a little gray hair and wrinkles, into its layouts. Meanwhile, fashion designers are recognizing that Baby Boomers' bodies are, of course, not shaped quite the same as a twenty-eight-year-old's. Recognizing this, Victoria's Secret, a company known for revealing lingerie, has accommodated its designs accordingly, but without sacrificing the youthful image or fashion sensibility. Comfort has also become a priority for many Boomers. Brands which are to prosper in the coming decades must continue to appeal to these and the new tastes which Boomers develop.

Brands need to think about how their customers perceive their age, and what products will enable the best of those feelings, as the cosmetic industry has done. Baby Boomers are the engine behind an explosion in the cosmetic industry that will be worth an estimated $457 billion in 2000. Fashion magazines are filled with ads exalting "age-defying" products. Since the introduction of alpha hydroxy acids that use natural ingredients to strip off layers of dead skin and provide a younger appearance, antiaging cosmetics have taken off. Renova, introduced in 1997, is approved by the FDA to market itself as reducing wrinkles. Any product that purveys a more youthful appearance is of strong interest. In marketing these products, those campaigns that emphasize physical and psychological benefits are more successful than those that focus on the problem being solved. For example, many men are concerned about aging because they realize they are competing with men increasingly younger than themselves in business. For these men, looking better may be part of feeling more confident in the workplace. If a brand can empower them this way, then a brand should.

Let's face it. Baby Boomers have, on the whole, worked pretty damn hard at their jobs. Whether in the workplace or the social agenda, Boomers are known for having battled for what they have gotten. Throughout their lives they have faced a highly competitive workplace as a result of their peers and, for twenty years now, the constant influx of younger workers. For all their antiauthoritarian noise in the sixties, this generation has developed a strong regard for status and achievement, and they are ready to cash in on the benefits. Boomers are becoming increasingly adept at maximizing the quality of their limited and elusive free time. Businesses of all kinds that provide much wanted rest and inspiring possibilities for leisure to this generation will thrive.

Gardening, travel, vacation homes—each of these has been flourishing with the Boomers because they offer what Boomers perceive as a simplified quality of life. They allow escapist indulgence. This taste for simplicity is invaluable knowledge in the hands of savvy marketers. It is not enough to say, "I sell computers. They are very good and they are competitively priced, therefore they will sell." *Brands must develop much more sensitivity to the symbolic values surrounding their product and image that are open to constant repositioning or embellishment.* A computer brand possessing the aforementioned data will identify the potential for computers to simplify life and free up leisure time. It will clearly and carefully illustrate its product's capacity to process tax returns quickly and easily, thereby freeing up users' time to go picnicking at a bright and cheery arboretum. *Such approaches enable brands to highlight both the real, tangible, and psychologically oriented solutions they bring to life. In order to succeed, brands must carefully craft these psychic identities* as well as the more concrete qualities quantified in *Consumer Reports.* Besides, I don't really care about how much RAM my computer has anyway as long as it gets the job done.

But what about the big change? Retirement? This generation will bring their finesse to bear on this as well. Even as they begin to downshift, Boomers will maintain remarkably active lifestyles. According to the U.S. Census Bureau, in 1999 there were about thirty million Americans over sixty. This number will jump to fifty million by 2015, and sixty-five million by 2030. Don't expect this tidal wave of elder Boomers to crash on Florida's shores though. According to a recent Gallup survey, 60 percent of respondents over fifty dream of retiring to a small town somewhere.[1] Projections indicate a disproportionate percentage of this group migrating to the Rocky Mountain states and Southeastern states such as North Carolina. Generic retirement communities that have flourished in Florida are being forgone for small communities, pleasant main streets, and polite neighbors. Many Boomers will

Why hire a thirty-year-old to understand sixty-year-olds when sixty-five-year-olds are lining up to give you the answers?

also supplement this lifestyle by reentering the workforce, whether out of boredom or a need for money. Lee Iacocca was one of the forerunners of this trend, retiring from Chrysler only to start up his own company, EV Global Motors Company, which specializes in environment-friendly transportation, such as electric bicycles. Despite the widespread prediction that Boomers are reentering the workforce in their sixties, most companies have not considered the rich opportunities posed by these experienced workers, or what it will take to attract them. Flexible schedules and virtual offices will be powerful draws for this generation. Perhaps some companies will institute "geriatric care"—the elder equivalent of childcare for the parents of these workers. They are certainly worth the extra effort, because hiring these elder Boomers will be one of the best ways to track and anticipate their needs. *Why hire a thirty-year-old to understand sixty-year-olds when sixty-five-year-olds are lining up to give you the answers?*

Understanding both these sides of Boomers—the desire to escape and downshift while remaining active—is vital for twenty-first century businesses. Products and promotions must sensibly cater to both halves of this mentality. Condescending branding strategies that connote easing them into inevitable elder oblivion will fail. The key is active and meaningful aging. The benefits of old age with none of the drawbacks.

With all this ambition and motivation, is there anything outside of death which will remain impervious to their influence? Actually, no, and that includes death. As one funeral consultant reported in a *USA Today* article, "Baby Boomers are living like no other generation in the world, and they are going to die like no other generation."[2] The costly and conservative funeral based on stuffy tradition is giving way to a more intimate one marked by poetry, contemporary music, and postfuneral parties, among other innovations. Some individuals are opting to be buried with their pets, reports the *USA Today* article. Mobile lifestyles and environmental concerns will make cremations more popular, while those still attached to burial can be presented to the afterlife in personalized "Art Caskets." WhiteLight, a Dallas company, sells such coffins as "Fairway to Heaven," marketed for the golf nut. Another one of their coffins appears to be made of brown parcel paper and is stamped with red lettering which reads "Return to Sender." Thus Boomer vitality and humanity is even applied to the final checkout.

Gen X to Gen eXcel: No Slacking Here

Let's clear up any remaining misconceptions about the so-called Gen X, born 1965–76, starting with that annoyingly persistent misnomer Gen X, and all that it conjures up. Sure, they got off to a rough start. Reared under the shadow of skyrocketing divorce rates, downsized parents, a sputtering American economy, the AIDS epidemic, and the horrifying new social problems such as the invention of crack cocaine, they were the first latchkey kids and they knew life wasn't perfect long before they saw the Challenger plummet to Earth in a ball of flames. However, their sobering youth provided a fertile atmosphere for fostering their take-control, independent-minded, pragmatic mentality which, aided by a booming economy, has effectively shed all resemblance to 1991's dispirited and dejected "slacker." Douglas Coupland, who coined the infamous term with his novel *Generation X*, now says of the phrase "It's almost retro now—it feels as far away as grunge."[3] Brands that continue to target the mythical twenty-something slacker are on the wrong track. However, brands which tap into the energy and spirit of today's "eXcel" generation will be able to forge a long-lasting partnership with this generation which is ready for some respect.

The eXcel generation clocks in with forty-four million members. At a mere 17 percent of the U.S. population, its numbers can't rival the mammoth Baby Boomer or Generation Y populations, each of which comprises about 30 percent of the population. However, they are a significant demographic which is in the process of building careers, buying houses, and preparing to people them with god-knows-what generation. Conservative and sensible in all matters pecuniary, 71 percent regularly save a portion of their income and 54 percent have started a financial plan.[4] While their Boomer brethren frivolously cavort in their second, third, or fourth youth, Gen eXcel is exercising maturity and prudence.

The ascendant eXcels' prosperity owes a great deal to their restructuring of family values. Dismayed by the collapse of stable families in the eighties, this generation views family life with prudence and caution. Like the pre-Boomer generations, they are averse to divorce. However, the eXcels' have tailored their own solution—wait till your career direction is set, and your youth enjoyed. The median age for marriage is twenty-five among women and 26.8 among men. Furthermore, when they do get married, eXcels don't feel restrained by marriage, and they renovate its institutional trappings from within. Whether they're using their virtual office to stay at home with the kids or going skydiving on the weekend to unwind, they're freely adapting marriage to their needs.

Brands with the flexibility to be appropriated by eclectic and individualized tastes will find in the eXcels a funky functionality which, by its mere unpredictability, is exciting. For example, while these budding family women and men aspire to owning traditional style homes, they view these homes foremost as a symbol of their individuality, rather than their status symbols, although more desire for status may well set in for this generation, as the eXcels stock portfolios plump up over time. But for now, the eXcels are planning their homes with that mix of frugality and personality that is their trademark. Urban Outfitters has been particularly successful appealing to their tastes. According to Melanie Cox, its creative director, "We sell a little bit of very inexpensive furniture and . . . [home] accessories. Our customer is somebody who has probably gotten a sofa from mom or dad, a table from grandma. None of it matches and [he or she] really wants to put his or her own mark on it by adding touches of personality and drawing it all together with some interesting things."[5]

Urban Outfitters employs this same sensibility in its focal point—clothing fashion—and the eXcels have responded in droves. By assembling an array of hip and inexpensive fashions, Urban Outfitters allows its customers to tailor a unique and hip wardrobe without hopping from store to store. Says Ms. Cox of the eXcels: "Predominately, they are looking for a particular look and that look can be provided by a multitude of brands. I think they have a particular comfort zone with some labels that that they know, that they've seen or their friends wear . . . [but we] think the customer is really interested in seeing a little selection from a lot of different people." That's not to say that the eXcel is a jumble of mixed patterns and appearances assembled on one collaged body, but rather that *they have a sharp and discriminating taste which freely adapts and subverts existing fashions and brands while meeting hip fashions and individualizing. In other words, your basic postmodern portrait.*

The eXcels have been a handful for stodgy Human Resources departments the nation over. These twenty- and thirtysomethings have been quickly absorbed into the tight job market and that's where they've worked some of their most significant and exciting changes. They saw job security and corporate loyalty fly out the window during the layoffs of the early nineties, and as a consequence, they are the workers most likely to leave the company they are with if they receive a better job offer. They are unwilling to sacrifice their personal lives on the corporate altar. They expect a healthy balance between personal and private life, and thanks to the high demand for workers and what amounts to a veritable generational coup, they've successfully rewritten corporate rules to their favor. *They favor work that offers variety and enhances their own skill set while allowing them to learn.* Further complicating the situation for managers and human resources, they are entrepreneurial and want to direct themselves, if not work for themselves. They account for 70 percent of new start-up businesses. Supplementing the eXcel's independence and drive is also a yen for teamwork. Unlike the more competition-oriented Boomers, among whom solitary work was prevalent at this age, the eXcels are accustomed to collaboration and enjoy being part of a team. They have abandoned the typical hierarchical mentality in favor of equality—in other words, they expect others, even their bosses, to treat them as equals. Being told what to do damages their morale, but being allowed to find their own solution and make their own mistakes is very rewarding for them. To top this all off, the eXcels seem to make pretty good bosses, and those that become bosses are likely to do so because they want to be a better boss to their subordinates than they themselves had. They are also equally accustomed to working for male and female bosses and show diminished concern for gender issues in the workplace, as in other realms. Wow! In another ten years Gen Y may be thanking these folks for fixing the place up. Businesses which accommodate the eXcels will be a hotbed for creativity and flexibility, the two most valuable assets in the market today!

eXcels have abandoned the typical hierarchical mentality in favor of equality—in other words, they expect others, even their bosses, to treat them as equals.

Brands definitely can't and shouldn't try to deceive these folk. Instead, businesses must provide accurate depictions in their media—appeal to the eXcels' individuality and their aspirations. Humor, particularly sarcasm, is a favorite of theirs. Anything irreverent has a good shot at stirring their sympathies and maybe, just maybe, their loyalties. Virgin Atlantic's campaign featuring Austin

Powers is one of the better and more appropriate Gen eXcel–directed appeals. Powers, a spoof of British sixties spy movies, is played by the comedian Mike Myers. Both movies featuring the character have been smash hits among Gen X, and his catch phrases, laced with sleazy yet endearing sexual innuendo, have entered Gen eXcel daily parlance. The eXcelers appreciated the amusing and subtly "naughty" ads linking the movie with Virgin Airlines, the spunky, hip airline. Additionally, the Austin Powers movies subtly poke fun at the Boomer generation, which spawned the original characters and culture spoofed in the films, which also appeals to eXcels.

Zippo's campaign to familiarize twentysomething consumers with their lighters also taps into the hip irreverence that eXcels are highly responsive to. Recasting the Zippo as an "ignition device" rather than a "cigarette lighter," the campaign's slogan is "Use it to start something." The TV ads are right up the alley of the young eXcels and elder Gen Yers. In each ad, a character named "Zippo guy" encounters strange and challenging circumstances with his Zippo. In one ad he tells the viewers, "According to recent studies, the ozone layer is rapidly depleting. The main cause for the phenomenon is the release of bovine gases. Igniting these gases early on will keep them from rising into the ozone. I will save the planet for the ages." Zippo guy is subsequently caught by two farmhands trying to light a cow's fart on fire. Crass? Tasteless? Brilliant? Yes, yes, and yes. Sure, Zippo could have explained the long history of their product and the refinement and personality embodied by its brands, and sure, that might have hit home with a Boomer, particularly with a few shots of James Dean with a Zippo. However, if you're going to try commanding one moment of an eXcel's valuable time, you better make it worthwhile. An amusing story with a great punch line and a good laugh is one way to do it. Offbeat, slightly off-color humor is often advised. For stumped and confused account executives, I suggest they sit down with my daughter and her friends and watch an episode of the show *South Park*. This show, hugely popular with Gen Xers, features irreverent cartoon characters who swear, fart on one another, and reference every bodily function known to *Homo sapiens*. By the end of the program, they will understand.

Campaigns that target the eXcels should strongly consider nontraditional approaches.

Campaigns that target the eXcels should strongly consider nontraditional approaches. Ford ferreted out the 120 coolest people in the thirty-five-year-old-and-under set and gave them each a Ford Focus to drive as part of the car's new campaign. Although accompanied by live ads on TV and the Internet, distributing the cars to these select 120 trendsetters, including DJs, concert promoters, and hip others, was a more underground means of generating buzz about the car without overcommercializing or overexposing the vehicle. Ford also prepared its dealerships for the customers who are expected to be mostly between twenty and twenty-nine years old and making $20,000–$35,000 a year. Car salesmen have been trained in the lingo and expectations of these customers and encouraged to rearrange their showrooms with vehicles appealing to a younger set. Ford has also been trying to loosen credit demands for these individuals who may not have substantial credit histories.

However, different brands will want to approach Gen eXcel in different ways, and traditional media should not be written off. As with all campaigns, Gen eXcel campaigns need to consider what each medium means to the consumer and how that medium and the content of its campaign adds to or detracts from the brand. A study conducted by BBDO New York of 104 adults reveals the media perceptions of this generation.[6] They describe the Internet as a means of escape and mental stimulation, as well as a way of gathering specialized information. They added that the medium gave them feelings of intelligence, accomplishment, and innovation. Users of the Internet were described as young and career oriented. As an interesting comparison, magazine readers were described as–attractive! Feelings of luxury, creativity, and sexiness were associated with reading magazines, and they were seen as a place to gain current information and to reward oneself. TV was described as a means for entertainment or ending the day, and largely was associated with homemakers and family. Watching TV was said to impart feelings of happiness, comfort, and fun. Newspapers were seen as a means of gathering in-depth information first thing in the morning, and readers were perceived as being middle-aged and, more often than not, male. Feelings imparted by reading the paper included security, stability, and respect. Radio was described as a background medium listened to in the morning or while doing other activities. It gave feelings of relaxation and youthfulness to listeners, and listeners were perceived as being young and hip. Based on these findings, one would assume that newspapers would be an excellent medium for advertising "serious" products, like financial related services, whereas TV would be seen as an excellent place for products associated with fun; however, such findings only provide hints and background information on how advertising can and will function in these mediums. Many of the most successful campaigns will take account of these traditional expectations and uses regarding specific media, and then subvert these expectations to grab the attention of bored eXcelers. Although seducing the eXcels is difficult, even for experienced and creative professionals, it can be done through a thorough knowledge of their life and lifestyles. To help provide this, I asked Peter Levine, executive creative director at my firm and director of d/g* Consulting, to lend us his expert knowledge on this generation.

The Generation that "'Tude" Built *by Peter L. Levine*

They all agree—"We hate the term 'Generation X.'" They can't be pinned down. Big surprise—they also haven't renamed themselves. Instead they wear the moniker X, Hester Prynne–like into the new millennium. X = void, X = placeholder for what is to come, X = naughty, rebellious X-rated. X marks the spot where the bomb is about to drop.

After studying this generation intimately (I've lived with a world-class Xer for five years), I have learned their badge is really one of possibility. The generation that was the first group of youngsters who were told, "Sorry guys, every American generation before you has had the ability to do better than their parents but the buck stops here. You guys have a whole lot of cleaning up to do." They were to inherit our debt. Social Security would run out. Job advancement would be scarce. Homes would be too expensive to purchase. They were angry—trusted no one except themselves, and this little group that forced schools to close because of their dwarfed numbers compared to the enormity of the Boomers, turned into the little generation that could. How? With a whole lot of "attitude." If asked what the single biggest impact Generation X has made upon the consumer landscape, I would have to answer thus: They were the first generation that said "What's in it for me?" Makes sense coming from the kids who heard "There is nothing left for you. The tickets to the American Dream are all sold out." "What's in it for me?" meant that brands could not sell the same way they once did. It was enough for many years for products to simply tell us how good they were. How well they were made. How affordable they were. How they would improve our lives. How much better they were than the other guy. How long they have been around, which meant that we should trust them. And, basically, how happy and content they would make us once they were in our lives. Our breath would be fresher, our ride would be smoother, and all of those wonderful ingredients would somehow brighten our boring lives. Generation X was brought up on all of those

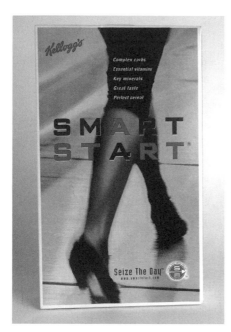

brands that told us how great they were against a backdrop of a openly troubled society: drugs, disease, a crumbling economy, broken families, and devastating unemployment rates, and razor blades in their Halloween candy! The response when they came of age was: "Yeah, so? I've heard how great you are my whole life and I know what phony advertising sounds like." This gave birth to a new paradigm of communication. The walls came tumbling down. We suddenly embarked upon a new era of relationship branding. Brands were forced down from the pedestal and asked to find a "handshake" between themselves and this newly desired consumer group that by their very nature defied definition.

These are some of the new rules:

Is It Hip/Cool?	Can I See Myself in the Message?
Is It Original?	Is It Honest?
Is It Flashy?	Is It Fun?
Is It News?	Is It Interactive?
Is It Creative?	Is It Cynical?
Is It My Community?	Does It Show I Have Style?
Is It Me?	Is It Humorous?
Is It Sexy?	Is It Real?

. . . Does it show I am one smart, brave, bad-ass success?!

Generation X is evolving into Generation lu"X"e as they break all of the rules and define the new economy. They are trading up to show they can afford it now! While sensible Boomers would "prolong" acquiring the badges that signify success until they had actually achieved a certain status—live-for-today Xers have demonstrated the opposite by donning the badges of success early and demonstrating that they are ever poised for such a state. This is the reason we see such heightened consumer activity at both high-end retail luxury brands and downscale mass merchants such as Target. "Hip and Cool" has suddenly become an important product feature and benefit. Evian water is a great example that sells itself today as a hip luxury rather than a connection to a natural source. Kellogg's Start Smart cereal broke every rule of cereal marketing to show a hip urban young person on the go rather than show crunchy flakes and juicy raisins in a bowl of milk. The Xers have managed to usher in the "alternative" to everything. Independent films, the Internet, cable TV, alternative music, alternative medicine. They will continue to show their entrepreneurial spirit as they age. Unbelievably smart (the most-educated American generation so far), they are savvy and pragmatic and exchange information as bargaining chips.

Raised on television, I'm convinced that they are the first true pop-culture generation. I have ferreted out some of the childhood influences that make up the Xer's DNA.

Recipe for a Gen-X Cocktail

1 part Scooby-Doo. The first cartoon that was anti-Archie. A wandering band of misfits that traveled the world solving mysteries with a talking dog, a stoner, and Velma, the first lesbianlike cartoon character. This gang banded together to roam the world, have adventures, get in trouble, and survive in the end.

1 part Wonder Woman. She was one tough girl who looked great but could kick ass with a single magic spin. She demonstrated that to break free meant being superhuman.

1 part Jan Brady. Stuck between the beautiful, popular Marsha and lisping, adorable Cindy, Jan the middle child was the misunderstood heart and soul of Gen X.

1 part Teenage Mutant Ninja Turtles. They were flushed down the toilet and had to survive in the sewer on chemical waste. The perfect representation of the times they were growing up in. It meant growing a tough skin for survival.

1 part Sammy Jo. She infiltrated the Carrington dynasty as poor white trash and showed those rich people who was boss. She represented the generation's desire to win against all odds.

1 part Luke Skywalker and Princess Leia. Even light years away, the Xers could identify with the overwhelmingly outnumbered youngsters who had to save the empire by using their wits to fight for good against evil.

1 part Supermodel. Fame and fortune and looking amazing from head to toe were a new form of competition.

1 part Madonna. She never let a lack of talent stop her from her ambitions of being a world-famous celebrity.

It's all there in the Gen-X DNA. They will be the easiest generation to forget again, as the aging Boomer population steals the limelight and redefines what it means to age in this country, and as Generation Y redefines what it means to be young and discover a new world. But Gen X has gotten our attention, seized our psyche, and forced us to change the way we speak about what we sell. They are perhaps the most tenacious generation yet. They refuse to adhere to any road map and can turn on a dime to acquire a new strategy or skill set to win with. Their next chapter can only be a hypothesis and written by them alone.

Generation Y: Coming Right at You (at Warp Speed)

The seventy-six million members of Generation Y, born 1977–94, compose a tidal wave poised to redefine America in general and branding in particular. The sweeping social changes which spawned a new world before the eyes of Generation X and the Boomers–the fall of Communism, technology's ubiquitous presence, a spiraling Dow Jones–have been the positive backdrop for their entire lives. Although still evolving, this generation's emotional palette and passions are entirely unique and comprise a fascinating challenge for Emotional Branding. And, considering that today's twelve-to-eighteen-year-olds get an average of $50 a week from their parents, winning their hearts and minds has very real rewards. Furthermore, estimates expect their current $70 billion in spending power to grow to $180 billion by 2025. Brands need to understand this generation today if they plan on serving them tomorrow.

The "warp-speed generation" would be a fair title for this group.

The "warp-speed generation" would be a fair title for this group. They are going faster and doing more than any previous generation. A November 1999 study conducted at the University of Michigan found that 75 percent of kids' time is preprogrammed today. Soccer leagues, homework, and family responsibilities have eaten away at this group's free time–today's average twelve-year-old has less than three hours of free time a week, ten less than their 1981

Hangtags for Mudd, the Gen Y fashion brand.

counterparts had. What little free time they have is heavily multitasked like the PC software they are so adept at using. It's not uncommon for them to be surfing the 'Net while talking on the phone and listening to their favorite CD. The activities which absorb them fully do it through demanding and concisely packed content. After all, this generation has been reared in the era of the sound bite. When trying to reach this generation, advertising needs to be brief and sans fluff. One popular ad campaign by Arizona Jeans, which was directed at this generation, featured teens mocking flashy ad campaigns and demanding "Just show me the jeans."

Targeting this age group is complicated because they have a tendency to reject the "mainstream," and as soon as a brand becomes big it is in danger of falling into their disfavor. Success = sellout = bad. Hence, brands must walk a fine line between prominent exposure and overexposure. Many have attributed Abercrombie & Fitch's recent lower stock evaluation by analysts to overexposure within this generation. Hampton Carney, **Brands should never talk down to these consumers as "kids."** an Abercrombie & Fitch spokesman has refuted this, telling the *Wall Street Journal* that "I have celebrities calling me all the time for free clothes and I turn them down. We don't want to be too out there."[7] However, considering that customers are truly the most significant form of publicity, A&F's customers may be the biggest source of overexposure. By displaying its logo prominently on many of its articles, it invites consumers very publicly to join the A&F fashion club. One of our interns, a twenty-year-old male suburban-raised college student (A&F's main customer), reports having been to parties where over half the men in the room were obviously sporting Abercrombie duds. This is great for building a Gen Y brand, awful for sustaining it. As my intern said, "I would rather believe that I have the strength of character to define myself than rely on a brand written across my chest to do it for me." Ouch. In other words, make your brand present, make it accessible and available–don't shove it down the public's throat and know when to temper its ubiquity. A little bit of exclusivity is always good.

Brands should never talk down to these consumers as "kids." These are the most adult teenagers since the birth of the "teenager" concept; by the time they have reached twelve they have achieved a notable sophistication and aware-ness of the world. These latchkey kids have grown up with an unparalleled access to information coupled with an absence of omnipresent supervision. Consequently, they have developed responsibility and awareness early in life. Having seen the horror of the Columbine killings, metal detectors at school, and the president of the United States testifying about oral sex, they are aware of the hypocrisy and danger that prevail in public (and private) life. Similarly, the high expectations put on them–from family, school, and friends–have developed precocious maturity in a large body of this generation. It follows that branding strategies that underestimate the sophistication of this generation will fail. However, brands that respect the mature identity of these youngsters and supplement that identity are among the most successful. Surveys among teens have uniformly identified intelligence as an important value in their lives and brands aimed at them should recognize and showcase their acuity.

The Bubblegum Crew, a group of cartoon characters with their own line through American Greetings' cards, taps into the complex identities and b.s.-piercing self-conception of Gen Yers, as well as their elders, the Xers. Based around twenty-nine characters such as Dancing Queen, Diet Slave, and Sun Junkie, these cartoon characters playfully poke fun at the personality stereo-types which populate the Gen Y social scene. Is it a little odd to send your best friend a card which implies that she resembles the "Fitness Freak" character? Not for Gen Y that disdains romanticized depictions and the traditionally sappy nature of greeting cards. By depicting the characters with big, goofy faces and bursting with neon colors, American Greetings has accessed Gen Y's gentle cynicism and provided an easy, convenient, and, most importantly, amusing way for them to interact in a medium which they normally would reject

(American Greetings has found that the typical greeting card customer is female and fifty years old). American Greetings is following the launch of these characters with stationary, key chains, plush dolls, and other related products. Aimed at seventeen- to twenty-three-year-olds, this line is one for which I anticipate success, based simply on the fact that two hip young employees at my office in New York City have adorned their workspace with characters from the Crew.

Gen Y demonstrates an unprecedented sensitivity to global issues, such as poverty, war, environmentalism, as well as race, gender, or sexual orientation discrimination issues. The sense of empowerment and knowledge that marks this generation's outlook on life has also reshaped social activism, revealing not only their intelligence, but also their altruism. But unlike their Boomer parents who challenged the status quo and took the streets for change, this generation is more apt to volunteer. All their lives this generation has been praised and told it could do whatever it wanted, and with that encouragement they have chosen to apply themselves to improving a screwed-up world. *They hold civic responsibility in high regard and whereas their Boomer parents fought to topple society, today's youth would rather fix it up.*

The Nickelodeon Big Help campaign, more than any other Gen Y "cause" marketing, has made an exciting and meaningful connection with young Gen Yers. Having recruited the aid of such cultural luminaries as Mariah Carey and Shaquille O'Neal, Big Help provides a conduit for youth across the country to channel their energy and aspirations toward helping the public good. Since Nickelodeon started this program in 1994, over twenty-eight million kids have joined forces to clean up the environment and improve their immediate community by pledging community service hours–262 million hours as of 2000. According to the Big Help Web page, "Like everything at Nickelodeon, it started with kids! Kids told us they were concerned about people, animals, and the environment. They wanted to make a difference in their communities and the world. And with each new challenge they tackled, they succeeded."[8] The program features a Helpmobile that travels the United States promoting civic-minded behavior wherever it stops. Within the twenty-four-foot converted Airstream trailer are interactive computers which teach kids how to improve the world, and each stop invites community groups such as the Lions Club and Rotary Club to teach the kids more about community service. For the past two years the tour has gone to those cities where the most kids pledged to work on revitalizing community parks. Once there, Nickelodeon donates money and workers to help the kids who show up. A stunning example of Emotional Branding, Big Help emphasizes that it's about the kids and what they want to do, connecting them to their aspirations, forming a community in the process, and achieving their goals.

Value-driven behavior among Gen Y is also linked to an increase in traditional values. Like their elder Gen Xers, Gen Yers has seen enough of divorce and strongly intend to avoid it in their lives. However, while they may not wish to emulate their parents' marriages, they still hold their parents in high regard. A survey by Yankelovich Partners in 1999 found that 94 percent of teenage girls consider their mothers to be friends. Eighty percent claimed that their mothers understand them. Mothers and daughters alike characterized one another as intelligent, honest, and attractive.

This fits into the overarching trend among these youth that exhibits integrity and respect for authority, as well as disdain for arrogance (seems like a diet of Bart Simpson and rap may not be as subversive as was expected). Hence, when approaching this generation, brands should recognize that trashing their parents and other elder influences is a big mistake. There is also an interesting dichotomy between this generation's individuality and its conformity. Although, like most youth, they have a profound need to fit in with their peers and are keen on being part of the latest, most hip trends, they also consider themselves to be autonomous individuals and express a desire to customize fashions to meet their personal needs, regardless of the trend. This desire is matched by an increasingly fragmented market, ranging from the media to consumer goods, which caters to individualized tastes. And with the Internet at their disposal, they can freely and independently of their parents develop their own tastes. Whether it's Pokemon fan clubs or a passion for snow boarding, there is a broad cultural offering at their disposal. Increasingly, with the advent of mass-customization technology, they will be able to create their own product lines and further develop this yen for individual expression.

The Internet may not, despite the hype, necessarily be the foremost venue of the Generation Y's consumer demands.

Bubble-yum has attempted to ally their brand to the teens' individuality sensibility via the "Blow your own bubble campaign" which stars a duck who sports a Mohawk, spiked collar, nose ring, and anklet. The nonconformist cartoon character blows bubbles that, literally, blow away all the other average, normal-looking ducks. Bubble-yum, whose Gen Y sales had been slipping, have found that twelve- to seventeen-year-old males seem to identify with the foul fowl. The campaign has also reached into cyberspace, where screen savers featuring the duck are available for download.

On that note, it's worth saying that the Internet may not, despite the hype, necessarily be the foremost venue of the Generation Y's consumer demands. This generation, more thoroughly versed in and accustomed to computer technology than any other, exhibits ease with the Internet and it would seem that they would also be natural techno-shoppers. It has been projected that the sixteen- to twenty-two-year-old group will spend roughly $4.5 billion online in 2000. But for Gen Y, it is a means of staying connected that provides a feeling of empowerment—it is this feeling of empowerment that has proved one of the greatest draws. *In particular, Generation Y enjoys using the Internet as a social space. However, until now they have shown a dislike for shopping on the Internet.* Although some Gen Y businesses have had marked success with Internet sites, this generation is nothing if not experience driven. Uninterested in two-dimensional substitutes for the real thing, this generation craves a more direct interactivity and sensorial experience in marketing. In addition, they crave speed. When it comes to shopping—the experience of experiencing of perusing, evaluating, and selecting consumer goods with their friends—the Internet has been a bit of a turnoff. They recognize the hype surrounding e-commerce and they're not particularly impressed. In one instance, *USA Today* provided teens with $500 to spend as they pleased on the Internet and the participants uniformly complained that they missed the mall experience—even those teens that were not fond of malls. They also complained about the slow loading time.[9] For this generation, ten seconds is often too long. Their desire for immediate gratification is frustrated by the delays of slow-loading Web pages and weeklong shipping waits. Web sites may be most useful as a means of furthering the brand identity—a space for previewing new fashions and interacting with others who have the same interest.

dELiA's forays into Internet have shown such foresight and Gen Y understanding that has become this company's trademark. When CEO Stephen Kahn first sought support for his plan to direct-market teenage girls, he was roundly rejected. Undeterred, Kahn used his own savings and the money of family and friends to fund dELiA's, which now boasts over $150 million in annual revenues. According to CFO Evan Guilleman, "Within three years we had cornered 100 percent of the direct-mail market."[10] dELiA's then turned to the Internet and bought out *gurl.com*, a popular Web site for girls, and linked it to its own Web page. *Gurl.com* boasts frequently updated articles on important issues to girls, such as sports and dating, provides services such e-mail accounts and personal Web pages, and, of course, access to *dELiAs.com*. Although there is a wealth of fashion and beauty information on *gurl.com*, it is not commercialized or designed to directly stimulate shopping. Instead, sections like "Looks Aren't Everything" deflate overblown conceptions of beauty through honest yet tongue-in-cheek columns like "The Boob Files" and "On Being Hairy," or games like "Messy Girl" and "Blemish Remover." All the info is highly personalized, often in the mode of testimonials, and visitors to the site are asked to provide their own input that is commonly represented on the site itself. Highly interactive and reaching visitors as sentient, emotional, and complex beings rather than customers, this Web site is a model of how to interact with youth respectfully on that medium which, for all practical purposes, belongs to them. By dealing with the whole person first, dELiA's gets a shot at their patronage later. Gen Y appreciates this.

In what other ways can brands catch the attention of these youngsters who, perhaps more than any other generation, have "seen it all"? By approaching them directly and putting it in their face, on their back, in their hands or the hands of someone they admire, brands can intimately connect to this generation. American Eagle outfits the cast of the popular teen show *Dawson's Creek*. Tommy Hilfiger put its clothes on rappers. Guerrilla marketing efforts are enormously successful with Gen Y. The advantage of this style of marketing is the ability to directly target clients and communicate with them in their own language without confusing adults. By selectively and personally targeting consumers, particularly the most influential and trendy members of this generation, this approach has an edge and appeal unmatched by other forms of marketing.

The biggest challenge with Generation Y will be to keep abreast of their fast-moving lifestyle and quickly evolving taste.

This is the main reason why promotional events are gaining popularity in marketing, but I believe they are still a relatively unexplored territory in terms of the powerful contribution they can make to an Emotional Branding strategy. Events are a great way to showcase brands in a festive, emotionally charged atmosphere–particularly to experience craving Gen Yers. Krystal Co., a sandwich chain with about 365 stores, has done some wonderfully appropriate work in this category. Its events are simple–college burger-eating com-

BABY BOOMERS
(36-54)
APPROX: 30% POP. BORN 1946-64
81 MILLION PEOPLE
SPEND OVER 900 BILLION ANNUALLY

Generation as Icon

"US"

DEFINING GENERATION

EXPERIENCED:
Rock and Roll
Television
Protests / Riots
Space Exploration
Vietnam War / Hippies / Protests
Racial Divides
Sexual Revolution
Yuppies
New Definition of 50

RESPOND TO:
Cues of Achievement / Status / Heroes
Iconic Authority
Heroes / Trailblazers
The things that are earned
Comfort
"I've earned it luxury"
Perks
Anti-Aging

GEN-X *or 13ers*
(24-35)
APPROX: 17% POP. BORN 1965-76
46 MILLION PEOPLE
SPEND 125 BILLION ANNUALLY

Generation as Individual

"I"

REBELS / INFLUENCERS

EXPERIENCED:
Disappointed Children of Divorce
Driven To Independence
AIDS Era Maturity
Crack / Gangs / Violence
Downsized Parents
Pop Culture
Information Explosion

TODAY:
Defy Traditional Structures
Entrepreneurial
Highly Educated / Money Driven
Taking Charge to show the power of their voice

RESPOND TO:
Themselves Reflected in Images / Messages
Fierce Sarcasm / Imagination, Creativity
Stupid / Smart Messages
Deconstructed Paradigms
Style
Luxury Goods and Mass Market

GEN-Y *or millenials, echo boomers, baby busters*
(6-23)
APPROX: 28% POP. BORN 1977-94
75 MILLION PEOPLE
SPEND 35-100 BILLION ANNUALLY

Generation as Philosophy

"ALL"

CONSCIENCE

EXPERIENCE:
Integration
Understand Multi-Layered Info.
Brought up in the Era of Brands
Unity
Optimistic
Reared in the Era of Psychology
Birth of the Future
Recycling

RESPOND TO:
New Ideas
Companies with a Philosophy
"Multi-Sensory" Experiences
Multi Generational Messages
Messages that acknowledge they are smart
Fun / Learning
Parents as their Heroes
Interesting People
Sense of Community

EVOLUTION OF ATTITUDES △	EVOLUTION OF ATTITUDES △	EVOLUTION OF ATTITUDES
ICONS-ROCK & ROLL, MOVIE, SPORT & POLITICAL, BUSINESS FIGURES	ALTERNATIVE MUSIC / FASHION IDOLS / CELEBRITY	BREAKTHROUGH VOICES / TALENT WITH MESSAGES
MARKETING INFLUENCED	ANTI-MARKETING INFLUENCED	MARKETING SAVVY
RACE DIVIDED	MULTI-ETHNIC	GLOBAL CULTURE
REALISTIC	PESSIMISTIC	OPTIMISTIC
TECHNOLOGY FEARFUL	TECH-NOLOGY PROFICIENT	TECHNOLOGY INDOCTRINATED
RELIGION	SPIRITUALITY / CONSCIOLSNESS	MYSTICISM
FORTUNE / PROSPERITY	FAME AND FORTUNE	FUN / INTERACTIVITY
ESCAPE / FANTASY	EXPERIENCE / REALITY	SOCIAL RESPONSIBILITY
ASPIRATION	INSPIRATION	FUN NOSTALGIA
WARM NOSTALGIA	HIP NOSTALGIA	SEXUALITY
SEX	SEXINESS	HEALTHY ATTITUDE
ANTI-AGING / LONGEVITY /MENTAL HEALTH	PHYSICAL HEALTH / WELL BEING	EXTREME SPORTS
MALE / FEMALE	UNISEX	PEOPLE

The information contained in this document was gathered from research books, articles, interviews, focus groups and web sites. @2000 DG Consulting petitions. Students who can scarf the most burgers in sixty seconds win prizes while their peers cheer them on. These events supplement traditional TV and radio campaigns and have the particular advantage of directly reaching their core audience. During the competitions Krystal Co. employees distribute coupons and other promotional items. Marketing that provides this all-encompassing brand experience may be the most novel best way to reach these young consumers. Another excellent example is the Pepsi-sponsored "Joy of Cola" tour, which appeared at twenty-nine major malls across the country offering entertainment, prizes, and, naturally, free Pepsi, to an estimated five hundred thousand consumers who attended.

The biggest challenge with Generation Y will be to keep abreast of their fast-moving lifestyle and quickly evolving taste. Some publications describe this group as "prosumers" because of their power and willingness to dictate what they will and won't buy. As the Internet brings more and more offerings to their doorstep from around the world, and spreads trends at unprecedented speed, businesses that once planned fashion aesthetics and purchasing plans six months in advance must learn to accommodate fashion evolution within a month. As demanding, optimistic, informed, individualistic as this generation is, I must admit that all the clever branding schemas only succeed in providing a pale sketch of their character, and vague hints of their future. The best advice I can give you is stand back and let them lead the way. They'll tell you what they want.

2

Disconnection Alert:
The U.S. Melting Pot Is Hot!

A surprising lack of awareness and some major communication gaps still exist today between the U.S. corporations and the consumer market. We are on the verge of major demographic changes that are already affecting the country and much of corporate America still seems to be, in many respects, dozing. Latino-American, Asian-American, and African-American populations are becoming highly influential groups with new sets of aspirations. Statistically, it is projected that the buying power of these three groups will triple in the next twelve years.

These groups contribute cultures and values that are very different from those of white European immigrants who have dominated the political and sociological landscape in the United States for the last two hundred years. Although we are already seeing the contrasts inherent to today's rich mosaic of population in the marketplace, most businesses don't yet have a **That is, people want to deal with corporations that are responsive and sensitive to their unique needs.** management that reflects this diverse population. In most cases, companies are still run by a very homogeneous Caucasian male leadership. This has created serious problems for companies in terms of a complete disconnection from the market and, in some cases, the fostering of corporate environments where racism can exist, as in the deplorable case of Texaco where African-American employees were discriminated against by top management that made racist jokes behind closed doors. In today's corporate cultural landscape this is viewed as inexcusable and highly dangerous; in the future it will be, quite simply, a company's death knell.

There is a new expectation out there, and it has everything to do with

Emotional Branding. That is, people want to deal with corporations that are responsive and sensitive to their unique needs. They want a relationship with brands that understand them. Smart consumers of the future, with powerful smart money, will discriminate between the companies that reflect their values and those that do not.

African-American Consumers

The disparity between the popular media's portrayal of African-Americans and their actual state, coupled with affluent isolation and misunderstanding within the corporate world, has unfortunately led some corporations to overlook opportunities with African-American consumers, perpetuating stereotypes instead of the kind of understanding that leads to real emotional contact with a brand.

Understanding the African-American culture means tapping into a market representing 12.2 percent of the population, half of which belongs to the middle class. This demographic is gradually becoming more affluent and educated and this year will have approximately $400 billion in annual income, which is indeed quite a sizable force.[1] This group's financial clout is considerable and seems to be only beginning truly to flex its muscle.

Despite the fact that most African-Americans have only known life in America, and parity with whites is creeping their way, they retain a sense of identity that separates them from whites and other minority groups, as well as independent and identifiable value systems. Both formal and anecdotal evidence indicates that African-Americans are proud of their culture and history. Nearly 70 percent of African-Americans feel the need to sustain ethnic traditions and symbols, as opposed to 46 percent of all other Americans. Seventy-eight percent of African-Americans believe that "parents should pass on ethnic traditions," versus 62 percent of all other groups, and 90 percent of African-Americans agree with the statement "I am proud of my ethnic heritage."[2] African-Americans spend more time at church, do less housework, and more child care compared with their white counterparts with comparable education and wealth. The African-American population is also younger and more likely to have families than European-Americans. Approximately three-quarters of African-Americans reside in urban areas; however, as they grow more affluent, many more African-Americans are migrating to the suburbs. Although there is a slow but sure rise to greater affluence in this population, the African-

American population remains highly sensitized to the economic disparities in America. According to a *New York Times* poll of 1,003 adults spread out across America conducted in March 2000, 69 percent of African-Americans feel that the growing income gap in America is morally wrong.[3] African-American businesses have been growing at rate exceeding those of whites, approximately 7 percent annually, as opposed to 5 percent for all other groups, and American society is witnessing the emergence of African-American enterprises in many skill-intensive areas of business and professional services. African-Americans have also been showing greater increases in college attendance and completion than Caucasians, Hispanics, and Asians.

African-Americans have consumption patterns which distinguish them from other groups, and brands should be aware of these patterns, even as they apply to industries which have no direct bearing on their own. For example, African-Americans have shown an increasing propensity in recent years to travel to places that have a history of their roots, such as the Caribbean, Africa, and South America. For that reason, an ad campaign that intended to appeal to the aspirations of African-Americans, even if it was touting the advantages of a particular investment plan, might be more successful depicting an African-American family visiting the Virgin Isles than Prague. That being said, some other trends worth noting include:

- Cars: the growth rate of African-Americans purchasing new cars is twelve times that of non-African-American auto purchases over the last decade.[4]

- Health and beauty: 10 percent of all dollars spent by African-Americans are spent on health and beauty aids. Most cosmetic companies in both prestige and mass-distribution categories do not market their products in a specific way to African-American women and there are surprisingly few product lines created specifically for African-American women (or other women of color). This is an opportunity begging to be developed since the ethnic makeup category is expected to reach $224 million by the year 2002.[5] African-Americans account for 30 percent of all hair-care products sold. In particular, the U.S. Census has noted that the African-American woman represents the greatest segment growth in consumption in this category. This demographic has very specific hair-care product needs and tends to be less straitjacketed by typical Western conceptions of beauty than other American women.

- Food: big purchasers in a whole array of food categories, African-Americans accounted for 25 percent of Coca-Cola's sales in 1995, as well as large portions of candy bars, corn, sausage, coffee, canned meat, and tomato sauce. Particularly fond of sweets, African-American households spend, on average, 54 percent more on sugar than the average white household, and African-Americans account for a whopping 50 percent of the Cognac market![6]

- Retail: African-Americans often spend a high amount of their income in retail, particularly clothing. That includes $380 million on men's suits and $377 million on hosiery in 1998. African-Americans also spend more per capita on children's apparel than whites ($266 versus $186 in 1998).[7] This also holds true in footwear. African-Americans also spend 75 percent more on boys' clothes than their white counterparts.[8]

Many African-Americans report that shopping is their favorite activity, although few are loyal to any one retailer. In the past they have exhibited brand loyalty, although they are becoming increasingly critical of brands, marketing, and advertising, and less willing to blindly embrace a brand. However, they will offer brand loyalty in return, if brands remain attentive and respectful to these consumers. Over 60 percent cite "respect" as the reason they choose one retailer over another.[9]

Just look at the success in the African-American community of FUBU, the highly popular, fast-growing African-American-owned-and-targeted clothing company. These consumers know that they are recognized and respected by this brand, which continually contributes to their lives in the most sincere and effective ways, by promoting education and nonviolence initiatives in the African-American youth community. This is why they were the very first company to win an Essence award for humanitarian achievement. When FUBU accepted the award, it was with the words: "Remember that the black dollar has power!" The audience cheered like mad. Why? Not just because they were happy to be reminded of their power, but because they *are* remembering!

Although African-Americans see much of the same advertising and promotional campaigns as other Americans, they often interpret these campaigns differently. Many commercials may come across as irrelevant, particularly those directed at white suburban families. However, it is to the credit of many brands and advertising firms that minority representation in advertising is more and more frequently prominent. There are specific means and methods that African-American consumers are particularly responsive to.

For example, African-American consumers have a strong favoring for personal contact, as opposed to direct mail.[10] Churches, shopping centers, and sporting events are all excellent venues for approaching them. The advantage of face-to-face marketing is that it attaches a real person to a brand and establishes greater credibility. As I just mentioned, FUBU is a master at this. The owners still frequent their home places in Queens, New York, and make a point of not appearing "distant" or changed because of their wealth and success. FUBU also stays active in community service, and has handed out turkeys during Thanksgiving and filled the wish lists for needy children at Christmastime. When companies such as FUBU are active and involved in the African-American community, demonstrating their investment and authentic interest, African-Americans communities clearly respond to this kind of commitment. Partnerships that raise money for local schools or sup-

Marketing will be more relevant to these communities when it is managed by agencies that either are African-American-run or else have a great deal of experience with African-American communications.

port community events are also an excellent means for a company to illustrate its interest. Of course marketing will likely be more relevant to these communities when it is managed by agencies that either are African-American-run or else have a great deal of experience with African-American communications. Volvo, which has received criticism in the past for neglecting minorities, formed a "minority diversity business council" in 2000 that consults with African-American and Hispanic business and community leaders in order to place future marketing and advertising. Also, advertising aimed at African-Americans must establish long-term relationships with African-American media, such as newspapers and radios, rather than present a sudden burst campaign that quickly fades. General Motors achieved this through an agreement with BET Holdings Inc., holder of Black Entertainment Television cable network, as well as the African-American-oriented print publications *Emerge, Heart & Soul*, and *BET Weekend*. This agreement provides an outlet for GM advertising in print and television, as well as on *BET.com* and possible BET-produced films. Although GM has been working with BET for some time, this one-year deal struck in 1999 created a long-term multiplatform arrangement that provides deep and consistent penetration into the African-American consumer market and varying demographics of African-American consumers. However, big-budget buys are not necessarily the key to success. Because marketing to African-Americans is most often about creating resonance in smaller communities, grassroots work through small local newspapers should not be underestimated, and often offers some of the best-priced media buys available.

One of the dangers of marketing schemas and demographic sketches is that they often reduce complex, multifaceted audiences to stereotypical simplifications that lack the original groups' rich diversity. Most crucial is an approach that is based on respect and emotional relevance. Ploys to sweep up a generic African-American consumer with a burgeoning income may very well fail, because they seem (and are!) insincere. However, *carefully crafted campaigns that articulate a brand's interest in serving and empowering individuals and their surrounding community will succeed, regardless of race and ethnicity.*

Hispanic Consumers

If there's one thing marketers, advertisers, and the media in general love, it's hype, and in the past year and a half there's been absolutely no shortage of hype about the growing power of Hispanic culture in the United States. "Latin U.S.A." proclaimed one cover of *Newsweek* in 1999, while Ricky Martin graced the face of *Time*. However, while the subjects of media hype will come and go with whatever frequency is necessary to keep the public stimulated, the phenomenal growth and impact of this burgeoning Hispanic affluence, matched by increased political and cultural clout and sustained by a population explosion that will soon make them the major "minority" in the United States and, in time, enable them to reach population parity with Caucasians, make the importance of this population impossible to dismiss.

According to the U.S. Census Bureau, in 2000 Hispanics composed 11.4 percent of the U.S. population, putting them only 8 percent behind African-Americans, the largest minority group in the United States. With immigration and high birth rates, in 2005 Hispanics will number approximately thirty-six million, putting their numbers just over those of non-Hispanic African-Americans. In the last fifty years, Hispanics have accounted for almost a quarter of the population expansion in the United States, and today one out of every nine Americans is Hispanic. Currently, the United States is the fifth largest Spanish-speaking country in the world; by 2020 half of American youth will be Hispanic, and by 2050 nearly one quarter of the population will be Latino.[11]

Brands that want to serve this expansive community will have to work hard to meet its needs and earn its loyalty. Businesses that start today will have an advantage over later entrants, but still must realize that Hispanics are not a new phenomenon in the United States, nor is their consumer muscle. It is behind groups like Procter & Gamble, Sears, Philip Morris, and Toyota, which have been aggressively courting these consumers for years now. Fortunately for marketers and advertisers, particularly those which use Spanish language, the Hispanic population is heavily concentrated in just six states: California, Texas, New York, Florida, Illinois, and New Jersey, and more than 60 percent live in just ten cities.[12] In all, 90 percent of Hispanics live in major metropolitan areas and a full two-thirds of Latinos in the United States live above the poverty line.

Although they share a common language and may appear to many uninitiated Caucasians to be relatively homogeneous, Hispanics are a complex composite that varies by nationality, age, and economic class, to name a few factors. Estimates have identified seventeen Hispanic subcultures based largely on approximately twenty-two different countries as places of origin. The resulting kaleidoscope of individual Hispanic communities across the United States includes every hybrid possible. These major communities are: Californians (primarily immigrant Mexicans and middle-class Mexicans), Tejanos (Mexicans and Guatemalans who have created a cowboy culture primarily in Texas), Chicago Latinos (primarily Mexicans and Puerto Ricans; this group comprises 27 percent of Chicago's population), Miamians (primarily Cubans, Nicaraguans, and South Americans), New Yorkers (3.6 million Latinos in total, comprised mostly of Puerto Ricans, Dominicans, Colombians, and Cubans).

Hispanics have accounted for almost a quarter of population expansion in the United States, and today one out of every nine Americans is Hispanic.

Of equal or greater import in understanding Hispanic subcultures, however, are degrees of acculturation among Hispanics. Over a quarter of the Hispanic population in America remains unacculturated (28 percent). A determined and hardworking immigrant population, these individuals remain Spanish-dependent. Largely impoverished or working-class, these Hispanics are working their way up from the bottom of American society. Although some conservative movements in the eighties and early nineties directly and indirectly disparaged these men and women (and sometimes their children as well), their tenacity is admirable and their commitment to "making it" deserves the recognition and respect of brands which may now, or in the future, have the fortune of providing products and services for them.

The majority of the U.S. Hispanic population (59 percent), however, is partially acculturated, having been born in the United States or spent more than eleven years here. Largely middle-income and bilingual, these are the Hispanics who have successfully carved a niche in American society and cruise between American and Hispanic culture, watching Telemundo at home and telling jokes in English to their friends at work. Their children will, in turn, compose and enlarge the slice of Hispanics in the United States described as highly acculturated (13 percent). Generally United States–born and raised, this group is primarily reliant on English and tends to be upper-income. They are the most well-educated and affluent Hispanic group, and their numbers will swell dramatically as Hispanics become more fully acculturated.[13] *If integration and advancement proceed at current rates, Hispanics can expect to occupy almost four million positions in professional and managerial roles by 2020*, dramatically increasing their power to influence and determine national directions and agendas, as well as national identity.[14] It is highly likely that future Hispanics will play a definitive role in rendering constructions such as "ethnic majority/minority" and "race" irrelevant in the public mind. In order to speak to this audience, marketers must recognize the varying degrees of acculturation and English language.

It's also crucial that marketers remember that the Hispanic market is very young, its median age merely 25.9, versus 33.2, the national median. Many of these young Latinos, called "Generation Ñ" by *Newsweek*,[15] in part because of the prominence of stars like Jennifer Lopez, Salma Hayek, and Ricky Martin, are trendsetters and widely emulated by segments of white suburban youth. Their rich cultural heritage, which may extend from Long Island to El Salvador, encompassing many gradations of Anglo- and Hispanic-American culture, puts them in a unique position to influence American society and appropriate trends and fashions from different cultures.

Estimates of Hispanic buying power for 2000 vary, although $275 to $300 billion estimated by the U.S. Census Bureau, derived from per capita income population projections, is a fair estimate. By 2015 that figure will balloon some 65 percent to approximately $450 billion. Los Angeles, New York, and Miami claim the greatest single-city shares of Hispanic buying power, holding $57 billion, $35 billion, and $15 billion, respectively in 1998. These figures are still handicapped by the lower per capita income and higher rates of unemployment. However, that should be recognized not as deficit but rather as growth potential, both among newly arrived Hispanic immigrants and their offspring.[16] Again, the sooner brands recognize this potential and the cultural trends surrounding this growth, the better they can position themselves to cater to this market's current and future needs.

Although nearly all industries can and should tap into Hispanic consumers' needs, there are eight key areas in which Hispanics spend as much as or more than their non-Hispanic counterparts. These are:

- Food consumed at home
- Apparel
- Telephone services
- Rental housing
- TV/radio and other equipment
- Personal-care products
- Public transportation
- Cleaning supplies

Among the spending patterns that distinguish Hispanic consumers is their high spending on personal-care products. They consume greater amounts of shampoo and conditioner than Caucasians, and Hispanic girls spend 60 percent more on makeup than all female teens.[17] There are also higher rates of spending for food eaten at home. Even breakfast patterns are distinguished by ethnic demographic. According to Strategic Research Corporation's survey in 1998, Hispanics were less likely to have eaten cold cereal and more likely to have eaten hot cereal than African-Americans or whites. Cultural influences act in their expectations of services as well. According to Insight Research Company, for 53 percent of Hispanics and Asians, as well as 44 percent of African-Americans, customer service is the most important factor in choosing a phone company.[18] For whites, customer service is a priority for a mere 36 percent of customers.

Because brands play a role in how consumers construct their identity, brand managers must understand what aspects of identity are most salient and influential among Hispanics in order to better serve their aspirational interests. Relative to fashion, Hispanics consider celebrities important trendsetters, and 18 percent of Hispanic-American woman turn to stars for clothing ideas, versus a mere 10 percent among non-Hispanic women. Hispanics generally hold family, religion, and tradition in high regard. The women tend to have more traditional aspirations regarding family and child rearing. Children are seen as precious, and elderly parents are given particular respect and honor. Multigenerational households are common, and Hispanics emphasize their desire to retain traditions from their countries of origin. As is frequently the case, the best way to avoid making an offensive mistake is to constantly monitor lifestyle and inspirational cues from these groups and make diversity a priority in selecting men and women to shape a brand.

Buick began seriously marketing to Hispanics for the first time in 1999 and, despite its inexperience, has shown acuity and sensitivity. It unveiled its first dedicated Spanish-language commercials on Telemundo and Univision. Buick had previously aired Spanish-dubbed versions of English commercials that improved brand awareness in Latino communities but lacked genuine resonance. Viewers knew it was a second-rate appeal to their culture and language. In contrast, the Spanish original ads, which were managed by a Hispanic ad agency and taped in Mexico with local talent and crew, have boosted sales of the featured vehicle, a Buick Century. Hispanic customers have previously accounted for 1 percent of the Century's annual sales, even though they account for 5 percent of national auto sales. Although many businesses have used a low rate of Hispanic patronage as a reason for writing off that demographic, Buick had the insight to recognize that this demographic could become a very important customer for their brand. Research showed that Hispanics seek comfort and amenities in a family car at a reasonable price—exactly the same positioning as the Buick Century. Their efforts have been supported by a Spanish Web site (*www.centurydebuick.com*). Finally, Buick planned a miniature version of the Hispanic-dominated Florida Carnival that GM currently sponsors. Buick's version will tie in to the vehicle and also feature Hispanic celebrities and visit twenty to twenty-five markets. Buick now expects Hispanics to jump from 1 percent of Buick sales to 8 percent by 2010, surpassing the national car purchasing rate among Hispanics. Detailed and far-reaching plans like this are the key to any serious attempt at attracting the Hispanic markets.

Asian-American Consumers

Although slight in their population numbers, Asian-Americans are the fastest-growing ethnic group in the United States and, considering that these 10.5 million people have the highest per capita income of any American ethnic group, including the white majority, they are a force to be reckoned with and a market to crave. Asian-Americans outspend other ethnic groups in important categories like computers, insurance, and international long-distance telephone calls. Many marketers remain confounded by the diversity of Asian-Americans and the absence of detailed research, but this is all the more reason for companies to jump into this market now, thereby gaining an advantage over their competitors. Precisely because so few companies are advertising to Asian-Americans, those that do are able to build incredible brand loyalty.

According to Admerasia, Focus USA,[19] out of today's Asian-Americans:

- 93 percent live in metropolitan areas
- 60 percent have an income of $50,000+
- 50 percent hold professional positions
- 37 percent of Asian-American adults have a bachelor's degree or higher
- 63 percent have credit cards

It is important from the outset to be aware of crucial cultural faux pas in terms of marketing to Asian-Americans such as the fact that most Asian-Americans follow numerology, and combinations of numbers in marketing messages may have undesired meanings for Asians. For example, six and eight are lucky in several Asian cultures, but four rhymes with the Japanese word meaning "good-bye forever" and is associated with death (a good reason why one airline's toll-free telephone number, 1-800-FLY-4444 did not go over well with this market segment!). The same goes for colors: white in many Asian cultures connotes death.

Although there exist at least seventeen different ethnic and linguistic groups in Asia, 90 percent of Asian-Americans belong to one of six groups:

Chinese-Americans are often broken down on the basis of whether they are foreign or native-born. Although the latter are usually more integrated into American society and wealthier, all Chinese-Americans tend to place family and education as high priorities. Particularly among foreign-born Chinese-Americans, advertisers must recognize the distinct meanings associated with symbols and colors otherwise innocuous within American culture. Chinese-Americans generally shop for the best price on goods, but will not sacrifice quality.

Japanese-Americans have been broken down into the less acculturated first- and second-generation residents, and the more acculturated third-generation residents. Of particular interest: the seventeen-year-old female is the fundamental image of advertising within Japan. Plastered on everything from toothbrushes to computers, she embodies the future.

Filipino-Americans are diverse, culturally and linguistically, and because many of their names are of Spanish descent, they are difficult to identify. However, they are largely concentrated in five urban areas: Los Angeles/San Diego, San Francisco/Sacramento, Honolulu, New York, and Chicago.

Korean-Americans are a very aggressive minority, recognized for their business savvy and commitment. A full 80 percent of Koreans in the United States are business owners. Half of Korean-Americans are Protestant churchgoers, and findings indicate that 90 percent are active in ethnic, business, and church-based social organizations. Traditionally Korean-Americans have shown a higher regard for brand name–recognition than price.

Vietnamese-Americans are generally recent immigrants who have little familiarity with American culture. The traditions of their native culture are especially strong because they have so little distance from them. These values include a disfavor for public displays of affection, high regard for family and elders, and although women are regarded the stewards of household budgets, men tend to make the decisions regarding very expensive items.

Indian-Americans are usually very well educated and fluent in English, the mother tongue of their former British colonizers. However, India hosts an array of subcultures, among which Hindi is the dominant second language.

California, New York, Hawaii, Texas, and Illinois are home to over two-thirds of all Asians in America. California alone hosts 40 percent."[20] The *DMA Insider* magazine, in their Winter 2000 issue, classifies Asian immigrants based on three factors:

- Ethnic identification
- Degree of assimilation
- Language dependency

Although these factors can create a complicated number of categories, and eventually illustrate the disunity in supposed "Asian-American" demographic, there remain values that generally unite Asian-Americans. Family and community are of powerful import, much more so than in Anglo-American culture, and most Asian-American households tend to be multigenerational as well as multifamily. Whereas American ads focus on personal choices, Asian-targeted ads may want to put options in the framework of family and community. Ads that flaunt personal status or undermine traditional hierarchies within these families will be ineffective. Ads should also recognize and respect Asian-Americans' desire to retain traditional values yet prosper in the American environment. By some estimates, a full two-thirds of Asian-Americans prefer to speak their own language at home, and studies have indicated that Asian-Americans see it as a sign of respect for companies to market to them in their own language.[21] AT&T concentrates on marketing in seven languages to Asian-Americans from six countries. Advertising that emphasizes this love of traditional cultural values yet avoids stereotypes is effective. The importance of service is also pretty consistent across the various Asian market segments. This means a more polite, formal tone with customers (AT&T, for example, bluntly tells Caucasian Americans "We want you back," but informs Japanese customers, "We are waiting for your call") and a perspective which shows an understanding of the post-sales experience.

Ads that flaunt personal status or undermine traditional hierarchies within these families will be ineffective.

As commercial interests recognized the affluence of this group, there has been an increased presence of Asians in commercial advertising, as evidenced by the campaigns of Merrill Lynch, EveryCD, L'Oréal, Sprint, and Goldman Sachs Group. As research on this group grows, so will advertising budgets. Already blue-chip companies such as Sears, Apple, Hallmark, MCI, Charles Schwab & Company, and the Seagram Company are jumping into the waters. The results of the 2000 Census are sure to spur many more big investments from major categories in this market. Greater efforts than ever before were made on several different fronts to stimulate participation. Thirteen percent of the Census Bureau's $165-million marketing budget for creating awareness was spent on the Asian-American population, and for the first time the questionnaire came in four Asian languages in addition to English and Spanish. There were also efforts organized around getting an accurate count within the community itself.

The San Francisco Asian TV station KTSF has made some advances by funding research of their viewers' consumption habits. These recently published findings indicate that certain brands have been successful at reaching these customers. The brands that topped their consumer-preference survey had either made strong investments in uniquely "Asian" marketing and media, such as AT&T, or they were brands that enjoyed a strong presence in the Asian market and were carried over from the "homeland," such as Coca-Cola,

Pantene, and Tylenol.[22] This survey is reminiscent of similar ones conducted by the Hispanic networks Telemundo and Univision in the eighties that were largely responsible for igniting widespread commercial interest in the Hispanic-American community. As research on Asians grows, it is likely that marketing and commercial investments will also flourish. However, this is no reason to delay investing in these communities. By tapping into the expertise of organizations like the Association of Asian-American Advertising Agencies, based in New York, successful Asian-American forays are fully possible now.

Although I have found few large-scale, well-executed, cohesive campaigns directed at the Asian-American population, I am impressed by the sensitive and thoughtful efforts made by the *New York Times* at attracting Chinese-Americans. They started in February of 1999, when the *Times* distributed Chinese folk-art calendars during celebrations for the Lunar New Year. Subsequently the *Times* pushed for an increase in dealers selling the *Times* within Chinatown. Although all of the *Times'* vending machines had been blue until that point, the Chinatown machines were changed to red because blue is considered a color of mourning among many Chinese, but red indicates happiness. Finally, ads were aimed at Chinese via print, commercial, and direct mail. The commercials aired on local Chinese-language channels, and the direct mail was printed in English and Chinese and featured toll-free numbers for Mandarin and Cantonese, the two dominant dialects of Chinese. The *Times* is an ideal product for this market because it is well-established and positioned as the most respected and authoritative source for well-informed news. Alyse Myers, vice president of promotions and marketing, said of the campaign: "Culturally there is an emphasis on education as the road to success"[23] Chinese-Americans hold education in great esteem and aspire to success for themselves and their children. Consequently, the campaign specifically targeted professionals and the parents of precollege children, who would most appreciate the *Times'* content, and advertisements emphasized the theme of parents' pride in watching their children excel scholastically. The campaign, designed by Asian-American marketing specialists Kang & Lee, New York, has been so successful that it has been expanded to San Francisco, Oakland, and Silicon Valley. Other campaigns directed at New York residents of South Asian and Korean descent are also under way. It clearly pays to pay attention to the needs of the growing Asian-American market!

3

Women: the New "Shoppers in Chief"

The consumer is not an idiot, she's your wife.
–David Ogilvy

I heard another one: She's not an idiot, she's your boss!
–David Lubars, BBDO West

On the gender front, for some time now women have been increasingly influential consumers. It makes me think of the line in the Woody Allen movie *Mighty Aphrodite* when Woody's son asks him who the boss is at home, "you or Mommy?" Woody's now-famous, very telling answer is: "I am the boss, your mom is just the decision maker." Women have long been a powerful but little recognized economic force; they represent 51.2 percent of the U.S. population and they influence or buy 80 percent of products sold;[1] spending close to $3.5 trillion each year![2] Today they not only have more and more buying power, but there is a whole shift in what they are buying and why. For starters, they are buying more products and services traditionally sold to men, like cars, computers, games, hardware, liquor, and cigars.[3] According to the Consumer Electronics Marketing Association, women are great influencers in 50 percent of all consumer electronics purchase decisions and for the past several years computers have topped the holiday gift wish list for women.[4] For some time now these changes have been recognized by many of the smarter corporations, but it is still a whole new way of thinking to some!

Home Depot is built around the premise of making a friendly, attractive, "non-macho" hardware store women would love, and it works. Sears's highly successful campaign, "The softer side of Sears," was an insightful recognition years ago of the fact that most of the in-store purchases–including automotive products–were made by women! Ace Hardware stores are jumping into the game and are now attempting to expand their retail spaces to accommodate and attract more women—who represent a full 50 percent of Ace's annual $13 billion in retail sales—by expanding kitchen, housewares, and garden sections of the stores and increasing the level of service to include, in some cases, even gift wrapping.[5]

In the automotive industry we see that women are the principal buyers for 65 percent of all cars and trucks in the United States,[6] and yet Saturn is one of the few car manufacturers to make a concentrated attempt to woo women. Much of Saturn's advertising is aimed at women, and it makes a conscious effort to hire women salespeople; 17 percent of Saturn's sales staff is composed of women, as opposed to the paltry 7 percent in the rest of the industry. This has paid off for the company: Saturn claims that women buy 64 percent of its cars.[7]

No company today can afford to ignore women. Period.

Ford has attempted to pull more women into its consumer base in an interesting way: by having women design its cars. Ford's 1999 Windstar minivan was designed by fifty women Ford employees, thirty of whom were mothers. These women used their firsthand experience for the implementation of a myriad of special features such as a special low-wattage "baby-mode" light, which would keep light from blaring in a baby's face when a car door opens, or bins with space for folded diapers as well as CDs, and a switch that prevents the driver's door from automatically locking when the key is in the ignition in case the driver has to jump out to tend to children quarreling or crying in the back . . . [8] Still, despite these examples, a surprisingly large number of companies continue to ignore female consumers or, when they do pay attention to them, it is often still through one-dimensional, stereotypical approaches with little understanding of their true desires and needs.

The truth is that no company today can afford to ignore women. The rising influence of women in our world extends far beyond their consumer power and evolving buying habits. Women are a veritable force to be reckoned with in the new economic landscape, and they do and will continue to shape this landscape in ways we can only imagine. Although on the whole women still only earn seventy-six cents to every dollar men earn,[9] and in 1999 they made up only 3.3 percent of the top earners in a selection of 2,353 U.S. companies assessed by Catalyst[10] (holding only 10.6 percent of the total board seats on Fortune 500 companies), a leveling of the playing field is beginning to be in sight. We are seeing significant, if symbolic, progress, such as the appointment this year of a woman as CEO of Hewlett-Packard Co. The fact is that there are vast new opportunities for women in our economy of rapid technological change and globalization. *The new economy has engendered a business atmosphere that requires problem solving, communication, and the manipulation of information, skills in which women are highly developed.* Not to mention the growing importance of creativity, flexibility, and humanism in business today. Women have long been in the entrepreneur mode–the key business model of our time–often working outside of the system as a way of avoiding the glass ceiling. Close to nine million women in the United States own businesses, employing some 27.5 million people, and this figure has risen 78 percent since 1987. Women today own 40 percent of all U.S. enterprises![11]

The Internet revolution is opening more doors than ever before to women because it is an unstructured format with no "old-boy network" to be dealt with, making it easier for women to either strike out on their own or reach higher levels more quickly in companies. The Internet has created an enormous demand for seasoned marketers and media experts, many of whom are women. Also, as a communications medium in the business environment (i.e., virtual conferences, and so on), the Internet does not make gender differences immediately apparent; the focus is instead on content. In 1999 women were chief executives in 6 percent of Internet companies and held top management posts in 45 percent of start-ups. As Gayle Crowell, the president of e.phiphany.net put it when speaking about success in today's market, "It is not about creating the best products or technology, it is more about brand building and knowing the consumer, and women are great at that."[12]

As women rise up through the corporate ranks, their influence on the business world is increasing enormously. Through different approaches to management and business strategy and by stressing the need for more quality time for the management of one's personal life, women are quite simply changing the way business is conducted and organizations operate. We are seeing companies, such as the software company SAS Institute, that offer a myriad of family-friendly flexible benefits to employees, ranging from on-site day-care and medical-care facilities to a family cafeteria. There are unlimited sick days and a thirty-five-hour work week. They are doing this because they want to be competitive in attracting valuable female employees.[13] At Pepsi-Cola North America, CEO Brenda Barnes surprised the corporate world in 1999 by leaving her high position to spend more time with her family after years of having to miss important family events such as her children's birthdays due to her intense itinerary. In the early nineties, Deloitte & Touche noticed the retention of women slipping in the company, instituted many widespread changes, and now says that over seven hundred employees use flexible work arrangements.[14] Deloitte & Touche and the SAS Institute are good examples of corporations that are listening and responding to the demands of a new work force. Eventually, these trends begun by women will have a very strong influence on the whole of the population. In light of women's growing power and influence in the new economy, these companies are certainly smart to invest in their female employees. They are ahead of the game. But we are still at the tip of the women's empowerment trend. *Women are not yet included in the top echelons of many corporations, and often diversity is a concept that reads well in mission statements but is not put into practice in any kind of meaningful way on a regular basis.* In the coming years we must recognize how truly formidable a force women are in our society, and adjust our organizations to reflect their importance. After all, if women are buying most of America's products, why wouldn't companies want to have women at their helms?

We are seeing growth of a much more effective brand of feminism from women who have given up trying to make it in "a man's world" and are going far beyond these narrow confines to create a business environment that corresponds to a more expansive vision. Businesswomen such as Anita Roddick, founder of The Body Shop, have been at the forefront of this movement for some time, using their businesses to make an impact on the world's environmental and social ills and to convey positive messages to women (e.g., "let's not lie about the miraculous antiaging benefits of this wrinkle cream; it's just a great cream and you're OK anyhow with nature's lines . . ."). The new media-convergence maven Gerry Laybourne, previously of Nickelodeon and now, of course, launching the Oxygen cable/Web-based network for women, is a more recent example of the difference an uncompromisingly feminine approach to business can bring. Laybourne, who has been described as "a nurturing Earth Mother, but a powerful infighter too,"[15] brings to her network concept a unique focus on high-quality content programming that is nonviolent, nonexploitative, and emotionally vibrant, with a predilection for shows about "real" women with "real" problems. Like Anita Roddick, she is motivated not only by a desire for business success, but also by a passionate belief in her mission to improve the lives of women and humanity at large. She has described Oxygen as "a grassroots movement."[16]

The old idea of developing products or brand identities around the concept of something for men that women, too, could have, such as the old "Strong enough for a man, but made for a woman . . ." deodorant ad for Secret, seems ancient today! *Women want products, ads, and businesses that are without comparisons to a man's world. They are creating their own world! Companies will do well to tune into this mentality.*

I predict that women will become increasingly valued in the Emotional Economy because they value and are highly sensitive to . . . emotions! Market research has proven time and again that the primary thing that women want, as people and as consumers, is relationships. Women prefer personal, one-on-one networking as a way of finding solutions to business problems, and this is often how they discover products as consumers (i.e., through talking to friends or reliable sources). Women are also largely holistic in their approach to relationships; meaning that they are less likely than men to compartmentalize a brand or company solely according to what it has to offer them in a specific situation. They want to understand the big picture; what the brand stands for on the whole, if the brand's image, philosophy and/or ethics are in sync with their own. They want to feel a deeper, more layered connection. Sounds familiar? It's what Emotional Branding is all about!

Let's take a look at these five key elements to women as consumers—*Respect, Individuality, Stress relief, Connection,* and *Relationship*—via several recent branding programs and ad campaigns. Although, as in the case of any successful Emotional Branding program, several or even all of these points are sometimes touched on in one example, I have for the sake of argument placed them in the categories that they seem to best embody.

* **Respect:** *Women know an awful lot more about carburetors and electric saws than you might think. Talk to them with respect!*
In addition to Saturn, Home Depot, and Sears, some other companies in traditionally "male" industries have begun to talk to women in interesting ways. Michelin targeted women in a clever way in their very successful 1999 ad campaign by showing women presenting tires to a friend at her baby shower. The ad plays with stereotypical images of women at a baby shower with the surprise element of a tire as a gift, and is meant to reinforce the brand's equity as a safe tire, giving a nod and a wink to the fact that they know women are buying more and more of these unconventional items.

What Women Want as Consumers

As consumers, what do women really want? The five most important elements of an Emotional Branding program for women are:

Respect: Women are well-informed. They research products well before buying. They read ingredients much more closely than men to make sure there are no harmful elements, and they are very careful about their decisions.[17] Acknowledge that they are intelligent and informed, and they will respect your brand.

Individuality: Women are playing multiple roles today and do not want to be talked to from only one, narrow perspective. They are feminine, powerful, nurturing moms or caregivers, independent, sexy, smart, and so on. Recognize their diversity as much as possible and resist any and all temptation to stereotype!

Stress relief: In numerous studies stress has been shown to be women's number-one enemy. Women today feel overwhelmed by taking an equal role as breadwinner and primary nurturer to the family. In a survey conducted by *Redbook* and Women.com, 43 percent of women said they felt frustrated in trying to balance their work life with parenting.[18] Offer solutions, or at least understanding, of the tensions that prey on them daily.

Connection: Women base most of their decision making on emotions as opposed to rational elements. Studies have shown that they don't like reading lists of numbers, specs, and stats. They want to know what the product will do for them, personally.[19] Find out what makes "your" woman tick!

Relationship: Women want dialogue, not just a transaction. Women are looking for brands to trust and will often remain extremely loyal to a brand that has built on their trust consistently—even beyond price. Part of the relationship a woman has with a brand has to do with that brand representing something important to her in her life. Brands that take a sincere stand for something and demonstrate it in real, concrete terms will do well with women.

A recent American Express ad, however, clearly does not get the notion of the importance of the concept of respect in marketing to women. The ad shows a woman in her fifties traveling in a foreign country. She has just left her wallet with $1,000 in cash—all her cash—in a cab. She appears hysterical and helpless. The solution would have been, of course, to have purchased American Express Traveler's Checks, but its woefully too late. Will women really be able to identify with the bumbling, fearful woman in this ad who exhibits very little foresight, resourcefulness, or street smarts? And even if they did, why does American Express want to position itself as the paternalistic "Big Company" with all the answers? Far better for it to attempt creating a relationship of equality with the consumer based on esteem. Why don't they show a woman celebrating with an expensive dinner after having lost her wallet because she was intelligent and organized enough to have bought American Express Traveler's Checks?

A recent Salomon Smith Barney ad nicely shows how to talk to women from a position of respect, making the point of their enormous responsibility in the lives of their families, by stating, "She manages a career, a family, and the household assets. Super woman? No, the average woman." The ad is not only acknowledging that many women are playing the role of family investors, but also all the other roles women play in addition to that of family investor, striking the note of *Individuality* as well. The fact that the woman shown in the ad is laughing in a relaxed manner is also a nice touch; it implies that although she may have a lot of responsibility, she is not always serious, and she knows how to have fun.

- **Individuality:** *Boss, mama, woman, worker, nurturer, girlfriend, biker, wife, business owner, seductress, friend, cook, volunteer, industry leader, activist, artist, sports fan . . . etc.!*

The luxury watchmaker Patek Philippe has captured the essence of women's multifaceted lives today in their new branding program. Patek Philippe recently introduced its first line of watches for women called Twenty-4. The watches are targeted to women in the twenty-eight- to thirty-five-year-old age group with emphasis on modern styling to fit in with every moment of the lives of busy women. Its ad campaign, which asks women "Who will you be in the next twenty-four hours?" reinforces an understanding of the many varied roles women play in the course of a day in a simple, intriguing, and eloquent manner.

In the cognac industry, traditionally vying for an older, often male consumer, Hennessy in its latest ads has been appealing to a more modern, aesthetic audience—young women in particular. The Hennessy ads attempt to capture an urban, hip young woman in all of her complexities.

A recent Corningware cookware commercial with the tag line "Find your inner chef," is a welcome relief from cookware advertising campaigns that show women in a state of Betty Crockerish kitchen perfection. This commercial shows a relaxed, young woman in a sexy, elegant cocktail dress having fun putting the finishing touches on dinner and laughing at her own "wonderful little blunders

Although we are starting to see a lot of finance branding aimed at women, many financial firms are not doing much yet to market to women in an emotionally sensitive manner. This is baffling since, according to the National Association of Securities Dealers, women now represent 47 percent of all investors, and they are savvy investors too. In a study of more than thirty-five thousand brokerage customers, the University of California at Davis found that women's portfolios earned 1.4 percentage points more than men's, with single women earning 2.3 percent points more. The reasons behind their success with investments provides interesting insight into women. Just as with other consumer decisions, women research their investment decisions thoroughly and are more consistent and patient with their choices. Men are risk takers and move around a lot in their investments, the cost of their numerous transactions bringing down their return rate. According to Brooke Harrington at Brown University, who studies the performance of male and female investors, women also ask themselves more personal questions before making an investment, such as whether their own personal firsthand experience with the company suggests that it is a quality product or service and if they would feel comfortable with the company on ethical grounds. Harrington also says that while men tend to base their investment decisions around the industry they work in or on outside information from the Internet or TV, women get investment ideas from their own direct consumer experiences.[20]

Text from a Women.com ad:

"A website for dolls. Also; women who played with dolls growing up; women who ripped the heads off dolls growing up; sugardolls; honeydolls; women who get dolled up; doll collectors; anyone who can hum Hello Dolly; women who wear babydoll pajamas; anyone who's seen the Dali Lama; and every women who's tired of hearing "hey doll" when walking by construction sites."

that only make her appreciate her final masterpiece that much more." By her dress and the lit candles we know she's expecting company and there is a sense of excitement and enjoyment. But instead of the focus being on the pleasure her cooking will bring to others (which is such a cliché in this category), it is on the great time she is having with the process of cooking itself.

The Women.com ad (above) with its wordplay around "doll" is a very ingenious, direct-line approach to the problem of stereotyping and a humorous, tongue-in-cheek look at just how varied women's interests are.

- **Stress relief:** *A woman's job is never done!*

Obviously the main reason stress is women's number-one pain today is because women have continued to be the primary family caretakers at the same time that they have vastly expanded their roles and levels of responsibility in the business world. Studies have shown that while it is true that men are doing more to help out around the house, women still shoulder the majority of the responsibility.[21] This is an incredibly important point for marketers to understand and respond to with sensitivity. Since Emotional Branding is about solutions, what can be done to help women find and feel more work/life balance and relief from stress in the brands in

What can be done to help women find more work/life balance and relief from stress in the brands in their lives?

their lives? A practical approach is never a bad idea. In response to women's busy schedules some supermarkets, for example, are beginning to group products in their stores around solutions, such as beauty sections, allergy, cough, and cold sections. Foods are beginning to appear grouped according to menu ideas—all this to make a woman's errands quick, easy, and fun. Grocery stores could and should do more to develop a relationship with women by offering more creative solutions to the mix, such as having health or beauty professionals on-site to offer tips, seminars or local speakers on important neighborhood issues affecting their daily lives in which they may wish to participate more actively but have trouble finding the time, or play areas for children.[22] The possibilities are endless. If the supermarket, or any retail space, could become a dynamic public and social space where women could see themselves reflected and their needs responded to, I don't think it would feel much of a threat from the Internet at all!

Eckerd's ad, which emphasizes the ease of its return policy, lets women know that it is well aware that they are pressed for time and would rather spend it with their loved ones than returning makeup products that aren't quite right. A new MasterCard commercial from the McCann Erickson "Priceless" series shows with humor how its debit card helps a modern Cinderella complete all her errands in time to meet her handsome prince for dinner. The L. L. Bean ad takes a different tack, responding to the fact of stress in women's lives by portraying a blissful moment of peace and relaxation. What woman would not love to be lying in that hammock?!

- **Connection:** *Give me a F-E-E-L-I-N-G (not stats or lists of numbers)!*
Philips has understood this principle and is using it wisely in the way it is marketing its home cinema collection to women. Instead of giving tons of specs for the system or zeroing in on performance, the campaign focuses on the pleasures (particularly social pleasures) of its home cinema. The print campaign features a young woman with the headline, "None of my friends go to the movies anymore. They come over to my place instead." This is a key element of the connection approach to marketing to women; tapping into a communal bonding, often between women, and often through humor surrounding women's issues.

Even makers of female-oriented products are also realizing they can update and improve their dialogue with women in some interesting ways. Always sanitary napkins recently launched a campaign to introduce their Always Ultra Quilted Maxipads that was very different from previous campaigns (absolutely no demos surrounding the efficacy of the product, for starters!). One of the humorous spots shows a group of handsome men in kilts dancing to funky techno-music as the female voice-over says: "Hey, guys. Guys. Stop! It's the new *quilted* pad from Always. *Quilted*, not kilted." The guys' expressions turn quizzical as they try to stop a gust of wind from lifting up their kilts. The tag line is: "Being a girl just got better." Another spot shows apparently naked men marching in tall grass, wearing helmets and guns to emphasize Always Ultra's superior protection. In surprising women with an unusual approach to a mundane product and giving them a chance to laugh at men in silly situations, these quirky ads succeed in emotionalizing a "serious" and highly practical product for the consumer. Andy Abraham, North American marketing director for Always says, "Consumers were tired of seeing women on sailboats out in the deep blue sea wearing white pants . . ."[23]

Also an amusing departure from the usual in branding a well-known "women's" product is a playful campaign in France for Mr. Clean, which seeks to connect with women on new ground, eschewing the traditional presentation of scientific data about germs. The ad shows the ubiquitous bald, muscled icon Mr. Clean bare-chested, without the usual white T-shirt, with the tag line, "There's nothing like a man who offers you his body." This is in the direction of Emotional Branding simply because in a clever, humorous way it recognizes that women are sexually empowered and may be amused by such a "come-on" from their friendly old housecleaning buddy who's been around since the invention of the television!

• **Relationship:** *It is a two-way street!*
Women will give their trust and long-term loyalty to brands that enter into a meaningful dialogue with them as opposed to merely focusing on the transaction at hand. Women want brands that reflect the values that are important to them. One of the major issues that top women's concerns today are mental, physical, and spiritual health, for themselves and their families. Middle-aged women are responsible for making 80 percent of all health-care decisions in America,[24] and in a recent study it was found that younger, twentysomething women also consider health issues to be of major (and growing) importance for themselves and their loved ones.[25] Their concerns surrounding safety and health cause women to view many products through a very different lens than men. Interestingly, in auto ads, for example, Langer & Associates found in a study that the word "power" conveyed excitement to men, while to women it was seen as a safety factor for maneuvering in tight situations.[26] Women are and like to see themselves as caretakers and nurturers, of themselves and others. And, by others, they are often including a wide scope of humanity as well as their "near and dear." It's important to talk to women from an understanding of this emotional perspective. Avon's long-term commitment to breast cancer, Target's work in education for children, and Liz Claiborne's fight against domestic violence are good examples of getting this right, among many others (see section on Cause Marketing in chapter 18, for more information). What is most important is that women feel they are dealing with a real brand personality that stands for something meaningful on some level, not an amorphous corporate entity.

While women *are* nurturers and caretakers, this is certainly not to the exclusion of their own needs. Of course one of the most meaningful causes for women is the one that has to do with themselves! In this era of feminine empowerment, women see themselves very differently today than in the past and yet much of our marketing is still playing to the "old woman." An *Advertising Age* article says, for example, that in commercials, "women like to see other women who are diverse, confident, and naturally beautiful. Women respond to emotional truth and real-life experience."[27] This, along with the fact of the aging Baby Boomer population, is surely the reason behind the trend of older and/or more natural (i.e., what was previously considered as "flawed"), non-airbrushed models we are seeing in the ads of Banana Republic among many others, which I mentioned in the Baby Boomers section in chapter 1.

Eileen Fisher has said that she's convinced that there is a consumer backlash against the androgynous young women who have dominated fashion. She says, "I want a new, more realistic image for women to aspire to."[28] In an informal poll of the women in our New York office, we found that across the board, the number-one offense of advertising for women was one-dimensional, unrealistic ads that objectify women.

This, of course, does not mean that women don't wish to see and be inspired by images of beauty. The Maidenform communications program of several years ago, with the tag line "Because inner beauty only goes so far," provided an interesting angle on this issue. This ad uses a humorous tone to point out that while women want to be recognized above all for the strength of their inner qualities, it is also important for women to feel attractive, so why not aim for both? Brands that avoid sexist imagery and build on positive, inspirational messages that recognize the multifaceted nature of women and the key challenges women face today will go far in building a relationship with women. And in today's age, this really goes for all brands given the fact that the stereotypical division of the sexes really and truly is going, going, gone. Consider, for example, the audience of Super Bowl 1999. According to Nielsen, it was 42 percent female.[29] How many brands recognized this fact in their advertising? Why, given the fact that women are buying more and more electronics, would Jensen want to alienate them with their April 2000 ad in *Spin Magazine* (women read *Spin Magazine* too; a woman pointed this ad out to me!).

As we progress farther and farther into an era of female empowerment, brands will need to learn to speak to women in new, inventive ways. Finding out how to create a loyal female consumer is probably the best investment a brand could ever make!

Today's Girls, Tomorrow's Women

Furthering that last thought, focusing now on the Gen Y female consumer and where she will be leading us in the future is an even smarter investment. Today's brand of feminism is rampant in popular culture, wed to the concept of a new kind of feminine empowerment that embodies the attitude of younger Gen Y women. "Girl power" is everywhere, as evidenced by a slew of celebrities, books, movies, and media (and brand!) images that portray sassy, sexy, extremely confident and successful women in a woman's world. These are girls who aren't afraid to take a stand for what they want (think Spice Girls lyrics: "Yo, I'll tell you what I want, what I really, really want . . .") and go their own way. They do not feel compelled to compete against men—they may, however, wish to seduce them! Then again, maybe not. . . . Girl power is, above all, about women being empowered without suppressing—or conversely, being compelled to prove—their femininity or sexuality. They are playing by their own rules, able to wear a mini-skirt *and*, like the Disney heroine in the 1998 movie *Mulan*, defeat an all-male military at their own game. Gen Y girls have begun to carve out a strong new definition of beauty that has more to do with personal style and health than size. This is probably in part due to the fact that Gen Y has had a very dramatic increase in involvement with sports over the past several years.[30]

As this generation of women matures, one thing is certain; they will bring their very distinct influences to the world of commerce, both from a business management and a consumer standpoint. As we saw in the Gen Y section of chapter 1, this generation equals the Baby Boomer generation in size and will surely exert the same kind of social muscle. We already know that these girls/women are and will continue to be much more likely to step outside of traditional stereotypes of all kinds, including buying products traditionally purchased by men. Studies have shown that this generation is more likely than their Baby Boomer counterparts to part with any and all tradition and make purchase decisions for cars, computers, and electronics.[31] This, of course, also means that they will be much less likely to tolerate stereotypes in branding programs for all types of products.

Brands mired in stereotypes, such as Barbie, have had to undergo some dramatic changes to keep up with Gen Y girls. It was only a few years ago that Mattel was lambasted for the talking Barbie whose comments included the insight "Math is hard," but Barbie has learned a lot since then. As showcased in the *Generation Girl* series, nowadays Barbie spends her time cruising the subways of New York City, studying to be an actress, and serving as the contributing editor for Film and Lifestyle at *Generation Beat*, the school newspaper. While hanging out with her multicultural friends, she's apt to shout out her favorite (and empowering) phrase "Go for it!" This new Barbie is intended to appeal to girls nine through twelve, who have been outgrowing Barbie earlier than their Gen X and Boomer predecessors. Mattel has also added more sports-oriented Barbies, such as NCAA Barbie. Yesterday's blonde bimbo Barbie is definitely a thing of the past. Her more intelligent and active counterparts have taken the stage.[32]

Maybe it's finally time to give up a good chunk of the blatantly sexist images in branding programs in favor of a more holistic view of women. Expecting nothing less than respect for being their multidimensional selves, Gen Y may very well be the ones to bring about this revolution as they grow and evolve in our society!

Women and the Web: An Incredible Force

Women are arriving online with incredible force. They currently make up 48 percent of the online population, and it is predicted that they will outnumber men by 2002. Because they handle 80 percent of all purchase decisions, obviously they will quickly surpass male online spending as well. Netsmart found that 53 percent of women made an online purchase in 1999, up from 33 percent in 1998. Women's online behavior and spending vary greatly from men's. Here is a look at what motivates women online.

Women's primary online activities are:

- Gathering information: (business/career/family/shopping/heath/travel/computer)
- Sending and receiving e-mail
- Chatting

While a large number of women do go online for entertainment and pleasure, women are increasingly dependent of the Internet to save time.[33] Netsmart found that 88 percent of women say that the Internet simplifies their lives.

A significant difference between men and women online is that women tend to go online for a specific purpose and men are more likely to be surfers or browsers. This means that user-friendly, intuitive design is key as well as tailoring sites toward convenience. Contests or helpful tips are more valuable to women than games.

What we already know about women as consumers translates well to the Web:

Respect: Women use the Web to conduct thorough research of products, services, and companies in order to make highly informed decisions. An interactive survey by Northstar Interactive demonstrates that for women the Web has surpassed newspaper, television, radio, and even their friends as a source of buying information; 67 percent use the Internet, 55 percent friends, 44 percent newspapers, 27 percent television, and 20 percent radio.[34]

Individuality: Women are using the Web to reinforce their sense of themselves as multidimensional people. They enjoy the power the Web gives them to expand their horizons in all the roles they play. They use the Web to do business and personal research and to explore current events, fashions, travel, and entertaining escape sites.

Stress relief: The major reason women shop online is convenience. Twenty-four-hour availability means that midnight shopping after the busy day is over is a real, viable alternative. Women also find the Web to be a great resource for a little relaxation and self-gratification. Ninety-six percent of the women in the Netsmart survey found the Web to be entertaining and pleasurable.

Connection: Content sites such as Oxygen, Women.com, and iVillage are increasingly popular with women. These sites have become successful by offering free, easy to navigate information and content that is highly relevant to women in a way that fosters a sense of community. They also offer resources such as free e-mail, weather, and stock quotes.

Relationship: Women use the Web to help themselves and their families. Eighty-three percent of the women interviewed in an online study by Netsmart said that the Web helped them to help their children (69 percent said they use it to help their children with homework).

4

Gay and Lesbian Consumers:
Sincerity Is the Best Policy!

IBM, Subaru, Anheuser-Busch, American Express, AT&T, British Airways, Allstate, Starbucks, Levi Strauss, Waterford, Philip Morris—these companies all share at least one thing: each has had the sensibility and intelligence to identify that gays and lesbians compose an important segment of its market *and* that they merit the kind of individualized attention that meets their cultural specifics. No longer is targeting homosexuals reserved for daring companies with specialized or marginal goods. As the preceding list attests, American society is at long last recognizing homosexuals' claim to legitimacy, and even the most mainstream companies are now courting these consumers with sizable disposable incomes. These companies have perhaps even begun to realize the enormous importance of the gay and lesbian population as key cultural influencers of our times.

Companies that ignore this audience not only lose valuable business, but also reveal themselves to be unfortunately ignorant.

Companies that ignore this audience not only lose valuable business, but also reveal themselves to be unfortunately ignorant, and our society, most notably the soon-to-be monetarily empowered, highly discrimination-averse Gen Y, is becoming less and less tolerant of this kind of ignorance. In keeping with their overall widespread policy of tolerance for ethnic and sexual diversity, today's youth provides a glimpse into the future for gays and lesbians in America: according to a survey commissioned by *Seventeen*, 54 percent of teens are comfortable with homosexuality, compared with 17 percent in 1991.[1] I anticipate this trend will continue, and as more teens accept the gay and lesbian population, and these teens become adults, yesterday's archaic taboo against homosexuality will largely evanesce. And as this happens, more and more brands will make attempts to attract these consumers. In the sea of brands newly fighting for gay and lesbian dollars, those that have demonstrated a long-term and unwavering commitment to this community will stand out, and that, in turn, will engender a genuine emotional connection with the brand and, ultimately, loyalty–branding at its best.

Largely due to the prejudice and intimidation which confront many of the men and women of this demographic, statistics about the group's size and influence vary considerably. Most estimates place homosexuals somewhere between 3 and 10 percent of the American adult population. Estimates about their wealth vary as well. *Genre*, one of the nation's largest gay publications, reports that its gay male reader has an average income of $92,000. The 1990 U.S. Census reports an average income of $58,000 for gay men. However, Yankelovich Partners reports a mere $37,000 for the same group in 1999.[2] Which is the most accurate? It's difficult to say, and probably best not to generalize. On one hand, the urban concentration of many gays and lesbians, and their lower likelihood of raising children, increases disposable income for many. On the other hand, discrimination in the workplace poses an obstacle to many gays and lesbians, and those that live in more rural areas where income is lower, are less likely to reveal their sexual orientation for fear of persecution. Fortunately, with the rise of the Internet and the proliferation of gay communities, it seems likely that better and more reliable statistics will become available, concerning the size, affluence, and lifestyle needs that distinguish this population of consumers. Such data will empower gay activists and marketers alike, as they are better able to identify the wants and needs of these consumers. Sites such as *gay.com*, which throughout the later part of 1999 had up to 1.2 million hits a month (far more than the combined circulation of *Out* and *Advocate* magazines) and, according to audited traffic reports, was visited by 2.56 million people in June 2000 alone, are excellent venues to begin to better understand this demographic and for brands to begin a dialogue.

What is certain is that gay and lesbian consumers are among those most responsive to companies' positioning in their community, be it a positive or negative presence. This demographic is definitely paying attention to how they are being treated by corporate America and avidly searching for companies that know how to talk to them with respect. According to a tracking survey by Greenfield Online and Spare Parts, 77 percent of gays and lesbians have changed brands based on a company's positive stance regarding their group. Of that 77 percent, 76 percent stayed with the brand for a year or more. The response to companies which took a negative stance was even stronger: 87

A new version of the famous Grant Wood, *American Gothic* portrait of Middle America.

percent of gay respondents had changed brands based on a negative stance, and 79 percent of that number never purchased that product again![5] This, the power to piss off consumers, I consider to be one of the most striking illustrations of Emotional Branding!

To realize their full potential, brands must recognize from the outset that their emotional identity is not only a result of ads and products, but also corporate policy and stances. The Coors family has in the past contributed to antigay organizations and this, combined with allegations of the mistreatment of gay employees, has cast a dark shadow over that brand within segments of the gay community, resulting in boycott actions since 1977. Coors is clearly trying to rectify its image within the gay community, and the brand has made positive steps by advertising in gay media with gay-specific ads that are increasingly daring, incisive, and amusing. Coors has now clearly made a commitment to speak to gays in a targeted manner "on their own turf." Coors would be wise to follow up its marketing efforts with a more consistent, message-cohesive corporate policy.

An unfortunate and unnecessary result of Exxon's merger with Mobil in 1999 was that Exxon revoked health-care coverage it had previously provided to gay employees' domestic partners. Although Mobil had previously received little or no attention for denying these benefits, ExxonMobil attracted outrage and condemnation throughout the gay community for revoking them. Such a reversal, gay activists accurately stated, flies in the face of public and private trends. Today about 15 percent of major corporations offer domestic partner benefits[4] and that number is slowly but surely growing. Exxon Mobil's decision generated bad publicity within a small but sensitive minority without winning much applause or benefit in the way of PR or savings. Furthermore, in an industry such as oil, outraged consumers can easily switch to a competitor. Finally, the change in policy undermines company morale and illustrates ambivalence about supporting its workers. Worst of all, if ExxonMobil reversed itself again and returned the benefits, its waffling would draw the criticism of the right, which would accuse it of buckling beneath the pressure of gay-rights organizations, while homosexuals would probably remain uncertain about the authenticity of its returned support. It would have been far better for Mobil to have quietly adopted Exxon's policies, thereby showing its unwavering support for its employees, and it probably would have escaped unscathed by controversy.

To realize their full potential, brands must recognize from the outset that their emotional identity is not only a result of ads and products, but also corporate policy and stances.

Think of the consumer activism generated around American Airlines' openly supportive and nondiscriminatory policies toward the homosexual population. The fact that American Airlines has been criticized by right-wing contingencies for its humanistic, inclusive policies has only served to mobilize large numbers of people (far beyond the gay population) in support of the airline, creating a very positive grassroots PR campaign!

Additionally, because so many large companies have begun advertising in gay media with gay-specific ads, corporate policy plays a more important role in distinguishing a company's loyalty and interest. Howard Buford, president of PrimeAccess New York, specializes in gay and other minority media. As he told *Advertising Age*, "We're looking at a lot more companies coming into the gay marketplace. It's not so pioneering anymore; now they're just covering their bases."[5] The jump in advertising within gay publications attests to that; revenues have risen from $73.7 million in 1996 to $117.1 million in 1998.[6] The companies that have already started talking to this community have rapidly developed sophisticated and subtle ways of addressing them without condescension or pandering. Gone (or fading fast at least) are the days when heterosexual ads were pasted into the pages of *Out* magazine with their opposite-sex couples intact.

IBM has been lauded for its gay-directed ad in 1999 which showed a male couple in Irvine, California, who run a photo-processing business, with the headline, "We're not your typical mom & pop operation . . . We're not even your ordinary pop & pop operation." IBM received thousands of e-mails, phone calls, and letters from gay consumers praising the campaign. Maureen McGuire, vice president of worldwide integrated communications at IBM, says, "Our research found that the gay audience feels advertisers often talk down to them."[7]

Still, many companies seeking to win over the gay and lesbian market but afraid of controversy are trying to play it safe with ambiguous ads which leave consumers guessing in terms of the real sexual orientation of the portrayed models in the ad, such as a Chase Manhattan Bank ad which showed two handsome young men shaking hands with the tag line promoting bank services for "unique individuals." This "safety zone" approach has had mixed results, leaving some in the homosexual community feeling sought after for their wallets, but not truly accepted. In addition to homosexual-friendly corporate policy and unambiguous ads, another important sign of commitment can be running ads in the mainstream media. Paul Roux, who runs a gay-oriented marketing firm in New York says, "People in focus groups repeatedly tell me they want companies to show they are truly committed to the gay market by running a gay ad in *Time* magazine, not just in the *Advocate* or *Out*."[8]

Subaru has been one of first companies to take this step. Since 1994 Subaru has been relying on niche markets to drive sales of its vehicles, and its success within the gay community is noteworthy. Research indicated that their all-wheel drive vehicles were popular with a number of unique markets that, in addition to health-care professionals and educators, included lesbians. Subaru turned to the agency Mulrayn/Nash, which had experience advertising to gay and lesbian populations, in order to design Subaru's homosexual-directed media. Before releasing four or five ads featuring same-sex couples, Subaru prepared press releases and retained PR consultants to handle the anticipated public backlash. However, other than several dozen phone calls and a box of petitions from one church down South, the controversy was minimal. Since then, increasingly clever gay-directed ads have been released by Subaru, including some that are found on public billboards and buses. Featuring the text "Different Drivers. Different roads. One car," the ad was unwavering in its direct message to the gay and lesbian community and yet sophisticated enough that it was unlikely to raise the eyebrows of many heterosexuals. The ad cleverly speaks to gay and lesbians through encrypted, "insider" symbols that are highly recognizable to gays. One of the vehicles had a bumper sticker with a yellow and blue equal sign, the symbol of a gay activist organization. The other two cars boasted the cryptic vanity plates "XENA LVR" and "P-TOWNIE," the first referring to the program *Xena: Warrior Princess*, which is renowned for its popularity among lesbians, the second referring to the popular and almost exclusively gay and lesbian Cape Cod vacation spot Provincetown. Subaru's decision to place these subtle, clever ads in mainstream media sent a powerful message to homosexuals and proved Subaru's true commitment to serving that community.

Subtlety can, in many cases, be much more effective than an all-out embrace. It is important to really spend the time to get to know this highly perceptive, intelligent, and complex demographic and attempt to form a genuine relationship. Grant Lukenbill, president of New York–based G. L. Communications, a consumer relations and advisory company, and author of *Untold Millions: Marketing to Gay and Lesbian Consumers*,[9] says that "The message can be sent in subtle ways that a company is supportive of the gay community. The key components are inclusivity, sophistication, and subtlety; you don't want to toot your own horn too much."[10]

In creating a campaign for Gay Financial Network (*www.gfn.comm*), a gay-friendly financial news and information site, Mad Dogs & Englishmen supplemented the usual focus groups with their own creative internal research. The agency wanted to better understand what it feels like to be gay and the perspective of a gay person within the context of a traditional business environment, and so they did some role-playing. One art director had a fake "coming out" and told her mother she was gay. Two men at the agency posed as boyfriends applying for a joint loan at a Staten Island, New York, bank. Says account planner Spencer Baim, "We explained that we wanted to set up a home together, used the same last name and touched each other's arms a bit. We felt the embarrassment and discomfort of the woman behind the desk, as well as our own anxiety."[11] This effort to literally step into the shoes of the consumer is a terrific example of the Emotional Branding approach. The resulting groundbreaking campaign, which will run in major mainstream American media, is funny and sensitive, taking a gentle swipe at homophobia in the business world. Each ad shows a businessman who appears uncomfortable or unknowledgeable about gays. In one ad a balding, cigar-chomping man says, "You're GAY!!! . . . Well, I'm feeling quite happy myself." In another, a silver-haired man reacts to a same-sex couple by saying, "You're partners? Oh! . . . Then this must be a business loan!" In a third ad, a man jokes, "Two ladies living together? Look out, fellas!"

Naturally, the sooner companies venture wholeheartedly into the relationship realm with gay and lesbian consumers, the greater their capacity to show their cultural relevance, distinguish themselves from competitors, and, in the process, win the valuable loyalty of these markets.

section II:
sensorial experiences

the uncharted
territory of branding

A Sense of Strategy

Think about a bad experience you've had at the DMV licensing center or some other unpleasant governmental office. Surely the frustration of waiting was coupled with a stifling, if not downright oppressive, environment. Now re-imagine that experience inside a bright and spacious foyer. The large glass windows lining the walls allow soft sunlight to flood the room, flattering the attractive and stylish interior. In the spaces between the windows, where faded three-tone "Buckle-up" posters once drooped, now hang colorful reproductions by famous modern artists. After completing your licensing forms, you hand them to a pleasant, engaging agent whose disposition puts you at ease. At her suggestion you stroll across the temperature-controlled room and help yourself to a glass of fresh orange juice. Subsequently, you retire to a comfortable–nay, *inviting*–lounge sofa and glance through a recent edition of your favorite magazine while serenaded by soft, soothing music. How might this change the DMV experience?

While this may be a very utopian vision as far as the DMV is concerned (!), questions such as this are invaluable considerations both for products and retail environments in the Emotional Economy. The nuance of an image, the delight of an unfamiliar taste, the memory of a familiar sound, the gentle caress of a soft fabric, the associations of an ancient smell–these are the cues which form indelible imprints on our emotional memories. Although we all have direct experiences of the powerful effects of sensory input, and their importance has been well documented, it has been given short shrift in terms of branding issues. Sensory experiences are immediate, powerful, and capable of changing our lives profoundly, but they are not used to their full extent in branding initiatives at the store level, in product development, packaging design, and advertising. This, despite the well-documented evidence illustrating the effect of the five senses on consumer behavior.

Given the competition among today's corporations, it is my feeling that no business can afford to neglect the five senses. Carefully crafted sensory appeals can create that consumer preference that distinguishes a brand amidst a sea of competing commodities. As commercial offerings of increasingly similar goods proliferate, sensory elements can be the key factors distinguishing one brand experience from another. As the authors of *The Experiential Aspects of Consumption* propose, "many products project important nonverbal cues that must be seen, heard, tasted, felt, or smelled to be appreciated properly . . . In the experiential view, the consequences of consumption appear in the fun that a consumer derives from a product—the enjoyment that it offers and the resulting pleasure that it evokes."[1]

Although consumers generally do value products' tangible qualities, the lifestyle and image of a product should never be neglected. Every product—from Kleenex tissues to opera at Lincoln Center—has symbolic qualities, many of which are conveyed through sensory associations rather than verbal description. But how does one interpret and apply abstract experiential elements such as "smell" through branding? The translation of sensory language is difficult, but Michael Pham from the Columbia Graduate School of Business has uncovered some of the keys in his own work, which states that "To select appropriate symbols, marketers must be aware of the current trends and fads of their target markets. This suggests that marketers who attempt to use mood-related strategies—especially at the point of purchase—must maintain intense, informal, contact with their consumers."[2] In essence, know your customers, find out what they like, what they want—and give it to them. Through the senses!

Sensory elements can provide a fertile and imaginative shopping experience for consumers—one which inspires what Osgood describes as "associative hierarchies." In this view, *"although product satisfaction certainly constitutes one important experiential component—the stream of associations that occur during consumption (imagery, daydreams, emotions) are equally important aspects of consumer behavior."*[3] Most consumers are not even conscious of the effects this stimuli has on them, and will *claim* independent reasons for their choices,[4] but it is essential that the seller be fully conscious of the effects.

Successful sensory appeals only occur through intelligent strategy. This raises a whole series of questions in brand design, such as:

- What music can be played on a Web site or in a store to convey the emotional identity of a certain brand?
- How can color set the appropriate emotional mood of my brand?
- What images on packaging, in a store or within advertising, enable customers to identify with a product?
- Can serving food affect the behavior of my customers?
- Can scent create desirable associations with a brand?
- How much is too much? Is there a point when customers are overstimulated?

It is my aim to answer these and many more questions about sensory branding but, above all, these chapters can only hint at the wealth of material and powerful branding solutions to be found in the realm of the senses. One starting point for further inquiry is the beautifully written book by Diane Ackerman, *A Natural History of the Senses*, which offers a plethora of social, scientific, anecdotal, and artistic inspiration for exploring the uncharted territory of the senses from a totally fresh perspective. Ultimately, however, it is up to all of us to do our own "sensory sleuthing" since sensory data must, above all, be experienced firsthand to be understood!

5

Sounds That Transport

I will never forget one particular Saturday I passed with my parents at a golf club in Paris. We were casually sipping cocktails on the terrace, wrapped up in a world seemingly insulated from the dilemmas and difficulties of daily life. Then, without warning, my parents became very tense and a look of dread overtook their faces. Confused and disturbed, I could not understand what had shaken my parents equanimity. It wasn't until later that they understood themselves and were able to tell me what had caused this reaction—*golf shoes on stone*. Or, rather, the memories this conjured. The clacking shoes on the patio reminded them of the German soldiers' boots marching down French streets during World War II. This sound evoked memories of terror nights when the Gestapo took people from their beds and no one ever knew who would disappear next.

This anecdote, albeit a dramatic one, reveals what numerous studies have confirmed—sound has an immediate and, to a large extent, cognitively unmediated effect on recall and emotions. A friend's voice, a song from the prom, waves lapping on a beach—these are only a few examples of the sounds that can set off an uncontrolled hierarchy of associations within the brain. In fact, studies indicate that activities, such as listening to music, encourage the release of endorphins in the body, activating the very powerful pleasure centers of the brain. Although we have an intuitive awareness of this, most branding programs do not take advantage of sound (that is, beyond poorly chosen Muzak used to placate callers and numb shoppers). But with well planned application, sound is not simply a means of occupying consumers but also of engaging their emotions. And there are many, many ways to do this. I am fascinated, for example, by the way the Japanese brand, Nagusakiya Mera Chan, sells chocolates to kids with a musical instrument integrated into the packag-

ing, inviting children to explore the product through the senses of touch and sound before or alongside that of taste (above).

Let's start out by reviewing some theoretical aspects of sound and then examine some of the cutting-edge applications of sound in branding.

Sounds Like Good Marketing

Generally, when consumers are exposed to products and their advertisements, they don't perceive a personal "need" for the product, nor do they intend to buy it. Because so many individuals are not actively seeking information about products, stimulating emotion and affect is a better way to distinguish a product and draw interest. Music is a particularly effective approach because it circumvents the rational mind and petitions directly to the emotional mind in which desire-driven shoppers revel.

Gerald Gorn demonstrates this in his study *The Effects of Music in Advertising on Choice Behavior*. By playing music while previewing products, Gorn found that subjects overwhelmingly (80 percent) chose products accompanied by the music they liked. Interestingly, subjects attributed their product preference to the qualities of the product (in this case, pen color) rather than the music. After documenting and observing this effect, Gorn concluded that "an audience may be largely comprised of uninvolved potential consumers rather than cognitively active problem-solvers. Reaching them through emotionally arousing background features [such as music] may make the difference between their choosing and not choosing a brand."[1] There are very real examples of the power of sound and music, such as a musical optic promotion created for Southern Comfort that increased sales by 112 percent![2]

The Canal Jeans Co. in Manhattan successfully puts this idea into practice. It has hired DJs to spin hip and trendy record mixes while customers shop. These DJs are elevated on the store floor, near the entrance, so that customers pass by them as they shop. This provides the edgy and exciting feeling of a club for the young shoppers. The in-store music at Abercrombie & Fitch also does this, although in a less theatrical manner. Abercrombie carefully selects music that appeals to its shoppers. Because its clientele **Particularly with Generation X and Generation Y shoppers, music is a device used for constructing an identity.** is relatively particular in its tastes, Abercrombie & Fitch has the advantage of being able to tailor its music to their particular preferences. The sound is fast and lively, brimming with youthful energy. This is consistent with the personality of Abercrombie & Fitch's aggressive, attitude-laden brand. Hence, the music not only stimulates customers, but also enables them to identify with the store. This is continued on the Abercrombie & Fitch Web site where these songs and many others are available as "A&F-Approved Tunes."

This brings us to a second valuable application of sound–identification. Particularly with Generation X and Generation Y shoppers, music is a device used for constructing an identity. By associating a brand with a particular genre of music, a firm can contribute to the distinction of its identity, which is vital for attracting consumers. A growing number of retailers such as Gap, Toys "R" Us, and Eddie Bauer are investing in customized music programs with AEI Music Network, a company that crafts music collections specifically tailored to a company's brand image from its library of over seven million songs. American Eagle Outfitters includes music reviews within the catalogs that it mails to customers, as well as profiles of select musicians. The selections range from rock to hip-hop, assuring that most visitors will find something suited to their own taste. Staples of hip youth culture, such as the Beastie Boys, are featured, as well as little-known emerging acts, thereby catering to shoppers' current pleasures but also providing means to develop new interests via the inside filter of their favorite brand. All music featured in the catalog is also available for purchase on the American Eagle Web site. For those shoppers who discover a new favorite band in the catalog, the band, as well as its image and sound, are permanently associated with AE. Such thorough and personalized service enables AE to transcend remedial product-oriented marketing, and reach into the much more sophisticated and satisfying realm of supplementing and enabling entire lifestyles for its clients.

The Discovery Channel has intelligently incorporated sound into its stores in such a way as to tailor an engaging and personalized encounter as well as enhance its own brand identity with consistency. For example, certain sections within the stores are demarcated not by partitions, but rather amorphous sound zones. Customers drift from one section of the store to the next, and the product changes are accompanied by corresponding changes in sound and music. This makes the experience of wandering through the stores into a fun adventure. Shoppers don't know what kind of sounds or music will surprise them next, which encourages them to explore the entire store as opposed to one area of interest. This exciting sound experience as well as tons of interactive devices, also entertain the kids, keeping the little ones occupied while mom and dad shop and explore. Kids and adults have a better shopping experience. The Santa Monica store has an attraction for children, which features representations of various animals that emit the corresponding sounds, as well as weight scales that indicate your weight on different planets in the solar system.

The media in the Discovery Channel stores is designed to be a function of the space; some areas have sound, some none, and some areas have sounds, music, and video all together, depending on what works best. All the music and sounds are available for sale, which adds to the pleasure of the trip since a part of the fun can be brought home, and this will contribute to the recall of the store and overall brand experience at a later date.

The Museum of Modern Art (MoMA) in New York City is another innovator in the use of sound and technology for creating stimulating, personalized service. For a $4.50 rental fee, visitors to the museum can rent Acoustiguide, a digital player and headset that provides a personal tour of the museum. Works and genres throughout the museum are labeled by numbers that correspond to tracks on the Acoustiguide. Visitors can pick and choose among these tracks, tailoring their own, personal tour. With this technology, MoMA (and certain other museums) are providing service that price considerations previously precluded from being available to the masses.

In addition, MoMA has turned the Acoustiguide into an independent marketing device. In MoMA's exhibition *ModernStarts* (fall 1999–spring 2000), the Acoustiguide tour was set to music from the late nineteenth and early twentieth centuries, which it encompassed. Other tracks were freestanding, only there to embellish the viewing experience. And, as the Acoustiguide informed listeners, the songs on the digital tour were sold as *ModernStarts*, a $14.98 CD compilation in the museum gift shop. In this way, MoMA has created, in its digitally recorded tour, individualized service, enjoyable atmosphere, *and* a vehicle for (subtly) advertising one of its product offerings. Incentive for attending the museum, learning about art history, and buying museum merchandise are cleverly wrapped up in one considerate, economical service.

Megastores should consider emulating the MoMA Acoustiguides with headsets of their own. The potential of such devices is immense. Headsets could offer shoppers musically oriented guided tours or simply be a way of relaxing and "tuning the world out" while they shop to the music of their choice.

Megastores should consider emulating the MoMA Acoustiguides with headsets of their own.

The research on sound, as well as its applications in branding, is so extensive that to provide a comprehensive illustration of its potential uses is impossible. Research has shown us that music most definitely affects the speed of shopping, the amount of time spent in the store, the amount of time people will spend waiting for things, and the amount of money people will spend. But in terms of the type of music, it is necessary to experiment. As a general rule, quieter, classical music calms; one store, Asada, even found that when classical music was played, people spent 20 percent more![5]

SOME SUGGESTIONS

In addition, I suggest incorporating aural considerations into the store design. Should the structure accommodate "sound zones," such as the Discovery Channel's stores? What about the product itself–if it makes sounds, can the customers hear those sounds inside the store? Any item that makes noises, from a blender to Tickle-Me-Elmo, needs to let the customers hear those sounds in advance. Additionally, build a library of music around your clients' preferences. By selling that music in the store, you can keep track of customers' tastes and capitalize on the promotion provided by the in-store music. As with all branding, the methods and devices are only limited by one's creativity, and each firm must determine the applications that best suit its needs.

Lastly, as with all branding, be creative! You must determine the applications that are most appropriate. In time, your brand will reap the benefits of this "sound advice."

Although it's difficult to distinguish instinctual perceptions from cultural ones, scientific research has confirmed the broad generalized responses that music can cause, and the connections between particular sounds and music and certain emotional states. Scherer and Oshinsky (1977), for example, tested different sounds on subjects who reported the following connotations:

Tempo	slow	sadness, boredom, disgust
	fast	activity, surprise, happiness, pleasantness, potency, fear, anger
Pitch Level	low	boredom, pleasantness, sadness
	high	surprise, potency, anger, fear, activity
Amplitude Modulation	small	disgust, anger, fear, boredom
	large	happiness, pleasantness, activity, surprise

Source: *Sound, Music, and Emotions: An Introduction to Experimental Research* by David Huron, featured in Meryl Paula Gardner, "Mood States and Consumer Behavior: A Critical Review," *Journal of Consumer Research*, 12 (December 1985).

In another study by Fried and Berkowitz (1979), subjects reported the following states associated with these particular songs:

SONG	CONDITION REPORTED BY SUBJECTS
Mendelssohn's "Song without Words"	Peaceful feelings
Duke Ellington's "One O'clock Jump"	Joyful feelings
John Coltrane's "Meditations"	Irritated Feelings

Interestingly, subjects who heard Mendelssohn's "Song without Words" were more likely to be helpful immediately afterwards than those who heard the other songs or no music at all.

Source: Meryl Paula Gardner, "Mood States and Consumer Behavior: A Critical Review," *Journal of Consumer Research*, 12 (December 1985).

6

Colors That Mesmerize/
Symbols That Captivate

From the age of ten on, sight is the predominant sense for humans' exploration and understanding of the world. Personally, as a designer, I have always held the sense of vision in great esteem. It is incorporated into everything I create. This is why I am often amazed by the optical neglect to which certain brands are subjected. (I suppose this is why I decided to enter design–I am on a sort of evangelistic brand "rescue mission"!) I would like to show such brands the alternative to dull and mundane design–*vision.*

Visionary Branding

Consider the following: red, white, and blue. Golden Arches. A red can of cola. Your favorite sports team. In each instance, the associations of color enable identification and prompt particular images and emotions. Every Emotional Branding strategy must consider the effect colors (or their absence) will have on the brand. When making such considerations, I suggest a need for something more than beauty, continuity, and vividness as components of brand experience. Color, among other elements, is a crucial vehicle of this experience.

COLOR THEORY

As I just implied, color branding is *not* about being pretty or aesthetic. Color is about conveying crucial information to your consumers (which may, in turn, relate to being pretty or aesthetically pleasing). Colors trigger very specific responses in the central nervous system and the cerebral cortex. Once they affect the cerebral cortex, colors can activate thoughts, memories, and particular modes of perception. This arousal prompts an increase in consumers' ability to process information. Properly chosen colors define your brand logo, products, window displays, and so on, and encourage better recall of your brand, as well as a more accurate understanding of what your brand represents. Poor color selection will confuse your message, confuse your customers and, in extreme situations, contribute to the failure of a brand. The most effective color-branding strategies will come from designers who are able to make use of the color palette and its meanings for consumers.

The effect of colors arises both from acculturation and physiology, and these influences are enforced by one another. For example, colors with long wavelengths are arousing (e.g., red is the most stimulating color that will attract the eye faster than any other) and colors with short wavelengths are soothing (e.g., blue, which actually lowers blood pressure, pulse, and respiration rates). This physiological quality of color lends itself to the development of cultural associations that reenforce this effect. Consider, for example, red lipstick. Although it draws on lips natural as well as the evocative qualities of red as a color, the social meanings of "lipstick" (sex and seduction) have acculturated us to consider red to be even more provocative. Similar determinants operate in other colors: yellow is in the middle of wavelengths detectable by the human eye—therefore it is the brightest and easily attracts attention. Hence, yellow is in objects that demand attention, such as road-safety signs and police scene-markers. This creates associations of caution around yellow that train us to pay even more attention to its presence. This is also the original reason for making the Yellow Pages yellow; to heighten the attention level of bored or sleepy telephone operators. However, the entire array of color associations is much more complex, and the subtle variations are endless. A few other color generalizations: true orange is friendly, pastel tints are gentle, yellow orange is welcoming, pale blue connotes calm, navy blue symbolizes dependability. Gray is generally perceived as a professional color, and often implies qualities of seriousness and anonymity. For this reason it is very popular in offices and with office supplies and hardware, although I personally do not think those qualities should always dominate in the workplace. Why not be daring and spice up offices with the energy of a bright red violet to energize employees, or ease stress with refreshing aqua that has connotations of the ocean and relaxation for many.[1] No one can fully explain why colors affect us these ways, but awareness of this effect enables designers to convey information and, more importantly, moods. A friend of mine told me a very interesting story about her experience working at one of the most prestigious art galleries in the world, a place that had been selling Old Master and Impressionist paintings worth millions of dollars for centuries. She was fascinated by what was called the "red room," a room that was literally red everywhere, carpet, walls, velvet curtains, even the ceiling, and once asked the owner why the paintings were always shown to potential buyers specifically in this room. His answer was that it was because red caused people to become emotional and that he needed to create this kind of intense emotion to make a sale!

Creative use of color can also be quite unobtrusive, and yet remain just as effective. I recently went to a private screening of a French movie (at the MoMA in New York) called *Hometown Blues* (or *Le Bleu des Villes* in French) by Stéphane Brizé, and in the question-and-answer session that followed the screening someone asked him why in a particular scene he chose to film the heroine next to a red teapot. He surprisingly answered that if you watch his film carefully you will notice that every time the main character is happy in a scene, she is either wearing red or the color appears nearby as a part of the set, and otherwise there is an abundance of blue throughout the movie's sets, the color of her uniform for her mundane and stifling job as a traffic cop. This is a brilliant artistic use of color!

COLOR AND BRAND IDENTITY

Color often sets the mood of a brand through logos and packaging. Generally, it is desirable to select a color that is easily associated with your product: John Deere uses green for its tractors. Green implies nature. IBM has a solid blue that communicates stability and reliability. The short wavelengths of its blue have a reassuring impact upon the mind. However, as Al and Laura Ries note in *The 22 Immutable Laws of Branding*,[2] "it's more important to create a separate brand identity than it is to use the right symbolic color. Hertz, the first car-rental brand, picked yellow. So Avis, the second brand, picked red. National went with green." The salmon color of the paper on which the *New York Observer* and the *London Financial Times* newspapers are printed is unmistakable and is a successful use of color branding in that it visually sets these newspapers apart from all the others, indicating perhaps that they offer a decidedly different perspective. FedEx chose the colors orange and purple for their logo, two of the colors in the spectrum that clash the most, precisely in order to grab the visual attention of consumers, hoping that the packages would be immediately noticed by everyone in an office every time a FedEx delivery arrived. The role color choice can play in brand identity is not to be underestimated.

PRODUCT COLORATION

Henry Ford invented modern manufacturing. His brilliant implementation of mass production created quality products at pricing and in quantities that made them available to all. The secret to his success: standardization. When asked what colors the autos would be produced in, Ford quipped, "You can have *my* car in any color you want–as long as it's black." This epitomizes the manufacturing mentality; brilliant in its time, but certainly very limiting in terms of a consumer-driven model.

Today modern manufacturing precepts have, of course, given way to postmodern consumer realities. People, not machines, determine what will be produced and how. The secret to success: customization and individuality. However, many would-be brands implicitly sustain the Henry Ford mentality when it is actually design-conscious thinkers like Andre Leon Talley, the current editor-at-large for *Vogue*, they should be listening to. Talley says, "There's a demand for color across the board. These are good times and people want to feel good. I'd like to see public transportation in hot colors. Trains, buses, subways in Peter Max colors: pink, yellow, aqua, chartreuse, and peach. Children ride to school on yellow buses, why can't adults?"[3]

People, not machines, determine what will be produced and how. The secret to success: customization and individuality.

Pink subways? Aqua buses? These seemingly outlandish suggestions are the types of considerations occupying the minds of the best designers because *bored consumers need bold options*. Colors can demand attention, incite responses. An orange, translucent, curvaceous iMac screams "fun" and "different." Contrast that with your typical, gray, rectangular desktop that communicates a "utilitarian" and "standard" (boring) identity. Neither computer is necessarily functionally superior, but the iMac is distinguished–the iMac is a brand (which does, however, make the iMac FUNctionally superior). This is a major reason why Apple's unit growth for the last quarter of 1999 was 2.5 times the industry average.

Why did it take nearly twenty years for a personal computer to make this relatively simple innovation? The less important reason: today's euphoric economic situation in the U.S. influences a consumer market particularly accommodating to color and fun. The more important reason: the prevalence of uninspired assumptions about what a computer is and how a computer looks. It took Apple, an underdog with the need for a big success and the *willingness to be daring*, to reveal what a computer can be–fun.

Actually, I don't think all dull coloration can wholly be attributed to unimaginative producers. In fairness, retailers must share a portion of the blame. According to Nada Rutka, the president of the color-consulting firm Nada Associates, "Many manufacturers who sell primarily to the Big Box retailers may have a colorfully diverse product line but are limited to what the store buyers will put on their shelves, which is really very basic, mass market." Consequently, manufacturers that rely on these mass retailers for their sales must conform to certain color choices and the consumer has no say. In the words of Nada, "With the significant amount of business that is done via these majors, we find the retail buyers are the arbiters of America's color taste, not the consumer." Retailers cannot continue to pursue this narrow direction– today's consumers want dynamic colors and excitement, and the Internet provides means for them to get it if their local stores refuse. Moreover, there's no reason for the terms "retail" and "diminished choice" to be linked, and in the Emotional Economy they are a fatal pairing.

COLOR AND DEMOGRAPHICS

Selecting colors is complex, and the interpretation of color independently of its product or without the guidance of a color designer is ill-advised. Pat Brillo, a consultant for Color Services & Associates in Huntley, Illinois, stresses that "Selecting the right color is about audience. Who's your audience? What's the message? Just picking a trendy color is not the answer. Different consumers are affected different ways by that color, and trends are constantly changing."[4] Well-intended coloring can easily have unintended consequences. For example, Americans, especially younger Americans, associate green with environmentalism, in fact, according to Cooper Marketing Group in Illinois, people aged eighteen to thirty-four are especially likely to link green to images of health, ecology, and nature. So, adding some

To choose colors without the consultation of a professional designer is like hiking the Andes without a guide.

green to your environmentally sound product for this demographic may increase sales. However, in Egypt green is the national color, and its use on throwaway packaging could be very offensive. Similarly, white represents purity in the United States, but as we saw in chapter 2, in certain Asian countries it is the color of death. Just as there are national trends in color perception, there are color perceptions associated with age, social class, gender, and religion. To choose colors without the consultation of a professional designer is like hiking the Andes without a guide. Maybe you'll get lucky, but don't stake anything too important on it.

VISUAL IDEAS FOR INTERIOR BRANDING

The Johnnie Walker in-store clothing shop we designed relies on nonverbal visual elements to convey the elements of the brand identity appealing to the sophisticated world traveler. For example, a backlit screen displays seasonal travel destinations and a series of clocks read different times around the world. Such nonverbal symbols carry multiple advantages. Particularly in the instance of photographs, images allow fantasy to carry customers away in a wave of pleasant associations mixing the brand identity and the lifestyle which they, as individuals, aspire toward. Furthermore, although words can often work wonders, pictures can cut to the point with an immediacy yet breadth often more useful than words. Finally, large images can remain alluring even from significant distance, whereas words are confined by the need to be legible. It is vital that store displays work from all directions and distances.

Lighting is also a crucial element of designing interiors. Generally, products simply look better with attractive lighting. Furthermore, with the mere change of a bulb and flip of a switch, lighting can transform any interior. When Victoria's Secret held a fashion show at the Plaza Hotel in New York City, the entire exterior of the building was illuminated–in pink. The sight for passersby was unforgettable. Although it's not often considered fully and creatively, lighting is a potentially inexpensive means of transforming any space, and an easy way for a store's color scheme to evolve from season to season and one product line to the next. However, lighting shouldn't and needn't be limited to mundane single colors or static displays. Recently I attended a party that had a small disc with patterns cut into it rotate over the lighting fixture, causing moving shapes to project upon the wall. The Appliance Design Studio, a part of the Royal College of Art, has conceived of a light called "DataLamp" that uses computer technology to project ambient, floating imagery with multiple colors onto the walls. Particularly when combined with the appropriate music, these methods can create a positively magical and mystical atmosphere that can easily be installed and manipulated at a moment's notice to create different effects.

This chapter can only provide the most cursory sketch of the interesting properties of color and vision, illustrating certain applications that will, hopefully, act as stepping stones toward creative and imaginative new uses. A profes-

sional guide is certainly eventually important, but first of all, the most important thing is that companies themselves begin to think about and see with new
eyes the visual aspects of the brand. The best starting place for a new perspective on the possibilities of color is to get a copy of the *Color Harmony Workbook:
A Workbook and Guide to Creative Color Combinations*, published by Rockport.[5]
This book is easy to use and beautiful, laid out in a series of highly descriptive
color categories, such as powerful, fresh, friendly, vital, magical, and so on with

a color wheel, themed color schemes, and tear-out swatches of color that encourage experimentation and allow for 1,400 color combinations.

Entering into the wonderful world of visual identity is also sometimes only a question of attention. Just a little bit of increased consciousness can, I promise you, dramatically inspire anyone's sensibility. Whether in New York City, the Sahara Desert, or the Louisiana bayou, stunning visuals confront us every day, and we can become numbed to them in the course of our daily exposures. Where does a shadow fall? What patterns characterize a particular tree's bark? In how many shapes do windows come? Simple observations of this type feed into great branding, believe it or not. These observations and awareness are vital and worthwhile—they provide a new sense of the world. Every time we walk out the door, there is a myriad of opportunities to discover and rediscover the subtlety and detail that characterize every day of our lives.

7

Tastes That Tantalize

One of my colleagues recently related to me the story of his psychology teacher's eccentric test-taking methodology. Before each exam candy would always be distributed to all the students in the class. Why? Well, the teacher, well versed in the theories of I. P. Pavlov and B. F. Skinner, intended to reduce the stress of test taking by attaching this positive stimuli to each exam. Hopefully, instead of associating exams with stress and worry, students would begin to associate the exams with tasty treats. More importantly, speculated my colleague, the candy illustrated the genial and kind nature of the teacher, which transcended psychological theory and instead relied on friendliness. Students appreciated the mere effort and thoughtfulness of their teacher.

How Customers Are Starved for Affection

Proffering food indicates kinship, makes us feel at ease, and even provides pleasure. If guests in our homes receive this basic courtesy, why do so few customers? Shoppers are looking for a place to escape from the demands of work and the responsibilities of home, a place where they can relax and interact pleasurably. In-store cafés and restaurants allow patrons to feel relaxed and enjoy tasty pleasures while accomplishing a few small errands. However, even a cup of coffee, a glass of wine, or some candies can make a difference. For many shoppers, these services are far more valuable than the price tag that accompanies them, both for their tangible benefit and for the symbolic value of the gesture. Furthermore, there is no cybersubstitute for relaxing with friends and having a bite to eat after a good shopping excursion. Despite all of these positives, although some businesses have caught on to the branding value of food, most have left their customers starved for affection.

Barnes & Noble is one of the first national retailers to exhibit true culinary savvy. Rather than throwing a hot-dog stand in the store corner (which more than a few retailers have done), Barnes & Noble assessed the meaning of its brand–the meaning of books. Some literature aficionado (I suspect) recognized the long-standing affinity between literature and coffee shops. Capitalizing on this association, as well as on the desire to sit down and enjoy a cup of joe and a pastry while leafing through a *New York Times* best-seller, the cafés have become inviting and profitable components of the Barnes & Noble brand experience.

Nordstrom, whose hallmark has always been high-quality customer service, also realizes that customers want and deserve food. Nordstrom has four different restaurant concepts, and at least one is present in most of its stores. The Espresso Bar, which is usually located outside Nordstrom entrances, offers a selection of gourmet coffees, Italian sodas, and pastries to customers and passersby. Café Nordstrom proffers a selection of salads, sandwiches, soups, pastries, and beverages in a cafeteria-style eatery. The Pub is an English-style bar serving breakfast in the morning, as well as food, stouts, ales, and cocktails the rest of the day, while broadcasting televised sporting events. Barbara Erikson, former vice president of store design explains that "When customers are spending the amount of time they do in our stores, you need a place for them to sit down and relax, have a meal, have some coffee."[1] For a long time coffee was provided for only twenty-five cents a cup because, as cochairman Jim Nordstrom said in 1992, he doesn't like restaurants "that charge a dollar for a cup of coffee when it cost only a few cents."[2] (Unfortunately–and unwisely, in my opinion–this has since changed, and now coffee is regular price.) Lastly, and I think the most impressively, if there is a wait to be seated in a Nordstrom restaurant, customers are given a beeper. They can continue shopping and when their table is ready, the beeper alerts them. This consideration for customers coupled with acute business intelligence accounts for Nordstrom's tremendous reputation for service over the years.

"When customers are spending the amount of time they do in our stores, you need a place for them to sit down and relax, have a meal, have some coffee."

Then there is the mecca of sensual marketing: Central Market, probably one of the most innovative and exciting supermarket in the United States. Its vice president John Campbell says that at Central Market, despite its enormous size and huge array of products, "It's about the shopping experience, not about selection. We want people to feel uplifted when they walk out of here."[3] One of the most popular tourist attractions in Austin, Texas, Central Market demonstrates that vivid sensual experiences make for great success. Central Market has hired a team of "foodies," comprised largely of ex-chefs, nutritionists, and so on, who wander throughout the store, talking to customers about cooking and eating. Besides engaging customers on a relevant and pertinent subject, the foodies help shoppers plan meals and special events, often developing personal relationships with certain customers who regularly turn to them for advice. The foodies are also authorized to open any package in the whole store and they constantly do so in order for customers to be able to explore new products and product combinations and to taste the foods before buying them. Delectable delights are available for the kids, too. Inside the store's entrance is the children's fruit counter where girls and boys can pick the piece of fruit they want for twenty-five cents. On the weekends Central Market hosts children's birthday parties at which children bake their own pizzas and participate in printmaking using cut up vegetables. Central Market provides classes on cooking and shopping and hosts cultural events, such as concerts, in the lovely parklike landscape outside the store. This area also attracts locals who picnic and socialize out front after buying their goods inside Central Market. Seeing the Central Market phenomenon, Ron Lieber of *Fast Company* was compelled to write: "Central Market lives in the experience economy—a place where stores offer experiences so vivid that retailers could probably charge admission for them."[4]

Most stores (even food stores!) are still neglecting food, however. Although Kmart, Costco, and other national chains are increasingly providing in-store restaurants, more often than not they appear to be a mere afterthought—a sort of watered-down version of fast food that merely enables longer bouts of shopping rather than the pleasurable and slightly indulgent experience of dining and discovering. Shopping should be an event, and brands—well, brands should be a celebration. And what celebration would be complete without food? Some opportunities that I think are being neglected:

- Having just noted Central Market, here are some other ideas for supermarkets: Supermarkets have become far too sterile. Cellophane and Styrofoam are pleasant assurances of any food's freshness, but it is still vital to make shoppers realize that they are in a food market. A symphony of smells should fill the air, and a sundry supply of samples should always be at the shopper's disposal. This is particularly true for those expensive specialty goods that consumers often need to discover firsthand before incorporating them into their regular shopping repertoire.

- Stores that specialize in home goods, particularly culinary implements (such as Kitchen, etc.) could have in-store chefs demonstrating how to cook gourmet foods (Orlots, for example, has implemented such a program). After watching the demonstration, shoppers could sample the food, speak with the chef, receive recipes, and purchase the corresponding kitchenware and cookbooks. Perhaps shoppers could even try cooking meals themselves with the kitchenware and the aid of an in-store chef. Not only would this increase sales of the kitchenware, it would help build a communal and personal environment, which is essential to branding.

- Although commonly overlooked, I think men enjoy shopping together if the right occasion presents itself. Hardware stores, particularly of the Home Depot variety, should hold pre– and post–Fourth of July barbecues. Painters, carpenters, and other professionals could provide instruction on home improvement similar to the popular TV program *This Old House*– only with hot burgers and cold beers, as well as the necessary building supplies available and on sale!

- No customers like idly waiting on lines. Certain establishments have begun providing finger foods to their waiting customers. When a wait threatens to stretch past three or four minutes, why not bring out chips and salsa? I think most customers would be so pleasantly surprised by the gesture, they'll all but forget about the line wait.

These are just a few ideas among millions of others. Even simple, relatively inexpensive gestures like complimentary coffee, soda, or a glass of wine will make a big difference and may be the final factor in drawing certain passersby inside, as well as in sustaining tired shoppers who may want to continue shopping but need a moment of refreshment first.

In Santa Fe some of the many wonderful galleries that line up one after another on Canyon Road serve sherry, coffee, or hot mulled wine in the winter months and cool drinks in the summer. This is a very inviting reason to visit one (as opposed to another!) of these galleries and could certainly help put people in the mood to buy a beautiful work of art. It is also certain to become part of the associative memory of the pleasurable time spent there.

Through well-done ad campaigns, even products not customarily related to taste can evoke a delicious sensory association all the same!

It's a known fact that if men are able to sit in a store, the woman they are with will shop longer (and of course it's also a known fact that the longer consumers spend in a store, the more they buy).[5] How much more time and money would a woman spend in a store if her "shopped-out" husband was not only able to sit in a comfy chair, but if he was also given a cold drink? Besides, if nothing else, it's basic courtesy. The Australian fashion brand Country Road is one of the few retailers to extend this courtesy gratis. When customers walk into their New York store, they are offered a cold glass of water or coffee that is also prominently displayed on a self-service table near two inviting armchairs. Each Thursday afternoon through the evening,

Food is a form of social exchange, and is imbued with special meanings in many cultures.

the customers are also offered a choice of red or white wine (Australian, of course!). When asked if there is an issue of spillage on the clothing or in the store, the charming saleswoman told me, "Oh no! We are very attentive to our customers and are always aware if they need assistance to find a place to set their drink down or someone to hold it for them while they handle a garment."

It seems that Country Road has carefully thought through the important details of the execution of this gesture of serving drinks and, most importantly, decided to ensure that its salespeople see that it is smoothly managed as a potential basis for social interaction between the customers and themselves. Psychologist Paul Rozin writes that "For humans, where the search and preparation of food and its ingestion at meals are social occasions, food is a very social entity. Ingestion of food means taking something of the world into the body, and that something typically has a social history: it was procured, prepared, and presented by other humans. Food is a form of social exchange, and is imbued with special meanings in many cultures."[6] Brands that recognize this and respond accordingly will never leave customers with a bad taste in their mouths.

8

Shapes That Touch

In my research for this book I encountered a puzzling problem: there is a remarkable absence of literature exploring consumers' tactile sense. Why is this? It is the most essential of the five senses and also the most immediate–consider the impact of a lover's gentle touch. How about the differences between linen, cotton, and silk? While most of the senses inform us of the world, most often it is touch that enables us to ultimately possess the world, to wrap our consciousness around it. Perhaps it is because the sense of touch is so integral that it is so frequently neglected in marketing.

I suspect that modern and particularly Western society has also suppressed our awareness and attention to touch. Public objects are usually considered dirty and bad to touch. But when we encounter one of those little signs saying "Please do not touch," what do we want to do? We want to touch it! Holding, feeling, caressing, these are all basic and pleasant ways of exploring and experiencing in the world. Additionally, studies have found that as brand recognition declines, customers are more likely to touch a product in the process of evaluating it. Presumably, this is because shoppers compensate for an absence of information by using their senses to gain more knowledge. Touch, whether it's the product itself, the store fixture, the room temperature, or even the floors or the front door's handle, is a dimension of brand experience. Particularly in this tactile-deprived world, which is becoming even further limited by the advent of the Internet, I think businesses that cater to touch will be rewarded by their customers.

> **When we encounter one of those little signs saying "Please do not touch," what do we want to do? We want to touch!**

Tactile Tactics: Branding that Feels Good

Although the proliferation of shrink-wrap, cardboard, and paper wrapping has made leaps and bounds in protecting merchandise, it has robbed us of the opportunity to touch and discover too many products. Within the limits of reason, just about everything in a store needs to be accessible to touch. We want to feel our clothing, pens, strollers, fiber paper, leather briefcases, shovels, towels, and lotions before we buy. This is not just for the most practical, obvious reasons, such as to test the shade of a lipstick, but for deeper, more primal reasons that have to do with the sheer pleasure of holding and playing with something and imagining it belonging to us before we take (or buy) it. If a woman is going to wear a lipstick, she wants to know the texture of the product; how it will feel against her skin, as well as how the actual tube will feel in her hand and how the top will feel to open and close! If there is secondary packaging, it should be designed so that we can touch the product. If an object absolutely needs to be wrapped, an example of the object should be on display. Sephora has built their retail success story on the touch, try, and play principle for cosmetics. Their stores are a fabulous example of what can happen when you give people the power to explore beauty products for themselves. Sherry Baker, Sephora's former head of marketing for the United States and Asia says of their "free to roam, free to try" policy, "Frankly, we get longer shopping time when people are left alone."[1]

I hate going to stores and finding that everything has been torn open because people wanted to see what the object felt like and someone wrapped it in plastic. Nobody wants to buy something that's been torn into and strewn all about. Consequently, packaging as well as unsold product both go to waste. If the product is unpleasant to touch, then something is wrong with the design. Even a cactus can have a lovely flower that is smooth to the hands no matter how prickly the plant itself. Unfortunately, many brands don't even consider touch.

However, some businesses do undertake inspiring designs with the express aim of making their brands pleasant to touch. We designed the Victoria's Secret Dream Angels line in smooth, arching, curvaceous shapes, specifically to be pleasant to touch and be held in the hand in a way that would convey the sensuousness of the brand identity.

Glass Coca-Cola bottles are another brilliant example of appealing to the tactile senses through a curvaceous bottle that is a pleasure to touch and hold.

PHOTO BY PAUL TILLINGHAST.

Victoria's Secret Dream Angels.

Obviously, the soda is not better when touched, unless it is being swallowed. But through the original design of the Coca-Cola bottle, Coke translates the identity of the brand to handheld touch. So well designed is the Coke bottle that it embellishes the identity of the whole brand–touch, vision, and taste all come beautifully together.

Since touch is a way of, quite literally, taking possession of an object, stores can really provide customers with an exciting emotional connection to products through an instant gratification of the desire to touch. Have you ever bought a new pair of shoes and worn them out of the store? A wonderful feeling, isn't it? As a child, I remember putting those new shoes on my feet–they felt so comfortable, they looked so good, I simply couldn't wait to put them on. Give your customers that tactile pleasure! Encourage it! That's what they're paying for.

A store is a product playground! Objects and interiors should be designed and laid out to be experienced, felt, unfolded.

A store is a product playground! Objects and interiors should be designed and laid out to be experienced, felt, unfolded. Remember the scene in *Big*, when Tom Hanks and his boss play "Chopsticks" on the piano in FAO Schwarz? Well, go to FAO Schwarz any day of the week and, I promise, you'll see that scene reenacted over and over all day long by a stream of customers. Is it because people love Tom Hanks? Well, yes, partly. *But* the rest of the reason is that it's fun and involving. The store becomes a playground meant to be touched, hit, jumped. That is vivid, and vivid is good. Additionally, any time a product combines two senses in a dynamic way (in this case, touch and sound), it becomes twice as pleasurable.

Although some brand managers have considered touch solely a matter of the hands, sometimes it's a matter of, well, the sole. Our shoes more directly come into contact with the store than any other part of the body and, as a result, so do our feet. Some stores need to put more thought into their floors and what they say about the store. Crappy tile floors are bad. True, they're easy to clean, but somehow those floors always look the dirtiest anyway. However, that doesn't mean lush carpeting is the answer, either. The Kitchen, etc. near my home has large ceramic tiles on its floors, just like a kitchen. *That* is brand identity. Other stores could do this. For example, why not have a gym floor at Sports Authority? Maybe even a small gym court for people to try out basketballs and try on sneakers, as the Nike store offers in its Chicago location? Maybe green turf could be laid throughout the golf section. These are the types of questions retail designers should be asking themselves.

But sometimes integrating a tactile sensory experience into a retail environment or product design can be incredibly simple (and inexpensive). Take Banana Republic's 1998 Stretch campaign, for example. To emphasize the elasticity of the fabrics used in their new clothing collection, Banana Republic placed large bowls of rubber bands in their stores for customers to take and play with. A fun, sensory, inspired way for them to get their message across!

Ergonomics: Designing Products and Retail Environments for the Human Race (Not the Rat Race)

We are moving into a world where people matter more than technology, and ergonomics has taken on an increasingly important role as a solutions methodology that connects emotionally to consumers. It not only says that we care, but *proves* that a brand is listening (after all, actions speak louder than words!). Designing products and retail spaces for humanity is beginning to come to the forefront of many companies' visions, but many important strides have not yet been made. How many products are too high or too low on shelves for an average person to access? Paco Underhill's retail research firm, Environsell, which has amassed fascinating data on retail behavior that can be found in his wonderful book *Why We Buy*,[2]has observed, among many other "ergonomically incorrect" retailing moves, that very often drugstores stock cosmetics that older women are most likely to use, such as concealer cream, at the very bottom of a wall display, forcing the customer who least appreciates it to bend down to reach the product![3] Think about that, then consider handicapped persons who every day must face retail environments that do not cater to their needs. With an increase in aging population, how important is it to use large enough copy on products to make information readable for that market segment? Have you ever tried to drive a car with so many blind spots that it is almost unsafe? Have you noticed older people in the cars where you can barely see their heads behind that big steering wheel? This uncomfortable situation occurs because very few cars have an "up/down" function for the seats in addition to the "forward/backward." Contrast that with lawn-mower manufacturers who have realized that the natural way for people to push is by vertical handles, not the traditional horizontal ones, since it is more efficient and better uses our body strength.

Because of my background as a designer and my personal interest in the way people experience their shopping environment, I spend hours watching people shop and have observed the difficulty they sometimes have in their buying rituals. One very obvious problem is that shopping carts are either too small or too large. Carts are difficult to maneuver in tight or crowded aisles, and baskets quickly become too heavy for everyone, but especially for older customers. Shouldn't we invent a modular shopping cart, upright on wheels, to which you can add the size of basket you need for that particular day? I think this is just the kind of thing that would make shopping more comfortable and would increase the amount of products people bought. In the same vein, shouldn't we have modular shelves that could be lowered or raised for convenience when a product is too low or high on the shelf? Sometimes I wonder what size of hand the manufacturers use as a standard to define packaging and bottle proportions. I look for the shelves surrounded by products that have been dropped on the floor—and for the ones that look messy. The problem is always caused by product, retail, or packaging design that does not take ergonomics into account. This makes customers uncomfortable and unhappy, and sometimes even embarrassed. It gives them one more reason to shop on the Internet instead.

Sometimes intelligent ergonomic design is a cultural issue. Because ergonomics requires an understanding of how products can be easier to use, it requires a knowledge of how products *are* used, which varies from one culture to the next. For example, many European companies have discovered that, in order to succeed in the American market, you need to think big. The President of IKEA said that until they realized that Americans put lots of ice in their glasses and therefore need bigger containers, they had a hard time selling their smaller European glasses. They also realized that Americans sleep in bigger beds, need larger bookshelves, and like to curl up on their sofas rather than sit on them! These are certainly sufficient differences to have made their now-booming U.S. business difficult at the start. In today's global economy, companies must take into consideration these sorts of cultural considerations.

Sometimes I wonder what size of hand the manufacturers use as a standard to define packaging and bottle proportions.

Which cuts to the heart of tactilely minded design—how does an individual use and experience any product? What constitutes added value and an enhanced experience for that individual? The question for designers should not be, how do we make this product work? That's a given—the only question is how do we make this product worth working with? More often than not, intelligent tactile design can contribute significantly to answering this question and subsequently become a constituent of brand personality. For a great inspirational source regarding ergonomics—products and information—see *www.ergoweb.com*.

9

Scents That Seduce

We have all known individuals who could be identified by a particular smell—*hopefully* a good cologne or perfume—or felt our emotions stirred by the faint smell on an article of clothing left behind by a loved one (the individuality of which was probably determined, in part, by a particular brand of detergent). But have you ever thought about the smell of Scotch tape? A new car? Or even the Galleria Malls? Each smell is unlike anything else and provides clues about subtle ways odor can be used to manage brand identity.

Better Branding Is Right Under Your Nose

Smell is arguably the strongest of the senses, yet scent is an oft-neglected tool for providing consumers with engaging and emotional experiences. A whole array of studies reveal that odor has the potential to evoke our emotions with more potency than any of the other senses.[1] This is probably because there are more connections between the olfactory region of the brain to the amygdala-hippocampal complex (where emotional memories are processed) than any of the other senses have. Scent is not filtered out by the brain; it is instinctive and involuntary. Hence, your customer's nose is actually a direct link to their memories and emotions awaiting your stimulation. *Where do you want your customers to be?* A romantic bedroom? A zoological garden? Or perhaps mom's kitchen? Regardless of the location, the richer the environmental stimuli, the better, and scent should be a vital part of your branding plan.

In a fascinating study by Susan Fournier exploring the relationships consumers develop with their brands,[2] it is shown that scents are used by some consumers to manage their own identity and, in turn, identify with particular brands. Viki, one subject of the study, says that "I am very, I wanna say, wholesome, pure, whatever, but I mean, to me, that's what's important. My hair, my scents, my clothes. Everything is very feminine and wholesome." Viki was compelled to buy many products based on their smell and its appeal to her sense of identity, and clearly connected scent to the construction of her identity, saying to the researcher, "Like, right now I can tell you used Aveda Elixir [shampoo]. I can smell the tree bark. I smell Aveda a mile away. Trying to be all earthy and responsible, are you?" Is Viki alone in her penchant for scents?

"Everybody tells you they hate scented products. They lie." This, according to Gail Vance Civille from Sensory Spectrum in Chatham, New Jersey. Her firm manages and designs product stimuli which appeal to the five senses. According to Civille, "people love scented products and will choose them over other products. People will give scented products other positive attributes based solely on their smell. You can give someone two identical paper towels, the only difference being one is scented, and he or she will tell you the scented one is softer."[3] In recent years businesses have become increasingly adept at deriving these benefits.

With the rise of aromatherapy (the use of smells to heal and relieve stress and illness and evoke spiritual well-being), many products incorporating scent have taken off. Robert B. Goergen, president of Blyth Industries, a company that owns Colonial Candle and is one of the largest candle manufacturers in the United States, said to me that "The rapid expansion of the candle business has been based on the possibility of creating scented candles." The expansion of scented products today is indeed incredible. In recent years, sales for aromatherapy products have increased approximately 30 percent annually, and scented candles have posted 10–15 percent yearly growth since the early nineties.[4] Scented clothing, hosiery, and even tires are being sold in Japan, and last year the British company Contour Mobel began selling "aroma" sofas that emit rose, lavender, and vanilla scents when their cushions are plumped. A spokesman for the company selling the sofas that start at $3,300, said that "the potential for scented products is enormous. Scents are very evocative and appeal to our emotions, and we think there is definitely a market out there."[5] David Easton, a New York interior designer, has an interesting point of view about why we are so enamored of scented products today. He says that "Artificial environments have developed our primal cravings for the natural,"[6] going on to point out the sealed windows in offices and hotels, fully air-conditioned houses, saying that these aromas of nature can summon up worlds we've fallen out of touch with.

Scent need not be limited to the product itself and should be considered the way other, more typical dimensions of product presentation are. Well-planned smells encourage sales, just like excellent color and lighting design. Susan C. Knasko, senior research associate at the Monell Chemical Senses Center, found through research that "customers stayed longer in two sections of a store when the areas were scented with pleasant scents, compared to when the areas were not scented."[7] Recognizing this, many companies have designed fragrances specifically for their stores. Robert A. Baron of Rensselaer Polytechnic Institute elaborates on the effects of odor, writing that "pleasant fragrances in the air influence human behavior by enhancing individuals' current moods. In other words, as informal experience would suggest, pleasant fragrances are one aspect of the physical environment that can make people feel somewhat happier–just as pleasant temperatures, attractive lighting, and the absence of distracting noise can produce similar effects."[8] In this same study, he finds that shoppers exposed to pleasant odors such as perfume, coffee, and cookies are not only in better moods, they also are more likely to engage in amiable and even altruistic behavior!

Well-planned smells encourage sales, just like excellent color and lighting design.

Fragrances may be one of the oldest marketing techniques around. Since ancient times open-air vendors have used burning incense to lure passing traffic over to their wares. Today many commercial spaces have jumped on the scent bandwagon, experimenting with the possibilities for branded scent, such as the London-based shirt maker, Thomas Pink, that scents its stores with the smell of "line-dried linen," the Rainforest Café that pumps fresh-flower extracts into its retail sections, and Jordan's Furniture stores in Massachusetts that uses scents such as bubble gum in the children's section and the smell of pine in the country-style section. Jan Hedrick, design director at Jordan's, says that sales have increased substantially since scent was brought into their marketing plan five years ago. Also, now there are systems available that can restrict a smell to within eighteen inches of the point of sale![9]

Dr. Alan R. Hirsch, neurologist, psychiatrist, and founder of the Smell & Taste Treatment and Research Foundation Ltd. in Chicago, is a specialist in developing scents for commercial use. Hirsch says that "If you're looking to increase sales, the best approach is an appeal based on the emotions, and the quickest way to reach the emotions is through smells."[10] Hirsch, whose 1997 revenues approached $2 million, says that his clients have seen their profits jump as much as 40 percent after going through his "odorizing process" that has designed scents for everything from jeans to the Galleria Malls.[11] Another great source for scents designed for commercial usage is the International Fragrance Foundation in New York that has designed scents for places like the American Museum of Natural History, where the smell of African grasslands was replicated, and specific smells to lend authenticity to amusement parks, such as the odor of a cave.

Gail Civille says, "I actually get upset over how often scents are chosen arbitrarily. Someone, usually the executive, will say 'I think our store smells like this,' and that's it." Good research, says Civille, should be used in choosing a brand fragrance. "Give your customers a product to taste, smell, feel, and then give them pictures, words, or logos. Ask them how much this scent goes with that image. Find the particular sensory stimulus that matches your brand."

The possible effects of well-designed scents should not be underestimated. In another study conducted by Susan Knasko it was found that among visitors exposed to various scents while visiting a museum exhibition, "A more positive mood was reported by visitors in the bubble-gum [odor] condition compared with those in the leather or no-odor condition. Visitors exposed to incense odor reported that they had learned more from the exhibit than visitors exposed to no odor. Visitors in the incense condition also reported that the odor of the room had a more positive influence on their enjoyment of the exhibit compared with visitors in the other odor conditions. Odor condition interacted in complex ways with a number of variables to influence lingering time." Other findings indicate that individuals born before 1930 more frequently associate natural odors, such as pine, with childhood, while younger individuals associate chemical smells, like Pez and Play-Doh, with their youth–an important fact for the designer targeting consumer's emotions because odors associated with youth possess the most emotive power.[12]

Fragrance choices take into consideration not only age but also gender and cultural differences. For example, researchers at Duke have found that fragrances, regardless of whether they're liked or disliked, improve the mood, specifically, of middle-aged women. Therefore, stores targeting that clientele certainly want to make a point of having smells distilled in the air. According to Dr. Hirsch, women have a better sense of smell than men, and Korean-Americans have the most acute sense of smell. Japanese have a relatively poor sense of smell, and American Caucasians and African-Americans tend to fall into the middle range. However, any brand that plans on using smell should *not* rely solely on this data to make choices. Rather, this complicated array of findings demonstrates the need for brands to experiment for themselves and develop an understanding of clients' specific tastes and qualities.

In the very near future, technology may put the ability to tap into these emotionally laden smells with unprecedented precision and even across great distances. DigiScents, a company based in Oakland, California, is currently creating a digital language that accesses a scent cartridge to recreate smells. Each cartridge can instantly create about one hundred different scents, and DigiScents hopes this technology will find application in Web sites, movies, and video games for starters. I think one great application would be on the Starbucks' Web site. Just think—Web surfers could log on to the Starbucks' Web site and immediately be enveloped by the smell of freshly brewed coffee. Consumers could then buy different coffees online and use the varying smells to aid their selection.

Just think—Web surfers could log on to the Starbucks' Web site and immediately be enveloped by the smell of freshly brewed coffee.

Organizations interested in sharpening their brand identity or simply improving their stores or showrooms should capitalize on the advantages provided by smells. Perhaps an in-store aroma system is the answer. Alternatively, fresh baked cookies might contribute to a gift shop's "homey" atmosphere while appealing to taste and smell simultaneously. The only limit is a creative one. Civille goes so far as to say, "What about refrigerators, televisions, furniture? Almost anything can be scented." In other words, scents makes sense.

Soothe the Senses:
Some Peace, Please!

Having noted the importance of sensory appeal, it's also important not to overdo it. Think of it this way: what's more seductive? A whisper or a shout? Generally, a whisper. A whisper carries a soft and subtle message to another. A shout is jarring and attention-getting. Throughout this book I speak about ways to get attention and surprise consumers pleasantly. However, in the Emotional Economy, sometimes the best way to get someone's attention is not to shout, but to whisper. In our wired age, it seems that many people believe strongly that everything should be action, motion, excitement, and saturation, while countless consumers want nothing more than a seductive oasis. It is a known fact, for example, that when we are bombarded by visual stimuli, the ability to assimilate the information is restricted to seven different messages at a time. We do not know very precisely what this number of messages would be for the other four senses or what are the combined effects of messages playing to too many different senses at once are. Hence, brands should be sensitive to our need for peace and relative quietness at times. Brands should know when to whisper. Consumers may not hear them the first time, but once they do, I believe they will listen.

In the retail world, Nordstrom recognizes that sometimes shoppers just want to relax, and it provides for shoppers' peace of mind with consideration and class. First, there is a wealth of seating within the store for shoppers as well shoppers' companions for those all important momentary breaks. "So what," you may say, but Nordstrom is no ordinary store. On the contrary, Nordstrom puts the customer first in all its considerations, and does not implement any changes without thinking about their valued customers. Nordstrom has selectively redesigned much of its seating, raising the chairs' height and thereby making it easier for weary shoppers to sit down and stand up. It is these most basic considerations like "Can we make our chairs better for the customers?" that are the mark of conscious brands—and these are brands with optimistic futures. Another wonderful aspect of the Nordstrom experience is its Spa Nordstrom. Located within the store, Spa Nordstrom provides facials, manicures, and massages to Nordstrom customers for a certain charge. Customers can just walk in or make appointments in advance to assure availability and certify that they are treated by their favorite masseuse or beautician. What better escape from the harries of life than an hour-long massage after several hours of shopping? Spa Nordstrom illustrates that shaping a brand identity is not about providing clothing and shoes. Rather, Emotional Branding is about crafting an intimate and reassuring experience for each customer.

In New York an excellent example of this approach to retailing is found in the Felissimo store. This luxury Japanese home-and-lifestyle brand has designed its store to create an "urban oasis" through a blend of minimalism and Feng Shui, the ancient Chinese philosophy of how to approach architecture and design in accordance with the earth's energy-flow patterns. The aim of the architect, Clodagh, in designing the store was to "incorporate surprising new finishes and features created to reawaken the senses without disturbing the calm within."[1] The store has a lovely rotunda called the Dreamgrounds, where among fountain sounds mixed with floral scents are plants, journals, gardening products, and an eclectic assortment of "grown-up toys." In their "tension-deficit" section one can find Felissimo's collection of bath products, incenses, soaps, and oils. On the store's fourth floor is a tea room with a fusion menu and Haiku tea. One more flight up, on the fifth floor, is a space entirely devoid of wares called Higher Ground, dedicated to lectures, artistic exhibits, meditations, and celebrations. Felissimo's Web site says its Higher Ground space is "not for selling, but for exchanging ideas and sharing good times," and that it is "not just a symbol of our dreams and aspirations . . . It is a place to nurture visionaries and their higher visions."

Another wonderful example of commercial architecture tailored to meet our need for tranquility is the new Ian Schrager hotel in London, The Sanderson, which has been called a "chic chill-out zone."[2] This beautiful hotel beckons to peace-craving travelers as a unique urban spa. Says Anda Andrei, one of the hotel's designers, "We want to create a feeling of being enveloped in calm comfort the moment you step through the door. It's a sanctuary."[3] Building-wide semi-sheer curtains, the postworkout "quiet zone," and the paintings of country scenes that hang above beds help achieve just that. Embodying the

Emotional Branding principles of dialogue and personal relationships, another one of the hotel's designers, Philippe Starck, says that "There is no style. Our job is to make people blossom, not to show *our* talent. It's giving them the minimum so they can find out about themselves as individuals."[4] However, design is carried into every corner of the building—even in the workout dumbbells designed by Starck himself. But in place of dictated environments that dazzle the visitors, beautiful but open-ended architecture and interior design aim to soothe and empower the hotel's visitors' introspection.

Another recent response to people's current level of overstimulation can be found in a current advertising trend. Some advertisers are realizing that in a media-saturated environment advertisements that use lush, relaxing visuals with music (or even sometimes silence) and a minimum of words either spoken or in typeface can be a much more effective way to get consumer's attention than traditional booming voice-overs with jingles and lengthy product explanations. While these ads may require that consumers pay extra attention to discern the brand message (or sometimes even what is being sold!), if done in an aesthetically pleasing, soothing way that speaks to people's emotions, they can intrigue consumers and build a stronger bond with the brands than more intrusive commercials. These ads prove that less can indeed be more.

As marketers and technology conspire to further infiltrate, accelerate, and complicate our daily routine, demand will grow for these soothing sources of stimuli. They will emerge in increasingly unexpected places. Meditation rooms in the rear of your favorite stores, art galleries within the office, ambient and abstract cable channels that feature flowing imagery and gentle sounds—all of these are possible, if not probable.

section III:
imagination

innovation is a brand's
best friend!

Thinking Out of the Box

After looking into the fascinating shifts taking place in the current demo-graphic landscape and delving into the untapped realm of the senses, we are more fully prepared to immerse ourselves in the dynamic world of Emotional Branding. The following chapters are the true backbone of this book because they explore the real everyday challenges of bringing a brand to life as a multi-dimensional, emotionalized entity that people will fall in love with and con-tinue to love.

Convincing people to buy a product or service in a very saturated, competitive environment is obviously fraught with difficulty. The key to success is to begin to understand the formidable and undefined emotional power that ultimately sways everybody's decision making. As with all worthwhile endeavors, there are no pat answers about the best way to do this. Creativity just doesn't work that way! It demands an ongoing commitment to building an open-ended, rela-tionship-oriented culture that encourages emotional sensitivity/understanding and the questioning of status quo, which, in turn, will inevitably lead to the most thrilling expressions of creativity.

The kind of inspiration that leads to innovative brand-design programs in product development, packaging, retail, brand presence, and advertising can-not simply be bottled or bought—but it can be sought . . . and eventually sold!

10

Sensory Design: The New Branding Power Tool

People need an escape and an experience that is different from their day-to-day
lives. I often use that analogy with our car designers; we're not creating great
automobiles, we're trying to create great experiences.
–J Mays, *creator of the Volkswagen Beetle, interviewed by Jim Blair for* Artbyte

What if manufacturers and retailers took this statement by J Mays seriously in
terms of viewing their products and store environments as, above all, creation
of an intense and wonderful experience? Imagine what could be done if corporations had this kind of commitment to design from the standpoint of creating an emotional relationship with consumers. As we progress toward an
economy that thrives on personal relationship, the value of designing consumer products and retail environments as sensory experiences will require,
more than ever before, emotion, imagination, and vision.

From Function to Feel: Welcome to the Twenty-first Sensory!

I believe that design is the most potent expression of a brand and that ultimately bringing powerful ideas to life through design is the best way to create
a lasting link between a manufacturer or retailer and the consumer. The
Volkswagen Beetle, the Gillette series, Issey Miyake's couture, and the Sephora
and Godiva stores are among a long list of examples of product or retail
designs that work. They are proof that at the end of the day design creates
emotions, sensory experiences, and, ultimately, sales.

I always believed that design would eventually belong to the twenty-first century; the emotional age, and this prediction is now starting to become reality.
Time magazine's March 20, 2000, cover hails the "Rebirth of Design" a little
over fifty years after Raymond Loewy, the much-celebrated French born

designer of his generation, made the cover. Such a mass-media tribute to a designer was unprecedented at the time and signaled design's golden age of the fifties. *Time* magazine now tells us that, once again, "Function is out. Form is in. From radios to cars to toothbrushes, America is bowled over by style." The *New York Times* has responded to this trend with a full issue of the spring 2000 edition of the *New York Times Magazine* devoted to home design with "Larger than Life" designer George Hansen, inventor of the swing-arm wall lamp, on the cover. We are seeing major, important design exhibits such as the Triennial Design Retrospective at the Cooper Hewitt Museum in New York. Catherine McDermott, the famed author and consultant curator at the London Design Museum has published a book called *20th Century Design*, which presents "a collection of the most important and influential pieces of design produced in the modern age."[1]

Today's broad media coverage of design has elevated the status and recognition of designers–such as Philippe Starck, the French "enfant terrible" of furnishing design; J Mays, the mastermind behind the Volkswagen; Jonathan Ives, the genius behind Apple; and Tom Ford, the multifaceted Renaissance designer for Gucci–to the heights of stardom in both the business world and with the general public in a way never seen before. Companies like GM are hiring star European designers like Anne Asenio who helped transform Renault into one of the top automotive brands in the industry.

It is encouraging to see that design is once again taking the driver's seat in defining the aesthetic of products that we buy on a mass level. Raymond Loewy, whose product designs became some of most successful marketing tools of his time, and who once said, "There is no curve as beautiful as a rising sales graph," would be proud of this crop of new designers with their finger so firmly on the pulse of the emotional and practical needs of consumers in a new economy. These are primarily needs for individualistic expression within the confines of a budget; the need for objects to have an approachable, humanistic feel in a cold, high-tech world. These needs are being answered with finesse and a ferocious creativity.

These are primarily needs for individualistic expression within the confines of a budget; the need for objects to have an approachable, humanistic feel in a cold, high-tech world.

But what happened from the fifties until the beginning of this century? There was a gap of time between the sixties and nineties when design faded quietly into the background and a bland industrial production controlled the aesthetics of mass products. What prompted this return to the popularity of design after such a long crossing of the desert for designers? What exactly are the changes in the world and in our economies that have encouraged such a renewed focus on design? These are interesting questions to ponder because they tell us a great deal about the Emotional Economy and why consumers desire great design today.

Obviously design was not dead during this gap, but it did not have the same impact and visibility as it has today. So what is it about the atmosphere of both the fifties and today that fosters a love of design? For starters, there is great similarity between the fifties, a period of booming economy following World War II, and the beginning of this century, which is witnessing the longest prosperity period in the history of this country. Today's new economy, fueled by the advent of breakthrough ideas inspired by technology as a new business model, is not at all dissimilar from half a century ago, when the industrial economy and the advent of consumerism had an incredible impact on the prosperity people enjoyed. Good economies encourage growth through imagination, risk, and rewards in business. Good economies, of course, thrive on people's seeking a better standard of living. The difference is that the fifties offered people the opportunity to get better jobs, and the possibility to acquire new homes, new cars, and new appliances that did not even exist before, whereas *in the twenty-first century the accumulation of goods is not as critical as the need to reach out for a better quality of life.* Yes, we are spoiled today . . . but that is not the only reason that we are becoming so choosy about the ways things look. Overall, this shift represents an evolution from the material to the spiritual.

Veronique Vienne, author of *The Art of Doing Nothing*, a book I will talk more about later, and one of the most respected journalists writing articles on design, told me that she felt that this design explosion could be attributed to "the nostalgia for times when things happened more slowly, and [to] our quest for the art of living a quality life."[2] In this new world where speed and computer screens are moving our life more and more out of touch with physical reality, the direct experience we have with the products we interact with on a daily basis can impact our moods and our feelings in the most profound way. The products in our immediate proximity, whether they include a portable phone, a palm anything, or the most banal objects from a dish scrubber down to the garbage can, need to bring with them a new sense of reassurance and pleasure. *In an out-of-control world it is the most human instinct of all to want to be able to impact our immediate surroundings with things of beauty and originality. This gives us a new sense of control.* "People need to be engaged emotionally, and design is proof of the presence of the human dimension" explains Veronique Vienne. Finding an element of personal human touch reconnects us to what's real.

A truly talented designer can tap into our universal need for permanence and beauty.

A truly talented designer can tap into our universal need for permanence and beauty. As we are leaving the old economy, its cold industrial ugliness might be leaving us . . . replaced by the warmth and beauty associated with a new art of living. Designers seem to have understood this emotional expectation from people.

THE RETRO-CHIC STYLE
By taking inspiration for their designs from previous decades, designers have foreseen our craving to anchor ourselves with known cultural values that are adapted to our time. The iMac computer looks like a TV set from the fifties, and the latest Jaguar aesthetics as well as the new Volkswagen Beetle design are a modern interpretation of past models. Philippe Starck recently redesigned Emeco's famous lightweight brushed-steel Navy chair from the forties in another attempt to bring continuity to new generations by translat-

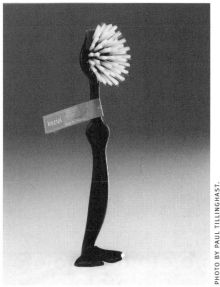

Even a dish scrubber can be personified and convey humor.

ing for today's tastes design successes of the past. Michael Graves's designs for Target take their inspiration from the Memphis postmodern design movement he helped create, and the list, quite literally, goes on and on!

The main thing these designs have in common is that they are created to become irresistible, pleasurable, sensory experiences that have both meaning and attractiveness. Design today has transcended the element of functionality so prevalent in the industrial economy to "embrace psychology and emotion" as Susan Yelavitch, the assistant director of the Cooper Hewitt National Design Museum says.[5] Bulthaup, the home design systems company, expresses this idea well in its advertising copy: "When you furnish your home with Bulthaup, you have arrived in your own conscious and sensitive world of design," a statement that design is a state of mind, which invites the consumer to enter into that state of mind.

And consumers are entering . . . in droves! *Design's past elitist association with high pricing and exclusivity has evolved to extend its definition of the profession to be also about design solutions for everyone.* The professional designer has been taking a more expansive and democratic route. Many design firms have recruited anthropologists and psychologists to help create designs that

Gift Wish No. 1

Blender from Michael Graves Design™
For the artful kitchen, a stylish blender that's
wonderfully practical, too. 400 watts with
five speeds, pulse and 40-oz. glass jar.
Only at Target. $59.99

are people-friendly, and mass outlets have used well-known designers to create and promote their brands. Target stores' former VP Ron Johnson, who masterminded the Michael Graves's line of products that has had a double-digit sales growth since it was introduced last year, said that "Customers really respond to products that involve new thinking and connect with their souls."[4] In the past, this comment may have surprised a lot of manufacturers who did not even consider until now that the mass market had a soul to start with! Design is all about personalization and customization. *Because well-designed products have real personality, it helps us identify a real person behind what we buy, and puts some aspect of our lives into a slower motion in a faster and faster moving world.* We can mentally imagine how long it takes a creator and a craftsman to offer us their artistic vision of the environment we live in and we can appreciate the time and care it takes to render the most innovative and exquisite products. Design can deliver on the promise of emotional and sensory experiences. It takes the edge off of standardization and mass production, destroying the robotic concepts of homogeneity and bulk to bring a new sense of humanity to our lives. The eternal question of whether design is about art or commerce is clearly answered by today's designers. It is about people and our role in making people's lives more fulfilling though beauty. The title in French for Raymond Loewy's book, *Never Leave Well Enough Alone* was *La Laideur Se Vend Mal*, or "ugliness does not sell," a much more appropriate title for today's business atmosphere!

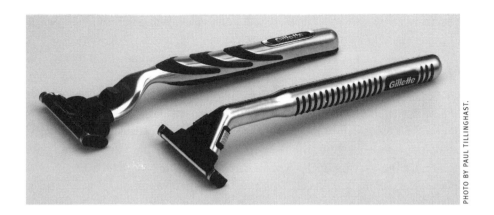

The Gillette Sensor, the father of the Mach III and the brainchild of Gillette's Phyl Symons and Peter Hoffman, is a case in point for the powerful role design can play in business. What makes this packaging great is not that the shaving system, the handle, and blades look pretty, but that the shaver's handle sends a strong message of the best technology any man or woman can get in the world of shaving. Blades are small and unconvincing unless their efficiency is explained to you in detail. Visuals communicate better than words and in the case of the Gillette razor, the handle is the messenger for the blade. But it is the packaging here that really sets the stage—a most glorified stage—for this innovative product. After all, the blades can only speak for themselves when you shave! It is no wonder that they are now clearly the worldwide leaders in the shaving category.

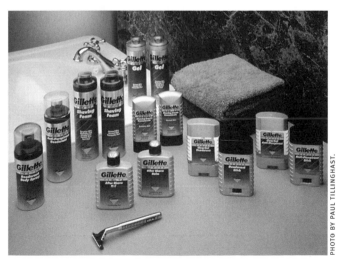

But there are still so many brands today that are missing out on this opportunity because they do not yet understand the difference design can make in their business and have yet to consider the meaning and power of design as a strategic tool. *Most talented designers are also challenging, and sometimes companies become frustrated by what they think is a designers' lack of pragmatism when, in fact, it is mostly a commitment to fresh, unusual solutions.* I will never forget the conclusion of the production department of Gillette when we presented our design for the Gillette Series, the grooming line that was launched following the success of the Sensor razor. It was a completely new way to package grooming products in this category. When we proposed very innovative designs with special finishes giving the effect of silver to build a feeling of freshness and technology in line with the core image of the Gillette brand, we were told point-blank by their production department that it could not be done. During an intense silence I watched the look of disillusionment sweep over the faces of my team, and I realized not only their disappointment but also their conviction that it *would* work! Knowing for myself as well that only bold thinking could make this project a success, I replied, "Well, if you can't do this, you can't be a leader in your industry, challenge yourself." A bold and gutsy statement that certainly could have gotten us fired on the spot! However, fortunately for us, in the room that day there were two great marketers who supported my assumption. And Gillette, a company that considers design to be the lifeblood of its business, found a way to help us do this project on time, on budget, and with the silver design we recommended.

On the other hand, an example of a missed opportunity for both us and a client was a fragrance bottle design we did for Procter & Gamble, which recommended an off-centered opening. To our dismay, this design was turned down by the company for technical reasons. Later we saw the very same concept successfully implemented by Estée Lauder for Tommy Hilfiger's Tommy Sport . . . guess who is one of the leaders in beauty products today?

We are now on the verge of a renewed partnership between corporations and designers. Corporations need innovative designs along with a strong understanding of trends in the marketplace to compete and reach a blasé consumer. This is something that connected designers can provide. *The smart companies have already understood that "trend-focused designers" can offer so much more than just "design!"* These are the companies that will succeed in the twenty-first century.

Global Design Sensibility and Taste

Inevitably the next question for designers and corporations alike is: "What really constitutes 'good emotional design'?" Does it have anything to do with the equally ambiguous concept of "good taste"? This is a debate that encompasses everything from personal perceptions to gender differences to national origin! I would argue that design is first and foremost about cultural and sociological values. Design that works in Brazil might not work in France. Different cultures very often have different aesthetic sensibilities borne of their distinct traditions of art, architecture, ways of dressing, and so on, which are reflected in their products and retail designs. In Japan, retail environments tend toward a sharp clean minimalism; in France an eloquent expressiveness is sought after. In Morocco themes are more colorful and visceral, and in the United States a kind of energetic abundance is often a basic rule of thumb.

In this new global culture full of diverse influences, our taste in design—just as our taste in food—has become much more varied and eclectic.

In this new global culture full of diverse influences, our taste in design— just as our taste in food—has become much more varied and eclectic. As we travel—either by plane, TV, magazine, or computer—our expectation is that we will experience the exciting influences in our "travels" at home or abroad. This presents a great challenge and opportunity for corporations to expand their vocabulary to speak to consumers in these new ways, and for us designers the world becomes a great source of inspiration.

Besides speaking for a culture at large, culturally sensitive designs immediately talk to us in a highly intimate language all their own, creating a brand personality that is expandable far beyond the product or store.

GOOD DESIGN IS COURAGEOUS

The iMac is clearly a design that is home- and people-friendly. Urban Outfitters, the growing Gen X and Y–oriented retail chain, is a thrilling, funky place to shop and feel connected to an "underground" New York fashion and furnishing sensibility. I sometimes wonder how the iMac could be used as an inspiration for a store, or what an Urban Outfitters computer would look like. Design is clearly more about inspiration and imagination than logic and analysis.

The late Bill Bernbach, renowned for his brilliant advertising for Volkswagen in the sixties, said, "Rules are what the artist breaks." The best design ideas are always immediate, consumer-enchanting, and, very often, they do break all the rules.

Good design *is* courageous. But apart from its aesthetic value, let's not forget that it represents a long-term investment that can increase a company's value tenfold and over. Can anyone dispute that Gucci's or Apple's turnaround is design driven? I am sometimes amazed by the financial risk CEOs take everyday with acquisitions, industrial investments, and even advertising, while design is left by the wayside—not a clear priority and generally not considered an investment in terms of potential return. Corporations will spend tens of millions of dollars on mediocre advertising year after year with sometimes poor results, forgetting about the single element that sells itself: design. In an article in *Advertising Age* about the outstanding campaign for the new VW Beetle, the author talks about the difficult challenge of creating the ads specifically because the car is, in his words, "a work of art on wheels, a 115-horsepower advertisement for itself.[5] The ads are remarkable because they show us the brand personality through emphasizing the product design itself in simple, clever ways.

Unless you have an innovative product, it will be very difficult to build brand emotion that will reach people and make a lasting connection. Take Apple's "Think Different" campaign as an example. While the advertising was arresting and original, I personally could not equate something so profound as the

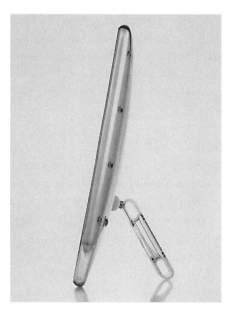

The new twenty-two-inch Apple Cinema Display is one of many product designs that attests to the company's commitment to great design.

116

larger-than-life personalities of Martin Luther King and Gandhi with a commercial brand. It felt to me like desperation at its best (or worst) from an advertising perspective—no product news to communicate, nothing else to say. Then came the iMac and suddenly "Think Different" made sense. I could see just *how* Apple was thinking differently about technology! The motto was validated by the product; an innovative, well designed, relevant one. The association between the advertising and the product was vivid, evident, and real. The communication concept and the product together made the message truly break through! Modern design could bring to the new millennium a whole new language for consumers to enjoy—a language of trust, elegance, and intimacy. Apple has continued this exciting design dialogue with consumers through other groundbreaking designs such as the new Mac Cube that encases Apple's most powerful technology yet into a clear plastic case about the size of a toaster with an eight-inch screen!

DESIGNING PLACES AS MUSEUMS

Brand-driven architects could also impact society by bringing a renewed sense of beauty to all places we visit. People are looking for experiences of newness, excitement, and fun in stores, museums, restaurants, offices, or amusement parks . . . well, maybe *all* these places should be amusement parks!

Frank Gehry's design for the Bilbao Guggenheim museum changed the economy of the town of Bilbao as well as the entire region. The innovative architecture of the building is so unique, compelling, and dazzling that the place is in and of itself an attraction, regardless of what is presented in the museum. Out of the four million people from around the world who visit this incredible structure of luminescent curved metal plates (made of titanium) every year, at least 40 percent say they are mostly coming to experience the uniqueness of the architecture. The museum has largely transcended its role as an exhibition provider to become instead a destination, with the work presented in the building partnering in enhancing the visitor's experience. What is more important here? The concept, the place, or the content? They all work together beautifully. The content is on the level of some of the best museums in the world. The concept is indeed powerful. The difference here, the reason why it works, is that Frank Gehry, an incredibly talented architect and artist, was successful in his *emotional* objective of mesmerizing people in a world built around art through design.

Frank Gehry's design for the Bilbao Guggenheim museum changed the economy of the town of Bilbao as well as the entire region.

The Bilbao Guggenheim Museum

Stores, even discount stores, don't need to be designed in a cookie-cutter fashion with a fixture book in hand outlining what has worked in the past. Brands like Old Navy have caught on, providing hip fashions at cut-rate prices in a delightful, concept-oriented environment (i.e., a retro "grocery store for clothing") and leaving more traditional discount retailers behind in the dust. As we move into a new age of globalization and cultural sharing, designers are really the interpreters, ambassadors, and visionaries of worldwide creative influences for consumers everywhere. Think about the most memorable store you ever visited and analyze what made it so great. I would bet that a really good design firm was involved. A very good friend of mine who is a professor at Columbia University once told me that, for her, going to "Pottery Barn or Crate and Barrel was like visiting a museum except that one can afford and buy the art presented in the store!" She told me that she felt that art has transcended its perception as only paintings on a wall or sculptures on a pedestal. She feels that art today needs to be found in all the things we buy in our private lives. I couldn't agree with her more!

Designing products and stores is first and foremost about understanding consumers and respecting their needs and desires. For a very long time, mass-distribution stores looked very "mass," as if saying loudly, "this is for poor peoplc, and the quality here is only what you can afford—style is not important." Well, a very smart designer has started to change that at Kmart. Martha Stewart's wonderful home furnishings collection is a total success. Innovation and fair price associated with style is something any consumer appreciates, whatever the size of their wallet.

TOMORROW'S TECH-DESIGN MAGICIANS

The future of design is as vast as the possibilities that new technology is bringing us. The burgeoning world of high tech is design's new frontier and the realm of endless, exciting opportunities. All of these fast-becoming-necessary objects—high-tech devices such as cell phones—will increasingly be differentiated by sensory-oriented, exciting, and fashion-conscious designs. Design will be the element that adds the all-important human element to our wired world.

Designing products and stores is first and foremost about understanding consumers and respecting their needs and desires.

Mitsubishi's portable convergence phone with Internet capabilities was specifically designed with a comfortable shape and a velvety texture to the silver exterior to give pleasure to the user. It is designed to stand out from the crowd. It is fascinating to imagine what the future of technology could be and how this future will be married to design as every day more and more ordinary, mundane objects are becoming infused with technology, and entirely new, inventive tech products are being created. Nike has now created a new division named Techlab to develop sports technology products, such as a digital audio player which plays MP3 files as well as Microsoft Windows Media audio files, high-tech walkie-talkies, and portable wrist monitors. The products come in shades like "fire warm," "green leaf," and "cool sparkle," and are most definitely designed to be fashionable.

IDEO, the innovative California-based product design firm, launched a six-month Project 2010 to visualize products ten years from now. Based on a continued evolution of our current technologies, they have predicted a new generation of cool products, such as flexible computer LCD screens of all shapes and sizes that can be pulled out from a cell phone for larger visuals or used in a portable scroll format (instead of a book), eyewear equipped with earphones that screens out the stimuli of the world but has interior displays for information or entertainment, and workstations and homes with computing and communication technology embedded in the furniture and walls for 3-D holographic information and entertainment. Already we see watches designed to double as cell phones, such as the great-looking ones by Swatch or Motorola. *Wallpaper*, the trendy design magazine, says of the Motorola watch, "A person could get tired of mobiles, but not when they're this cute."[6] And in fashion there is a hot new "cyber fiber" trend where fabric technology is allowing designers to create clothing out of "intelligent" materials that can protect the wearer from UV exposure, inhibit bacteria, perfume the wearer all day, or monitor one's heart rate.

Conclusion

Designers have an uncanny ability to define the future with their vision, bringing the most remarkable concepts to life. They can be magicians, creators, and real think tank and R&D resources for companies. *Design solutions will evolve toward design creations, which is a much more effective way of defining the profession.* Designers are transcending the realm of engineering and technology to embrace market-driven opportunities through product stories that are always much more emotionally potent than either of the former; this is what will make a real difference in the marketplace. In the Emotional Economy, the role of designers as assets to corporations is growing, and it will not only create surprising and great-looking shapes, but also act as incubators for new ideas.

Designers have an uncanny ability to define the future with their vision, bringing the most remarkable concepts to life.

Raymond Loewy designed for speed and efficiency—industrial-production speed and efficiency—key values for the culture of his time. Streamlining, the modernistic, motion-inspired design style he created was meant to help manufacturers win in the marketplace with high-functioning products that had an aesthetic edge over their competitors. Today, from the perspective of Emotional Branding, design must be responsive to people's emotional needs and desires for sensory pleasure. This demands passion, honesty, and, above all, commitment to a mission to improve the world we live in. Sound utopian and radical? Well, just ask those folks on the street.

11

Emotionally Charged Identities: Unforgettable Brand Personalities

There is a fundamental truthfulness and legitimacy in a brand that will never change, but its execution must always be defined by the market.
–Philip Shearer, President, Luxury Products Division, L'Oréal USA

There are unemotional brands such as Kmart and Compaq, and emotional brands, such as Wal-Mart and Apple. The difference between the two is the vision, visualization, and emotional connection the later have been able to convey to the world.

From "Dictated" to Emotionally "Connected" corporate-identity programs are the expression of a corporation's culture, personality, and the products or services it has to offer–the very symbol and signature of the values that should inspire trust with consumers, employees, clients, suppliers, and the financial community. Logos and their colors–whether expressed as symbols (like Nike), logotypes (unique typographic treatment of the name, such as the FedEx identity of upright Roman letters designed by Landor), or a combination of both (as in the case of the AT&T logo)–have been an essential part of all major branding strategies since the middle of the last century. Coca-Cola, IBM, and Mercedes are examples of successful identity programs that have withstood the test of time. Coca-Cola's particular typographic script and powerful red color are unmistakable and memorable; the IBM logo–in its distinct blue–is recognizable worldwide; Mercedes' three-pointed, encircled star logo is not only seen as a guarantee of superior engineering, but it acts as a signature of cachet value of the automobiles and translates easily to a sign of good taste and status for the cars' owners.

Powerful logo identities like these make advertising and public relations programs more effective by becoming a visual shorthand for the meanings attached to them and thereby influencing consumers to be receptive to a company's message. Products bearing the logo of a well-known, high-quality corporation benefit from the perception that they are also of superior quality. The products' appeal to the consumer is further enhanced by the comfort level that is evoked from a brand with which the consumer is already familiar.

Logos can be very memorable and can crystallize many different meanings. *A logo by itself is not necessarily a communication tool but it can most definitely act as a symbol of what a company represents (or hopes to represent) and the resulting consumer perceptions.* As the flag of a company, a logo is its most important visual asset as well as a catalyst for good and bad feelings and therefore needs to be managed with intelligent care. Today this intelligent care means becoming more flexible and far-reaching. Corporate identity programs in the new economy are far more vivid and effective if the identity has integrated elements such as *social sensitivity, cultural relevance,* and an attempt to find *a real connection point with people.* Creative solutions are necessary to help find this combined and crucial "human factor." A logo can be very visible, but without being humanized–that is, without "heart"–it is like a person without "heart": cold, uninteresting, a robot.

A logo without "heart" is like a person without "heart": cold, uninteresting, a robot.

Designing Logos for the Heart

In order to reflect a changing business environment, corporate-identity programs have evolved over time from an approach based purely on the concepts of visibility and impact (products of an industrial economy and in the language defined by corporations) to one based on the concept of *emotional contact* with consumers founded on interaction and dialogue (couched in a new language of a "people-driven economy"). As we have been moving into this consumer-driven economy, corporate identities have begun to expand the expression of their character, becoming more flexible and dynamic in order to bring levels of added meaning and soul to consumers' perceptions of them. Corporate identities are transforming from the "dictated" visual identities of the past (corporate-centric identities that "tell" us what will be the unconditional values they represent) to the "personal" visual identities (those designed around an emotion and whose interpretation is often different from one consumer to the next) of the present and future.

To balance a corporate-identity message today, it is also important to consider the power of its emotional message within the context of the strength of the visual message. Just as the *emotional meaning* of a brand needs to evolve from dictated to personal, the *graphic expression* of the brand needs to evolve from "impact" to "contact." ("Personal" identities tend to be more illustrative and imaginative, just as "dictated" ones tend to be more abstract in their graphic style.) Both aspects need to be managed to build the proper message. Clearly the dictated and

The *emotional meaning* of a brand needs to evolve from dictated to personal, from impact to contact.

impact models connote a more passive consumer stance than the newer personal and contact models do, which imply a closer, even bilateral connection. Indeed, logos are now being designed specifically to bridge the gap between corporations and people, and these "connected," branded logo designs can help to better define and communicate the desired personality of the company.

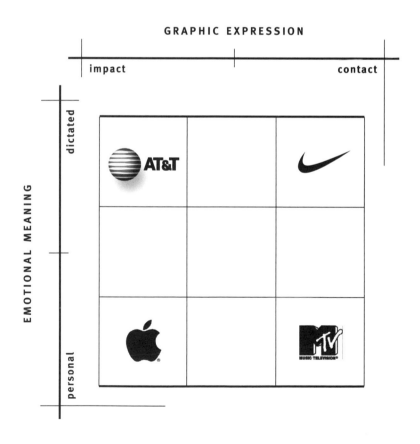

GRAPHIC EXPRESSION

Before the process of building a strong corporate-identity program from the perspective of Emotional Branding can be understood, it's important to examine the way the development of corporate symbols of leading corporations have changed over time, toward the successful "connected" logos of today. Successive generations indeed define their approaches with their own language, cultural values, ethics, idols, myths, management principles, and corporate logos; and three clear eras evolve: what I call the Pragmatist Age (roughly 1940–67), the Evangelist Age (1968–89) and, most recently, the Sensualist Age (from 1990 to the present).

THE PRAGMATIST AGE

Americans in the forties and fifties experienced an unprecedented economic boom based on the globalization of the American industry and new, more efficient distribution systems. Fueled by a strong postwar economy and America's newfound position as a superpower, this era saw the advent of single, large corporations producing multiple and multifaceted products and services—with an emphasis on function, reliability, and the pragmatic. As these corporations began to venture into the global market, corporate design began to be recognized for the first time as an important tool that could help address the need of presenting an unequivocal corporate voice through a cohesive visual identity to the world markets. Corporations realized that their identity needed to be the very emblem of their business through a simple, powerful, easily recalled symbolic form of a logo or logotype—one that would be retained and remembered by millions of people.

At a time when there was a global desire to own a piece of the American Dream (the United States was relatively prosperous compared to many of the devastated European nations), brand design strategies were created to help U.S. brands compete not only at home but abroad as well. Corporate images created by such brand-design experts as Raymond Loewy, Walter Landor, Paul Rand, and campaigns masterminded by American advertising agencies such as Young & Rubicam, McCann Erikson, and Leo Burnett were the voice of the entry of American products into the global market. These efforts left an indelible impact on the culture of our era, because these brand identities were themselves cultural symbols reflecting the corporate profile and pragmatic glory of this industrial age. Visibility, stability, and

Visibility, stability, and consistency were apparent in the visual expression of the corporate values of the time.

consistency were apparent in the visual expression of the corporate values of the time. Mass standardization and production were at the core of the business equation, and the typical corporate objective was nothing less than conquering what was truly now a global market.

The success of American brand icons such as Coca-Cola, McDonald's, IBM, Ford Motor Company, TWA, Marlboro, and Levi's, for instance, were largely due to communications tools that stood powerfully above their competitors'. The objective was to visually dominate markets with commercial messages supported by omnipresent advertising and unwavering corporate-identity programs.

THE EVANGELIST AGE

In the seventies and eighties, the Baby Boomers of the Western world went on to enjoy an even higher level of economic freedom than their parents, and the United States was becoming the most active consumer market in the world. At the same time, the soon-to-be-called Baby Boomer generation did not share its parents' view of the American Dream; the Boomers had a different perception of the ideal world than that portrayed in the fifties and sixties. The Vietnam War, the growing negative perception of the influence of international big business in local and foreign politics, and the realization that the same socioeconomic opportunities were not available to everyone, led business entrepreneurs for the first time in history to speak about righting political and social wrongs through business practices–to literally evangelize about values they believed in. Apple, for instance, created a corporate culture based on the belief that technology will give power back to people. Cesar Chavez–a Hispanic union leader–led an unprecedented boycott of California grapes to help negotiate better terms for Hispanic farmworkers. And the Vietnam War, with its dubious necessity, helped raise the social conscience of Americans and made people realize that they did indeed have power and could positively change the course of politics and the world around them. Corporations needed to appeal to this empowerment of the common man and woman on the street.

The most innovative and assertive entrepreneurs of this generation injected into their business practices new ideals representing philosophies of justice, equality, and sensitivity to the environment. For the first time, business practices and pragmatism were intertwined with a concern regarding the impact business had on people and the planet. Consequently, a new business language was formed. Benetton, for instance, started to preach to the world about injustice through its radical advertising campaigns that forced issues like violence, racism, and the AIDS epidemic into the forefront of social thinking. As I mentioned in chapter 3, The Body Shop, led by Anita Roddick, built its success by creating a business model that was extremely proactive regarding issues of the human condition, the environment, and animal rights. Patagonia, the clothing brand, was very strict in imposing the most stringent ecological standards on its suppliers. By implementing new management practices that were less rigid and more people-friendly, Apple computers spearheaded a new corporate lifestyle that influenced its time. Apple deliberately distanced itself from IBM by making IBM appear as an Orwellian Big Brother firm (in the famous "1984" television ad, quite literally so).

Nike broke all the rules by creating a counterculture marketing program that focused on people (in particular, women), motivating them to challenge themselves physically and spiritually. Virgin Atlantic caused an upheaval of the rules in the staid travel industry by promoting a more fun, friendly style and better responsiveness to consumers' needs. I still remember the innovative design of early Gap stores in San Francisco: they were places where you could find all the jeans you wanted in stores that were decorated in bold, modern, colorful graphics, a completely revolutionary idea at the time, and one that should be considered again. Taking another tack, Ralph Lauren gave us a very clear perception of the "American look" and broke open the doors of exclusivity by giving permission for people to buy into the private lifestyle of the upper middle class. Lauren personally introduced a level of pride into American fashion that eventually wooed the world.

Corporate symbols reflected these companies' innovative cultures. The Body Shop logo, with its open, curvaceous, freestyle design, used a typography that did not have the corporate, mechanical look inherent in the corporations of previous years. Benetton's green logo and round typography was unique in its graphic statement, while Apple's identity was a completely different attempt at connecting with people, with a graphic style clearly not expressed in the terms of the unemotional, corporate world. Virgin developed a logo that looked like a handwritten signature to evoke a personal and approachable feeling. The Ralph Lauren polo logo helped us aspire more to "the good life" in its expression than did, let's say, Levi's jeans.

These new strategies meant that new branding agencies were beginning to convey some of the days' new counterculture messages: Chiat/Day for Apple, and later Wieden & Kennedy for Nike, became the messengers and the voice of a new generation. Brand-identity programs reflected new logos, packaging, and store designs that were hugely personal statements about the brand's philosophy. This era was "teaching the world to sing," like Coca-Cola, to "just do it," with Nike, to share in spreading humanistic vision and responsibility with Benetton

Brand-identity programs reflected new logos, packaging, and store designs that were hugely personal statements about the brand's philosophy.

and The Body Shop, and to enjoy the "good life," as defined very precisely by Ralph Lauren. These lifestyle-oriented, "evangelistic" brands were true believers in their dual mission to build successful businesses and influence people's lives.

THE SENSUALIST AGE

The values of the nineties were geared more toward hedonism, glamour, fame, and individual expression. Through the social construct of Generation X, the emphasis began to shift toward the individual, toward seeking immediate, often sensual rewards, and toward a need for constant change. The Internet revolution is now introducing a new set of values (based on the premium of speed) and is whipping branding strategies into a frenzy, stirred up by the rush to take advantage of the enormous financial opportunities. The digital generation—among it the creators of Amazon.com, Yahoo!, AOL, Kozmo.com, and eBay—are immersed in a world of innovation and financial rewards that is unprecedented in the history of the planet. Never before have there been so many millionaires and so young.

This same generation is creating its own language, culture, and symbols that are derived from the energy associated with this unbridled, digital playground. Naming conventions for portals such as Yahoo! and Excite, e-commerce retailers such as Kozmo.com, digital communications firms such as Razorfish, and

magazines such as *Red Herring, Fast Company*, or *Wired*, are a few examples of the new and very different corporate vocabulary this generation of entrepreneurs is creating. Speed and the willingness to change are of the essence. Branding strategies need to work in six months or less, and corporate identities are often created at a moment's notice or even sketched out on napkins over lunch. A logo's two-dimensional role as a signature of the business has been diminished in comparison to the bigger role logos can play on Web sites. Digital identities operate by different rules: the online world is one of instant buzz, where the merger of wireless modes of communication with the Internet will bring a new era of online business, and where entertainment will add an entirely new dimension to commerce. This new economy is more like a Star Wars universe, where multidimensional battleships are always moving, always reinventing themselves through technology. Corporate and brand identities will begin to reflect this new business attitude, transcending forever the role of the logo as a two-dimensional property.

MTV was a pioneer in creating modular, interpretive logos which were flexible to the brand's expressive needs.

THE SHAPE OF LOGOS TO COME

Forty years ago, as we've just seen, an identity was required to look great on smoke stacks; it was designed to last forever and look appropriate in any context as a true reflection of the conservative values of the time. Today, corporate identities are changing to become consumer-driven, flexible, multisensorial expressions of not only what the company thinks it is, but also reflections of how a company wants to be perceived by people and how they want people to interact with it. When designing a corporate program today, designers manipulate not only graphics but also sounds and textures. One must animate the logo on a Web site and define its cultural connection to society. An identity program in the twenty-first century is a multidimensional expression of a brand vision brought to life in the most imaginative way. Identities need, therefore, to be more modular, continuing to innovate along the lines that MTV has done in the past with their varying and highly expressive logo presentations.

Companies are just now beginning to explore how a logo can become a living, breathing creature that can foster a great deal of awareness for a brand in a very positive way. *Logos can be a lot more than a minuscule corner portion of an ad! And considering the money corporations spend to develop a corporate identity, why not put them to work a little harder?* Target's use of their logo in so many creative ways in their advertising communicates the store's innovative approach and overall commitment to change. Target has created an entirely new story with its brand by leveraging the strength of their red bull's-eye logo to send a message of fashion, modernity, and fun. Some Gen Y–oriented brands, such as Bonfire (a snowboard label owned by Adidas), are beginning to take this trend of flexible logos a step farther by allowing con-

Target's logo based advertising.

sumers to pick from a selection of different logo designs available as stickers (Bonfire has a choice of seven) that are then displayed for them in a personalized way on the product. This is a concept that will continue to develop, particularly in the realm of mass customization.

Given the life span of some identities, there is currently in the marketplace a jumble of different visual languages reflective of different generations and economies juxtaposed in magazines, on television, and on the Web. Today, the business of creating corporate identities faces the challenge of how to stay current. There is the danger of being pegged as irrelevant because the corporate identity you created ninety-five or even five years ago is outdated, or the new name you built your identity around is suddenly . . . not hip!

Not surprising then, logo designs, the most important signature of a brand, have evolved to reflect the different philosophies of each generation of entre-

IBM is an example of the corporate-driven business approach of its time; Apple, as a name and a symbol, is humanistic; while Yahoo! mirrors the quirky spirit of the Internet generation.

preneurs. Even though established identities have had to adapt in order to remain relevant, most are still stuck in the past. Three technology logos that clearly epitomize their times–IBM, Apple, and Yahoo!–exemplify how corporate expression has evolved over the years. The IBM logo, designed by Paul Rand, is a strong example of the corporate-driven business approach of the time; pragmatic, industrial, and conservative in typography. Apple, as a name and a symbol, on the other hand, is humanistic, a trait consistent with the "evangelistic" values of the Baby Boomer generation. Yahoo! mirrors the quirky spirit of the Internet generation. It is sensual, expressive, fun, and uses the hip retro-chic style of the fifties that appeals to members of Generations X and Y.

In our new virtual world where rules are reinvented every nanosecond, logos are not merely physical markers.

In our new virtual world where rules are reinvented every nanosecond, logos are not merely physical markers, but serve as a cultural connection to people. In this unruly epoch where change is a constant, the priorities are different. The amateurish look of the AOL logo would perhaps make Paul Rand (the creator of the IBM logo) or Saul Bass (the designer behind the AT&T logo) cringe.

In the branding program we developed for IBM's new sub-brand, NetVista, we designed a visual vocabulary around a bold, personal graphic device as the sub-brand's icon to answer the challenge of ensuring consistency in extending the identity across all channels of communication, from the Web site (please see *www.pc.ibm.com/us/netvista/index/html*) to printed materials. NetVista's brand positioning is about "the next generation in computing," as

the products allow for ease of use for all Net-based computer devices. The dynamic, fresh look of NetVista is meant to convey the brand as a new way of looking at computing from a perspective of ease and simplicity. The program was designed to be cohesive, yet highly flexible with a three-tiered approach which emphasizes the N as the main graphic element in PR materials, the products as the main visual elements in consumer-oriented communications, and the NetVista brand icon as the main graphic element in communications addressing the overall program.

Typography Is about Personality

A computer has yet to be made that can cross-reference knowledge and interpret novel situations with the complexity and originality of the human brain. Even from the perspective of today's electronic age, it's hard to imagine machinery ever matching this human ability in its full and dynamic complexity. One of the most fascinating aspects of human processing is that it's often unprompted and subconscious—it just happens. I offer the following examples:

Reagonomics

Reagonomics

Reagonomics

What's the difference between these three messages? The word is the same in each case, but although the semantic definition is consistent, there is clearly a difference in the three representations. For me, the first message conveys seriousness and importance; the second indicates a comical repetition of the phrase, such as one might encounter in mocking satire; the third has a strange and ironic sophistication to it. Most of us, by the time we're fifteen years old, have been significantly acculturated by the world around us to interpret these relatively subtle typographical nuances of meaning. No classroom formally trains us in making these qualitative evaluations of lettering, but somehow the information is stored in our minds anyway. The ability to immediately and creatively reference stimuli is inherent to the human brain, and on this fascinating quality rests the power of typography.

The way letters conveying a message are designed is an important visual element of branding that can utilize powerful emotional connotations. It is a kind of science that can be used for a real strategic advantage, and it is unfortunate that it is not always given the attention it deserves. Typographic styles speak volumes about another kind of style: the lifestyle, that is, the Époque or character of a brand. In our design for the Coca-Cola Olympic City logo, we used the typeface Confidential—a typeface with a gritty, urban feel—to communicate the "For the Fans" positioning. We rendered the type in the soda's proprietary red and white colors yet far enough from Coke's classic scripted type that it gives the brand a contemporary edge—we expanded the brand meaning while not taking it too far from the original brand. People decode these kinds of typographic messages on a subliminal level, extracting subtle nuances of meaning that would otherwise demand lengthy and unwieldy explanations that defeat the message. (To see our work for the Coca-Cola Olympics, please take a look at Tool #3, Brand Presence® Management, in chapter 17.)

Many enduring corporate identities of monolithic brands have been built almost solely on typography. IBM uses typography that is modern, reflecting the bold character of the industrial world. The thick, solid, and calming blue letters convey the reliability and unwavering strength that the company aspires to project. Paul Rand developed the trademark logo in 1956 from an infrequently used, thirties typeface called City Medium. This geometric slab-serif font was designed along lines similar to Futura. Rand's orig-

The way letters conveying a message are designed is an Important visual element of branding that can utilize powerful emotional connotations.

inal logo was updated in the seventies with the stripes we see today. The positive association of these characters with the IBM brand identity, compounded by their consistency over the course of many years, contributes to the formation of "consistency" and "reliability" as associations with the company.

Magazine titles use typography to express something even more abstract: the values the publications represent to readers. *Vogue*, for example, connotes

The look of the IBM typography design is highly recognizable even when the "IBM" is replaced by ".COM".

a classic elegance with its Bodoni serif type. *Wired* magazine has an audacious, innovative, and dynamic typographic look that suggests the speed, energy, and unpredictability of the world of technology it covers. The *New York Times* uses a Gothic typeface associated with Gutenberg—the inventor of the printing press—for its title to get across the grounded heritage and authenticity of the newspaper. This typeface is a highly recognizable aspect of the *New York Times*' identity and is immediately associated with the newspaper.

While it is true that typography is often taken for granted, some firms do understand the power of typography and even develop their own proprietary typefaces for a stronger corporate identity and message consistency. In the advertising and print world, typefaces have been created to differentiate one company's message from those of its competitors and sometimes even differentiate its own new message from an old one.

In just such a way, Microsoft used the services of famous designer and typesetter David Carson to create a new look for one of its advertising campaigns. Many have credited Carson with redefining nineties typography and capturing the spirit of technology with his innovative work—particularly in his work for *Ray Gun*, the magazine Carson started with several colleagues and positioned as an underground alternative to *Rolling Stone*. Commenting on existing media, Carson has said: "Today it's about the information, and I happen to think that it's not enough to just present information with no thought about its visual impact. It has to have something more to it. It's like *Ray Gun*. If *Ray Gun* had been presented traditionally, I don't think we would have survived, because the writing wasn't that great, and we covered a lot of the same bands other magazines did, but in the end the visual language became as important as the content."[1]

Carson makes layout and typography elements themselves crucial vehicles of meaning. Form doesn't simply follow content; form is content. Carson's work is largely responsible for spawning the "look" of technology which now manifests itself in *Wired*, *Shift*, and other publications, both on- and off-line. Mattew G. Kirschenbaum—a professor of English at the University of Kentucky and an astute observer of digital culture and new media who also conducts applied

PHOTO BY GERI BAUER PHOTOGRAPHICS, INC.

research in humanities computing and informatics—has described this as a "distinctive visual aesthetic associated with information."[2] At the Massachusetts Institute of Technology's Media in Transition Conference, Kirschenbaum claimed that "information has now assumed visible and material form as a definable and even datable set of aesthetic practices; a visible spectrum of tropes, icons, and graphic conventions that collectively convey the notion of 'information' to the eye of the beholder."[3]

This observation is noteworthy on many levels. First, because technology and information comprise possibly the most exciting and influential force of the moment and are reworking the forms of countless industries, branding must adapt to these changes while adopting its methods. These methods are not simply about Web pages and digital networks, but about aesthetics. Additionally, as Kirschenbaum says, "information itself has historically been defined in abstract, intangible ways." But this has changed, I believe, as a manifestation of how everything becomes branded in a media-saturated culture. There is no "neutral" font. Even packaging a product plainly and using utterly generic labeling can become a point of distinction today.

The current electronically inspired revolution in typography reminds me of the revolution brought about by the playful and illustrative typography that blossomed in another period. Psychedelic posters, like the ones designed by Peter Max or the Pushpin Group in the seventies, made a strong statement that immediately signaled an epoch of mind-blowing change. I asked Seymour Chwast—one of the founders of the Pushpin Group—what gave them the inspiration to create this new look, and he mentioned that the music industry and the record albums were a tremendous medium for them to express their creativity. Remember the 1967 *Bob Dylan's Greatest Hits* album and poster designed by Milton Glaser?

This new look redefined the revolutionary language of the era's youth movement. Look at today's CD graphics for inspiration. The music industry is always ahead of its time in typographic trends and a true barometer of generational graphic expressions. Frank Kozik, whose colorful and explosive graphics have been used by up-and-coming punk-rock bands, is at the forefront of today's exciting and revolutionary rock imagery. Within his imagery a beautiful synthesis of typography, imagery, and colors conspire for a cohesive and stunning visual effect. The bands' unconventional spirit is inevitably conveyed, whether the portrayal is of Jimi Hendrix or a contemporary group such as the Red Hot Chili Peppers.

People's deepest emotions, aspirations, and dreams always need a new language that crystallizes their mind-set and sends their message to the world.

Brilliant typography can not only seize the moment (e.g., Solidarsnok—the political movement led by Lech Walesa against the Communists in Poland) but preserve its brilliance and vitality indefinitely. People's deepest emotions, aspirations, and dreams always need a new language that crystallizes their mind-set and sends their message to the world. Typography is an ideally suited tool for these times because it often delivers more powerful yet more subtle messages than images or lengthy explanations.

Nomenclature and Organizational Structure in the Emotional Economy

Connecting corporate ideas and the market in the simplest way is so much a part of the new consumer-driven economy that all corporate nomenclature systems–that is, the ways companies choose to name their divisions and products–should reflect an emotional model that has humanity at its core and allows for a free flow of ideas between corporations and people. In order to be relevant to our new economic order, corporate-identity strategies must evolve to encompass a larger social and cultural context through a dialogue-based approach–internally and externally–that encourages contact. Most corporate programs are top-down and internally driven with minimal input from people and reflect organizational charts that, in most cases, fail to indicate this all-important human factor of the company.

Taking this system to an even more–to me–puzzling and extensive level, is

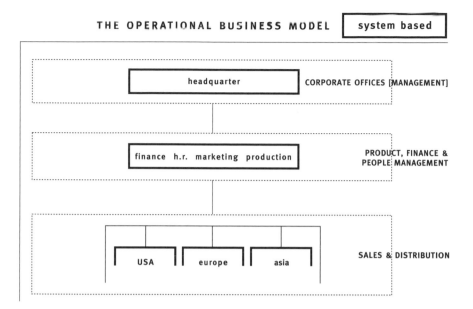

Ralph Lauren's brand architecture. It includes so many brands and sub-brands that it dilutes the power of the creator. From Polo to Chaps, to Polo Sport, Polo Jeans, Double RL, Ralph, Lauren, RLX, etc., the brand system is set up from a corporate and distribution point of view that could vastly benefit from being addressed from a market-driven perspective.

These identity programs are a pale reflection of the human dynamics found in the new economy companies based on the relationship model that encourages communication. The much more organic, people-driven model allows for simplicity of consumer contact as well as internal-external dialogue.

For one of our clients, a large, well-known Japanese corporation, we designed a new relationship-based model of nomenclature that captured their corporate organizational architecture. The objective was to unify the company behind a new business strategy and to simultaneously change perception of the company as an old-economy corporation in the eyes of the financial community, the public, and the employees. The company asked us to create a corporate identity that would communicate a new vision of it as a global entity. However, after months of auditing the company, interviewing employees, and analyzing the organization's brand equity, we realized that what was asked of us would have only been a short-term, cosmetic solution if the company did not funda-

THE CORPORATE IDENTITY OPERATIONAL MODEL | system based

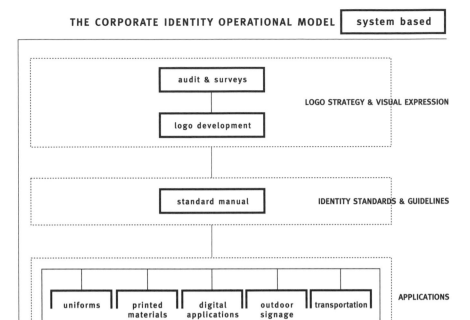

mentally change its overall philosophy. We began helping the top management of the company rethink their business strategy and to approach it entirely from an emotionally branded perspective. And a new visualization of their organizational chart proved to be very powerful in making the organization understand this new vision.

We felt that the company needed to evolve from a factory-based business to a "brand incubator." The idea was a very bold and challenging one since the core culture of the business was totally driven by industrial capabilities and the feasibility of their equipment. It was a hierarchical and traditional model based on the strength of their operations.

The company's enormous success had come from smart industrial ideas that were on the level of genius forty years ago. Starting out as a small company manufacturing glue for bicycles, the founder searched for ways to expand his business by finding other tube-based products to develop around this industrial expertise. They found it in toothpaste and, as a result, almost overnight this small operation became one of the biggest Japanese toothpaste manufacturers. The company went on to develop more than a hundred oral-care prod-

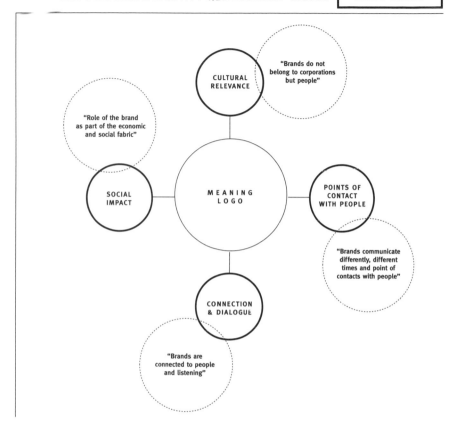

ucts for all population segments and distribution channels. They enjoyed tremendous growth in the Asian market until Japanese protectionist policies softened and new megabrands from the West began to infiltrate the market. Suddenly this strong, industrial-based business was threatened by brand-driven companies with the reputations and money to conquer them on their home turf.

The exercise for us went far beyond traditional identity charts, nomenclature systems, and good-looking logos—all of which would have been ineffective against the far stronger brands now challenging the company. Rather, our goal was to show our client the opportunities offered by a new brand strategy vision. We set out to help them leverage their strengths by using the power of their people to rebuild a dynamic, competitive global business. *We did this by focusing on moving from a culture of rationality (based on the functions and benefits of products) to one of desire (based on the emotional bond people have with a brand).* We wanted to help take them from a culture of creating brands that people need to a culture of creating brands that people desire. Our recommendation was to emphasize the company's branded "intellectual properties" beyond the limitations of their existing factory capabilities–in short, to change the company from an industrial mentality to a market-driven one. To communicate this idea, we devised an organizational chart and brand architecture that emphasized a *relationship model* that helped clarify roles and responsibilities as well as facilitate communications between all divisions.

The difference between the relationship model we created for the company and their existing structure can be likened to the difference that exists between algebra and geometry, 2D and 3D–between a flat earth and a round one! In trying to create a more dynamic model that would promote interaction–connection and synergy–we took our inspiration from the circling planets of the galaxy. We divided the roles and responsibilities of each group and defined the connections among the divisions and groups to headquarters, which was represented as the sun, a symbol of life and creation (the incubator). The brands and brand groups were seen as planets circling the sun that was seen as a provider and consultant, with financial, R&D, and marketing capabilities to assist the brands in evolving freely in their different markets so that they could consolidate their positions worldwide.

The language that we used made a difference in explaining the human and emotional dynamics needed to rally a corporation behind a new, powerful idea and vision.

The language that we used made a difference in explaining the human and emotional dynamics needed to rally a corporation behind a new, powerful idea and vision. This model clarified the corporate message and struck an emotional chord with our clients, helping them better envision the possibilities of their brand.

Corporate branding works when it is based on a total market-driven business vision. Emotional branding enhances corporate branding with a powerful point of view that can integrate the human factor to provide a more cohesive vision consistent with the financial, business, and marketing objectives of a company. The first step toward a new vision is an "emotionally driven" identity program that involves people at all levels of the organization as well as

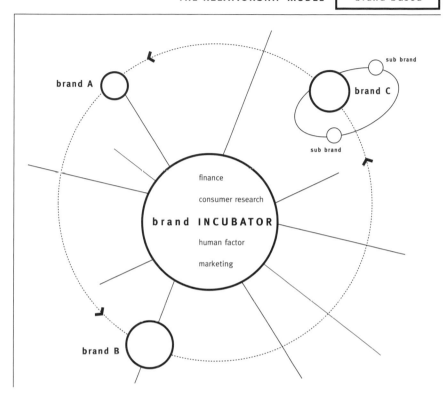

influences from the outside. It is about simplifying and clarifying the possibilities and charting new innovative paths.

Flexible Signatures

Abercrombie & Fitch in the United States and many fashion brands in Europe—such as Fendi and Gucci—have developed identities that help them carry their fashion signature farther, in a wider variety of contexts, expanding the expression of the personality of the identity to be more flexible and less "dictated" on their clothing products and accessories. Chanel's interlocking *C*s, the superimposed *L* and *V* for Louis Vuitton, the *G* for Gucci, and the famous Fendi double *F* designed by Karl Lagerfeld, are powerful visual signals that connect in a personal and emotional way with people on all their products. Corporate identities such as with Tommy Hilfiger's powerful flag-inspired logo, Ralph Lauren's polo player symbol, and the Victoria's Secret heart have developed intense brand meaning because those brands know how to manage the different expressions of their visual identity—whether it is a fragrance or an article of clothing—all in concert to bring a brand to life.

Heart-Stopping Brand Personalities

Corporate identity programs such as those for FedEx or AT&T are powerful, memorable, and dominate visually thanks to extremely well-designed nomenclature systems that are engineered to create ubiquity for the brand. On the other hand, fashion, retail, and Web companies have steered away from that path, building strong, flexible emotional personalities around their businesses and by designing brand identities that closely match the cultural and personal aspirations of their customers. The challenge to please people day by day, season by season, in these sectors requires flexibility in brand expression to

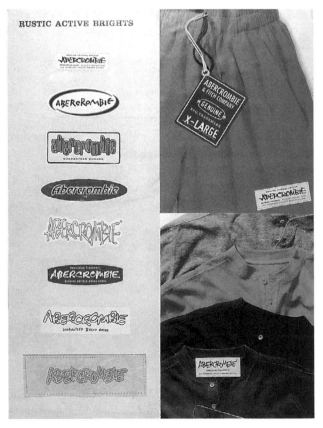

Abercrombie & Fitch's flexible logo expression.

match the cultural appetite of the time. This is why fashion, retail, and Web brand identities are some of the most powerful examples to study for building corporate identities that conform with the philosophy of Emotional Branding. They are about personalities that easily cross all boundaries of media expression. These are "brand characters" that are less about rationality and order than they are about desire and cultural connection. They are personalities that show more than just a superficial façade–they indicate a pulsing heartbeat and a lot of imagination behind their logos.

DEFINING A PERSONALITY

Commerce is, of course, all about selling more products and services, but people are all about desires and aspirations. We are constantly looking for brands that know what we want and we are constantly considering in what ways we may want to associate ourselves with brand personalities that possess charisma. We sometimes desire labels to express who we are (or rather who we want to be) to others, but most of all we want brands that offer us a variety of experiences. So while commerce simply wants to own our minds and pocketbooks, we look in the exchange for brands that understand our heart and soul.

Once again, branding should not be about company nomenclature and obscure systems, but about flexibility and emotional reach. A lot of companies have logos but no soul. In those cases, a logo is a meaningless and unempowered visual element of a company's vision. It is critical for businesses other than fashion and retail to craft and define a clear emotional personality that will make them stand out (although for a Boeing or a Goldman Saks it may not be as useful to be categorized by the good-boy-good-girl, bad-boy-bad-girl model!–see sidebar on next page). We all clearly understand Martha Stewart's message (of classy, domestic know-how) and what Calvin Klein stands for (rebelliousness and sexy chic). But, unfortunately, it is harder to clearly discern exact personalities for NBC or Winston cigarettes.

Emotional brands are most successful in extending their product offering to respond to their customers' aspirations. When you identify with a brand emotionally, you'll be more likely to buy varied products from it, even if your emotional connection was first forged around one specific line. Rose Marie Bravo's magnificent turnaround of the Burberry's brand was the right balance of emotion and product relevance. And, if you believe in Virgin, you believe in its culture and meaning first and foremost, and in its products secondly, whether it

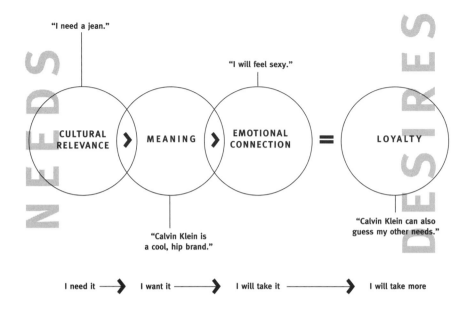

NEEDS **DESIRES**

"I need a jean."

"I will feel sexy."

CULTURAL RELEVANCE > MEANING > EMOTIONAL CONNECTION = LOYALTY

"Calvin Klein is a cool, hip brand."

"Calvin Klein can also guess my other needs."

I need it → I want it → I will take it → I will take more

be its airline, its cola, or its music stores, you are buying the brand first. Emotional brands have strong appeal that leads to growth potential through an extension of the company's offerings.

Bad-Boy-Bad-Girl Brands versus Good-Boy-Good-Girl Brands

When I am good, I'm very good, but when I am bad I'm better. —Mae West

In seeking new ways to look at and understand identities, I have discovered a way of clarifying and decoding brand personalities, which I find both helpful and amusing. When analyzing the effectiveness of Emotional Branding in the fashion and retail industry, it seems to me that there are clearly two separate camps into which these brands fall: what I call the good-boy-good-girl brands (GBGG)—think Brooks Brothers—and the bad-boy-bad-girl brands (BBBG)— such as Calvin Klein, for example). Based on the attitude—the rebelliousness and sexiness or well-mannered restraint—that companies project, it is often easy to place them in one camp or another. Gucci seems to fall squarely into the "bad" category, judging from its haughty ad campaigns that capture an on-the-edge urban lifestyle. Nautica certainly seems "good" in the sense of promoting conservative, good, almost family-oriented behavior.

This GBGG/BBBG polarity can also sometimes evolve over time for a brand. Did Estée Lauder buy a new product line or merely some much-needed sexy,

Lancôme's update of its brand imagery.

bad behavior associations when it acquired the hip young company MAC with endorsing celebrities such as drag queen RuPaul and hip-hop stars Mary J. Blige and Lil'Kim? How about Lancôme, the fabulous multidimensional cosmetic company that recently injected some new life into its brand by rejuvenating the look of its line with new models and makeup artist Fred Farrugia? It updated an image that tended toward the staid and that was beginning to seem dangerously too close to grandma's generation! But some brands lack clarity in terms of their GBGG/BBBG positioning. At first glance, the Gap and Tommy Hilfiger seem to be "GBGG" brands, since their brand imagery gravi-

tates around neat, clean, wholesome images that keep any sexiness within certain boundaries. Yet, the most recent Gap ads spoofing the world of *West Side Story*, a tale of gang warfare in New York, seems to be a stretch in the BBBG direction. And Hilfiger's clothing has found an undisputed niche among the BBBG world of rough-and-ready hip-hoppers. Both Gap and Tommy Hilfiger appear to want to play both sides of the paradigm. Gap gives us the GBGG/BBBG "khakis/jeans" dichotomy of the *West Side Story* ads, but the "jeans" contingency seems like a kind of cleaned-up "PG-rated badness." I believe that taking a clear stand and being at one end of the GBGG/BBBG spectrum is more desirable.

Should Abercrombie & Fitch be categorized as a BBBG? In its quarterly publication, *A&F*, it advises its Generation X readers to indulge in some creative drinking, portraying models in a frat-house kind of lifestyle—and very naked! In the consumer brand business, is IBM "good" because of the perception of

RALPH LAUREN
ROMANCE

Dior

A look at two different interpretations of romance via the BGBB/GGGB paradigm.

it as a serious, well-established business, and Apple perennially "bad" because it always finds a way to challenge the status quo? Is Coca-Cola "good" because it symbolizes Americana, and Pepsi "bad" because of its irreverent teen-driven communications? What about Victoria's Secret, the sexy lingerie brand, versus Playtex, the functional brand? Matching brands by association to a character classification is always an interesting way to identify the strength, relevance, and clarity of a brand. . . . Mae West, a very well-defined "bad girl brand" was definitely onto something!

GIVING MEANING TO A BRAND: VISUALIZATION
AND PERSONALIZATION OF A BRAND CONCEPT

During my continuing relationship of more than fifteen years with Les Wexner, the chairman and CEO of The Limited, and Ed Razek, his WCMO (that's my title for him; as in "Wizard Chief Marketing Officer"),[4] I had the great opportunity of collaborating on the identity creation and repositioning of some of the most successful retail brands in the world. Brands such as Express, Structure, Abercrombie & Fitch, Bath & Body Works, and Victoria's Secret were projects where our contributions had the most impact and where every drop of creativity was squeezed from us! Our goal was to reinvent corporate identity by infusing the elixir of emotion in order to reach an identity's most expressive limits.

One of those assignments culminated in the creation of the emotionally driven name "Intimate Brands," when Bath & Body Works and Victoria's Secret were spun off from The Limited and introduced in a very successful public offering.

It was in our work for The Limited that we first tested on a grand scale our new concept of Emotional Branding. *We wanted to find an approach to branding that raised the bar on how far you could go in connecting with a consumer on a personal level by creating verbal and visual stories around a brand through an illustrated script everyone wants to read and believe.* Our initial attempt at utilizing this concept involved the repositioning of Limited Express in 1985 as a brand with European flair, at a time in America when everything European was desirable. I had been living in the United States for barely even a month when Kevin Roche, a leading retail strategist (and one of the founders of FRCH, a well-known American retail design firm), heard of our company and asked us to meet with a firm I had never heard of–The Limited. My first meeting with Les Wexner was a lesson in humility and learning. I had never met anyone with such an intuitive feeling about brands, whose entire business model was brand driven . . . long before branding was a household word.

Our first assignment was to redesign the brand identity for Express, a new retail clothing chain they had just created. For research purposes, we traveled to Europe to observe the latest fashion trends. Once there, I realized that without some definite context in which the brand could evolve, I would never be able to direct my team of designers toward a groundbreaking solution. Frustrated and sleep deprived early one morning in Paris, I went to Café de Flore, a wonderful place on Boulevard St. Germain, where generations of artists, poets, and writers seeking inspiration have met since the beginning of the century. On the way, I bought an issue of *Paris Match*, a French magazine (similar to *People* magazine in the United States) that publishes the latest gossip on the "famous and beautiful people." In it, an article on Princess Stephanie of Monaco reported details of her "unprincessly" life as a fashion designer and singer under the worried supervision of her family.

I was immediately seduced by the independent spirit of this young woman, the strength of her character, her creativity, and her blue-blood upbringing. This was a beautiful story, and I could not help but think that if we could attract someone like Stephanie to a new Express store, we would be communicating to the right aspirational customer. I felt I had a story that could propel the meaning of the brand beyond graphics and provide a great brief for my designers–design an identity to reach Stephanie! Which is what we did. But first, we created a visual board that conveyed in an imaginative way the lifestyle of this potential customer, this pseudofictional and composite character, as a foundation and inspiration for our work.

I was so afraid to have my concept turned down by the staff of Express that I hid this concept board until I could show it to Wexner himself. It was a risky strategy–if it didn't work, I risked being sent back to France for good! But it was the only way to make an impressive statement and distinguish myself from my competitors. This certainly was not standard procedure at the time, and anyone but Wexner would have been put off by my approach. Actually, at first, I started to show several logo designs and packaging applications, unsure of when or if I would present the "Stephanie"-inspired style boards. The meeting was going well, but I couldn't feel any great enthusiasm or commitment to the concepts. Even though the presentation was strong in terms of the work and probably would have been approved, it did not get anyone's adrenaline to shoot up to the point of making them true believers in the ideas presented so far. I had not reached the standard I had in other presentations.

I decided to show the "Stephanie" boards, and immediately I could see a sparkle in the group's eyes: the boards had made a strong and immediate emotional connection. It worked well, and Wexner foresaw in it great potential for the future of the brand. His immediate decision (in the very same meeting!) was to ask his brand group to make a huge poster of my board to be placed in the buyers' conference room and to print postcard-sized copies for merchants to take abroad so they could buy or design clothing with "Stephanie" in mind as the ideal customer. The stores themselves were later redesigned to resemble in a quirky manner the palace in which Stephanie was living. The story of Stephanie, and all the qualities that we projected onto her, became the idea behind the brand.

This approach of inventing and romanticizing (or expanding imaginatively) a character as a "real person" and building details, characteristics, and emotions around them was subsequently modified and evolved into our SENSE® process, a unique technique for visualizing a brand, which creates imaginary brand lifestyles to better help define a visual platform as a basis for the development of a branding program. The SENSE® process was successfully applied to other divisions of The Limited (For example, "Kate," a fictitious entrepreneur dedicated to making wonderful beauty products from natural ingredients culled from the American heartland, was created as the inspiration for the Bath & Body Works brand), and became the branding technique for which we were best known. This idea of conceptualiz-

Conceptualizing a brand through personalization has become a very powerful way to build a brand identity.

ing a brand through personalization has now been adopted by other companies and has become a very powerful way to build a brand identity. It was reported to me that, at some point, I was one of the virtual subjects of this branding game. I never probed further for fear of finding out more—it might have been a story I wouldn't have liked!

VICTORIA'S SECRET: THE MAKING OF A SUCCESSFUL CORPORATE-IDENTITY PROGRAM THROUGH VISION, VISUALIZATION, AND EXPRESSION

In the early nineties, Victoria's Secret established itself as the premiere lingerie brand in the United States. The romantic English-inspired stores opened with great success all over the country and the catalog became very well known among both men and women. Victoria's Secret had in fact given American women the freedom to feel comfortable with sexy lingerie on their own terms, in contrast to competitors such as Frederick's of Hollywood, a California lingerie brand with a much racier attitude. Indeed, by 1995, Victoria's Secret was a successful brand that had achieved an enviably strong position as a catalog and store concept. But the modest price points that helped make the lingerie so attractive to shoppers also had a disadvantage: the line was seen as a mass brand. It had not yet reached the level of "status" symbol it enjoys today.

Vision

Les Wexner knew that in order to dramatically accelerate the business in terms of growth and profits, a fundamental element of the Victoria's Secret marketing plan needed to be changed. *He understood profoundly that the value of the brand was not in its product line, but in the emotional connection women had with the store.* By driving the business from an emotional perspective, he believed that the product lines could be evolved in a more meaningful way, that price points could be raised, and that women—younger women as well as the core customer base of women in their mid-thirties—would welcome a more meaningful in-store shopping experience with the brand. Wexner understood the potential of the brand and was determined to see it grow to its full potential. A team was immediately put together to create a new vision for the business: Ed Razek, Dick Tarlow (of Tarlow Advertising), Bob Ruttenberg (the imaginative CEO of Gryphon, a marketing and new product development arm of The Limited), Grace Nichols (the president of Victoria's Secret), and myself (as the brand design consultant).

Visualization

From an Emotional Branding perspective, creating a story around lingerie can be fun and inspirational, but focusing on a good idea that is sustainable was difficult. Dick Tarlow, whose ad agency had been one of the first to capitalize on the success of the supermodels in work for Revlon and Ralph Lauren, made an immediate connection between Victoria's Secret and the fashion credibility, modernity, and aspirational value of the supermodels. We all liked the idea. This was the beginning of a new and powerful brand story; The Victorian and slightly old-fashioned look of the existing identity was too narrow of a story and lacked the sex appeal star models could bring to the brand. What the brand needed was a major makeover!

In order to better define this new identity, we used the SENSE® process to bring to life the world of a supermodel. Not unlike the projective exercise we did for Express, we fleshed out in an idealized way what a typical month in the life of a supermodel would look like—where she lives, what her bedroom, bathroom, and kitchen look like, the restaurants where she eats, the night club she hangs out in, the look of her boyfriend, the sports she enjoys, what she does in her free time, and so on. We also considered decorative materials and music that we felt fit the brand, and we listed key words that built a creative language around the brand's concept. The objective was to add a level of sensory experience around a brand that would affect the overall look and feel of the identity—through packaging and graphics—and express this new, younger identity. A new heart symbol developed, and the Victoria's Secret logotype was defined.

A particularly bright shade of the fun, feminine color pink with associations of love was chosen as the corporate color, with stripes and the heart symbol to crystallize the whimsical romantic character of Victoria's Secret. Wexner asked us to design the now-famous pink shopping bags to be seen a mile away—to be memorable and to act as advertising for the store in the street. The high profile of Victoria's Secret bags subsequently contributed to a general "coming out of the closet" for lingerie brands (this was around the time when Madonna was showing us all how lingerie could be worn as a fashion statement in and of itself). American women no longer had to be bashful about shopping for lingerie and carrying the new Victoria's Secret bags was its own fashion statement. Eventually the bags became a status symbol of their own—

sending the clear message about the person holding them, "Look at me! I just bought some very sexy lingerie!"–and they became popular with men as well.

With our design help, Gryphon, under the leadership of Bob Ruttenberg and Grace Nichols, changed the total look and concept of the existing VS bath and beauty products line to incorporate the new identity. Our concept boards inspired new product ideas, and the creation of new bottle designs for fragrances with names such as Encounter and Rapture, all of which contributed to conveying a new positioning of romance and sensuality.

Such a dramatic change for a business that was already wildly successful would have been terrifying for many. A lot of managers run companies based on numbers and past successes. Not so with Wexner, who manages his company based–above all–on the meaning of his brands to the consumers. He has the courage to change and alter that meaning to better match the consumers' desires as time goes by, even if it means taking bold steps in a new direction.

Emotional Connection
The full impact of all this effort could not be realized without sustaining a powerful cultural connection to the consumers. And that's where Ed Razek came in full force. Razek has an incredible ability to translate and elevate the emotional value of a brand to an ultimate level in the most brilliant and relevant ways. He is a true communicator. His idea was to test the power of Victoria's Secret through a fashion show–something he believed would also generate a lot of coverage for the stores. It sounds uncontroversial, but I still remember him telling me that he went out on a limb doing this project. "But it is right for the brand," he said to me in a conversation I had with him just before the first show; an attitude that demonstrated his passion and commitment to the business even though his job could have been on the line.

The enormous success of this initiative catapulted Victoria's Secret into the realm of the most admired companies worldwide. The event got more media coverage than any fashion show in the world, including the ones produced by the leading European fashion designers. This kind of exciting thinking certainly did not stop there. Through the years, up until present, Victoria's Secret has continued to work hard to maintain this kind of unique edge in the market. Ed's 1998 Super Bowl ad that brought more than one million people to the Victoria's Secret Web site, will be remembered alongside the Apple's "1984" Super Bowl commercial as one of the most innovative and successful communication efforts

The old (top) versus the new Victoria's Secret branding.

of all time. This new awareness regarding the brand eventually fed into the success of the Victoria's Secret beauty division and its new hosiery business. Consequently, Victoria's Secret has been able to attract some of the finest executives in the world, such as Robin Burns, the former president of Estée Lauder, who now runs the beauty division. The catalog has also continued to be a phenomenal success, with supermodels now fighting to be in it. Ed Razek's latest coup was to organize the "Victoria's Secret Cannes 2000" event to raise money for amFAR, a foundation which raises money to support AIDS research. In partnership with Air France, Victoria's Secret whisked a star-studded group of supermodels and celebrities such as Elizabeth Taylor and Elton John, in a Concorde jet, custom decorated with Victoria's Secret identity details (such as Victoria's Secret logo decals on the aircraft doors, pink headrests and menus), to the French Riviera for a dinner and fashion show. This event,

The enormous success of this initiative catapulted Victoria's Secret into the realm of the most admired companies worldwide.

which was also Webcast, demonstrates not only the business savvy of Victoria's Secret, but an important a sense of social responsibility.

Emotionally driven corporate-identity programs need to be visionary, integrated, visceral, and reflective of a true commitment from corporations to share their values with the consumers. Connected identities are culturally relevant and endorsed by people, consumers, and employees alike. They are flexible, imaginative, and attractive. Dictated identities are only what they are, only another logo on the door. In one of my recent meetings with Wexner, a new visual merchandising director for Victoria's Secret was presenting a new version of the striped packaging. The director mentioned that this look would forever be the new look of the brand. Sagely Wexner replied, "As far as we can see."

Emotionally driven corporate-identity programs need to be visionary, integrated, visceral, and reflective of a true commitment from corporations to share their values with the consumers.

Just Call My Name

Names are difficult to find and even more difficult to register. Just spend an hour for the "fun of it" on *www.uspto.gov* and you will realize that almost all of the words in the English dictionary and all the word associations have already been registered! Name research has become one of the most challenging (and frustrating!) projects for consultants and corporations alike.

At d/g* New York, our naming department has developed a unique technique that helps create the name of a brand. We have found that it is best to start out working with a name list composed by people of varying backgrounds—creatives, copywriters, teachers, researchers, and professionals well versed in languages—as a basis for concept. As a parallel step, it is effective to have groups of people respond to visuals specifically selected to reflect the desired brand attributes in order to generate any relevant instinctual name ideas.

We are always surprised that very few people tend to like a name at first mention and generally have many rational, emotional, or personal reasons for disliking a name. The most important thing about naming is that a name takes on an entirely fresh meaning once it is associated with a business concept. Alone it could have little appeal. Who today would endorse names like The Limited, or Nestlé, for example, all by themselves? They are not so great-sounding. What would we think of Chase today if taken literally and in isolation? A lot has been written about the Chevy Nova saga of a name going awry in Latin America, where Nova translates in Spanish as "does not go." Procter & Gamble launched the Pert shampoo in France. Not a great idea in a country where the hair product's name translates into "loss."

A name therefore needs to be viewed in its total context. We always recommend looking at names in several typographic fonts—they can take on entirely different meanings when expressed in different typefaces. Then it is important to apply these varied looks to at least one element of the communications program, either a Web site, a storefront, or a letterhead. One test that really helps feel out a new name is to role-play: try being the receptionist and answer the phone by saying "Good morning, [New Name]" or repeat the phrase "I work for [New Name]." It really can lead to a different perception of the personality of the name when you hear and use it.

The objective of a name is to stand out and to distance itself from any formulaic or trendy expressions that could diminish the impact of the brand.

Of course the objective of a name is to stand out and to distance itself from any formulaic or trendy expressions that could diminish the impact of the brand. In 1999, within a year of each other, these three companies appeared, all with the same suffix: Novartis, Lactalis, Aventis. Sounds pretty old-economy to me!

Since the new economy has brought a new naming style to demarcate Internet brands from traditional ones, new possibilities in naming have opened up. Corporations are more willing to entertain concepts that would not have made even the first cut years ago. In this environment, risk taking in naming is sometimes required for success. Computer Literacy worked with Interbrand to find a new, unusual name that users would easily retain for an e-commerce book site. They eventually came up with the controversial name "Fatbrain.com." Although it had an incredibly high recall percentage in focus groups (nothing less than 100 percent!) it was highly disliked by a significant number of participants. Some employees of the company even threatened to quit if the name was chosen. After much debate, the company took the plunge and went with the name despite the misgivings. The result was terrific: six months later the average number of site visits was up 200 percent—and no one actually ever quit over the choice![5]

OTHER SUCCESS STORIES

I had the opportunity to discuss Lancôme, a brand that has benefited immensely from its corporate image, with the president of L'Oréal USA's Luxury Product Division, Philip Shearer, who told me the fascinating story of this brand that clearly has the necessary components of Emotional Branding we mentioned

LANCÔME
PARIS

before; cultural relevance, meaning, and emotional connection. The Lancôme rose and the accent on top of the *o* are two major signals that bring tremendous meaning and personality to the corporate image. The rose is obviously a symbol of femininity, but the circumflex accent on the *o*, which has no reason to be there from a purely grammatical point of view, connotes the French origins of the brand. The combination of both symbols brings a powerful cocktail of exoticism and promise, which have been at the core of a universal language that has struck an emotional chord with women worldwide for decades.

The most amazing thing about Lancôme is how it has evolved during its sixty-five-year history. I have always been fascinated by Lancôme and followed the growth of this almost $2 billion brand with great interest. There is no doubt that Lancôme's success is based on the quality of its product line, including what most professionals and consumers perceive as the best mascara in the world. But this organization is also driven by its people. I have been told that annual sales meetings at Lancôme are major events, company representatives dress up, bond, and show their pride in working for the company. People of different ages mingle together creating an oral tradition that helps newcomers immerse themselves in the wonderful history of the company.

The most amazing thing about Lancôme is how it has evolved during its sixty-five year history, always moving alongside trends and absorbing them into its brand identity without ever becoming dominated by them. The fact that Lancôme is as successful in Asia and the Americas as it is in Europe is another testimony to its great flexibility and ability to speak to women in a universal language.

As distinct from Estée Lauder, where the spokesperson, Elizabeth Hurley, in my opinion, has dominated the meaning of the brand, Lancôme has always retained control of the voice, the reason, and the signature behind the products, regardless of who the company's ambassador is. Lancôme is warm and approachable, yet classy and elegant. It is about "la femme," the universal woman, and it crystallizes this universal woman's aspiration.

The Lancôme identity reflects this multidimensional brand character through its powerful visual symbols. The Lancôme identity is an identity that is "personal" and designed for "contact" through its flexibility. Myths need symbols, and Lancôme's layered graphic expression creates a bridge between the brand and women worldwide. It puts the final accent on a wonderful story . . . the eternal beauty of the rose.

The story we created for Ann Taylor was the personalization of the fictitious "Ann." Sally Frame Kasaks, the president of Ann Taylor at the time (1992), was convinced that in order to turn around a retail brand that had lost a great deal of its cachet, consumers, as well as everyone in the organization, needed to be turned on by a new concept. Our SENSE® program this time was a collaborative exercise with the top twelve managers and buyers from Ann Taylor. It injected a new spirit and passion into the company and steered everyone involved with the brand in a clear direction. The story we built around the brand was so developed and realistic that people in the organization associated themselves in a very personal and emotional way with the independence, truthfulness, elegance, and approachability of the Ann Taylor character we created—even internalizing some of these perceived qualities. Often, managers would review products in the new collection and comment, "Ann would never do this," or, "This is very consistent

We updated the Bodoni typeface logo and added in handwritten script the tag line "Destination." Details, such as new box shapes, navy grosgrain ribbons, and a photograph of a purposeful, multifaceted real woman on the bag made from recycled materials, add character and personality to the total image.

with her voice"! On the basis of this visual strategy and story, we developed a new logo, a unique packaging program, the flagship stores in San Francisco and New York, and an ad campaign that resonated successfully with a new, younger consumer group of professional women who started to shop at Ann Taylor again. This identity program was one of the most integrated programs we have ever done, and it made Ann Taylor one of the premiere moderate-priced clothing brands for professional women in America.

Conclusion

People are usually afraid of change, and corporations most often hate change, but our lives are, of course, about change and human experience. The success of a corporate identity program resides in its flexibility; not so much to evolve and stay ahead of its market as to be meaningful—on many levels—to consumers and the company. Putting the word "forever" in a corporate identity program is like locking up the personality of a company that might not mean a lot to future generations. Some of my clients' major fears, I found, revolved around their questions "Is our logo

If the identity of your brand is not well defined, you may have visibility but no personality.

going to survive trends?" or "Will certain graphics age gracefully?" The real question is, How can I ensure that my culture and consumer connection will stay relevant? The Apple logo was the antithesis of the "business-driven" logo, and it still lives. The Virgin Atlantic logo is still relevant, and the Bloomingdale's round letters seem to withstand the passing of time, even though they could have been perceived as trendy at the time they were invented. These identities are still relevant because they reflect a culture that is still relevant. The logo, again, is the badge and the visualization of an emotional reality, and as long as this connection exists between a brand and people, the identity will keep its positive meaning.

If the identity of your brand is not well defined, you may have visibility but no personality. A logo is but the tip of an iceberg in a corporate expression. If it is not supported by the passion of a corporation's leadership, if it is not about meaning and shared objectives, it will fast become generic and familiar, not loved. Through the process of vision, visualization, and expression that I have just described, identities with character and personality forge connections with consumers through unique, evocative, and multidimensional messages; the expression of the brand is without limits. If it is couched in these processes, it will remain relevant, almost updating itself.

12

Retailing with a Passion: Sensational Stores of Tomorrow

Raised in a family of retailers, I realized firsthand and very early the truth of the age-old maxim that the key to continued success is the level of relationship you are able to build with your clients. The retail business does not stop at 5:00 P.M. but is an ongoing relationship process that continues long after the sale, which must constantly reinforce to your customers the idea that you are committed to providing them with the best products at the best value.

Retailing the Old-fashioned Way

My grandparents were clothing retailers in a small French village in the west of France. Since they met their customers every day in the street, at church, or during social occasions, their personal credibility was under close scrutiny at all times. They made sure that their reputation was one of integrity.

In those days, particularly in rural France in the first half of the twentieth century, traveling was very limited and done mostly on foot, horseback, or in horse-pulled carts. Villages were mainly commercial centers where every Monday an open market allowed farmers to sell their products, trade cattle, or buy necessary items such as clothing, agricultural equipment, or even food. Apart from the market, the other important gathering place was, of course, church on Sundays. The men would pack into the back of the chapel in order to demonstrate just enough presence to be saved, meeting afterwards at nearby cafés where they would trade or make business deals among themselves or with passing salesmen. In those meetings much was discussed, including arranging marriages and sharing human resources for harvest.

My grandparents understood the needs of this population intimately. One of the things missing from the community was the idea of a "general store," and my grandparents saw an excellent opportunity to make a decent living. Descendant of bourgeois landowners who had never worked, my grandparents had seen their own version of a "new economy" with the advent of the industrial age and the flight of the rural population toward cities and new jobs in factories. This phenomenon literally wiped out the value of land and forced them to find another source of income. They created a retail concept that included a grocery store, a restaurant, a café, and a clothing store all under one roof.

In this clever idea that was ahead of its time, they saw the potential value in providing a place that would offer rest, clothing, and great food and drinks for a hardworking rural population. They created an environment that was relaxing, cozy, and cheerful. The restaurant and café was a place where people could find an atmosphere of friendliness and comfort and that enhanced their mood for shopping. They created the perfect state for potential shoppers to shop. In those days, farmers dressed up for Sunday church and special events such as christenings, communions, and weddings, and my grandparents' store offered not only the appropriate clothing for these occasions, but also the facilities in which to celebrate some of those events. My grandparents store became an important place for social interaction and an integral part of the fabric of the village community.

There was an incredible attempt in the store to give every patron the utmost personal attention. My grandparents had a heightened notion of respect for their clientele. They felt, I was told, that if someone paid you for a service or for products, a moral contract existed between the vendor and the client—a contract that went beyond return policies to deliver the best level of quality on all fronts. It was a contract to never, ever deceive the client. The "brand promise" was made . . . and kept.

My grandparents felt keenly the significance of sharing what was important to their clientele on all levels. This is why they made it a point to go to church every Sunday. Similarly, they participated in all the village's seasonal fairs. They also were always available to meet customers at their own homes if work kept them there. This relationship with the town's people was reinforced further in times of crisis. The shop was used temporarily as a communication relay for the Resistance during World War II. They profoundly cared—and they showed it.

I have always referred to my family's retail history as a standard-bearer of a responsive, highly interactive, and ultimately extremely successful consumer relationship model. Our lifestyles may have changed enormously, but people haven't really. People still have urgent needs and beliefs stemming from our different social, cultural, and political backgrounds . . . and we still want to believe in a commercial landscape that will support and enhance those needs and beliefs. In a nutshell, we still appreciate when the people we do business with care about the same things we do! This means being able to find out what your customers really care about and

My family's retail history is a standard-bearer of a responsive, interactive, and ultimately successful consumer relationship model.

telling them that you support the same causes they do and have the same interests. Tell them that you appreciate the same music, the same values, the same dreams. In short, become a best friend. This is the way to create loyalty.

A COMMON-SENSE APPROACH TO RELATIONSHIP

My grandparent's legacy was carried on as my parents entered the restaurant business. I remember vividly some of the business conversations they had around the dinner table with friends or family. Most of those discussions obviously seemed very abstract at my age, but still they fascinated me to the point that I would stay until I dozed off when other kids or cousins had already left the table to play.

One topic that always was discussed with great seriousness when describing a competitor or someone's success centered on the *sense du commerce*–commerce sense . . . or business savvy. One either had it and was blessed, or did not have it and was destined to terrible luck–a life of hell, as I interpreted it. Having this "commerce sense" is, as I found out later, a quality that is very much overlooked in today's megaretail corporations. It simply means making the customer first in everything you do and constantly bridging the gap between your business and the end user.

The sense of commerce is about personal relationship, starting with the president of a company. It is about trust and commitment. Sally Frame Kasaks, the former CEO of Ann Taylor, when working on revitalizing the Ann Taylor brand with us, implemented a card system that allowed each of her customers to communicate with her personally from the store, and she would answer each card in person. The great Lee Iaccoca once said, "The dealer franchise system set up by Henry Ford is a damn good one. You want to buy from the guy who goes to the Kiwanis meeting and is part of the community."

In my business I sometimes meet high-level businesspeople isolated in their ivory towers and incapable of making a real connection to the people to whom they sell their products. Some retailers won't even wear the clothes they sell! Maybe they are above the market or have a "superior" taste? But in reality they could be the best representatives or ambassadors of their brands! At a time when hats were a must in church, my mother's role in my grandparent's store was the millinery business. She was a very elegant and beautiful woman, and always wore a fabulous hat to church in the most dramatic way, which was, of course, the best promotion she could have done. Their business became successful to the point that people traveled long distances to shop at their boutique.

I sometimes meet high-level businesspeople isolated in their ivory towers and incapable of making a real connection to the people to whom they sell their products.

Understanding the day-to-day life of your clients and catering to their wishes is the key to success and something that can be achieved today with the flexibility that new technologies offer. Meeting each and every one of your customers on a regular basis today is obviously impossible, but through technology companies can interface with them in some very unique ways; through personalized Internet sites or customized promotional initiatives. Basically any sincere attempt to become involved in answering people's personal needs will help maintain this crucial emotional bond of human contact that can exist between companies and their audience.

Evolving Retail from Service to Relationship

In the Emotional Economy, there is little room for buying. True, buying takes place every day across the globe, but the Emotional Economy heralds a much more rewarding and engaging activity–shopping. Buying is an activity understood by economists. Shopping is a phenomenon of interest to anthropologists and sociologists. Shopping provides opportunities for dreaming and playing–it's an escape and, ultimately, an art. There is much greater demand, value, and, most of all, potential inherent in shopping than in its remedial counterpart, buying. Vendors who create an atmosphere conducive to shopping give their customers a good reason to leave their homes and, in turn, create opportunities to buy.

We can learn a great deal about ways to inspire the art of shopping by borrowing ideas from the customs of age-old cultures. For example, in Marrakech,

Morocco, the Souk, the Mediterranean Arabic version of our department store, brings magic to the shopping experience by awakening your curiosity and desires at all levels. It is recommended that you pay a guide to take you through this immensely complex amalgam of outdoor shops. The idea of a guide is already enticing, conjuring a mysterious world of shops. The guide coordinates your tour according to your desires, and he serves as both a translator and quality-control person. On your tour music and exotic aromas constantly surround you. Each shop offers you a flavorful mint tea that reinforces your sensory experience of the place. It is truly an experience to relish, on the same scale for tourists as visiting a monument or a famous site. Some years ago we were doing a project for Ethan Allen, and Farouq Kawahari, their president, explained to me how much he enjoyed Oriental markets—similar to the open markets of Kashmir—and how his aim was to bring that sensation to his stores. His point was that the experience that people had there was so powerful that it sometimes bordered on the sacred. Even capturing a mere shadow of the richness of these experiences could transform most retailers into exciting destinations worthy of visiting simply for the atmosphere.

In contrast to this experience, consider the state of retailing in the United States today: a glut of offerings accompanied by the proliferation both of homogeneity and increased specialization. Department stores, most notably JC Penney, which have long been the mainstay of American families, are fighting to keep their competitive edge. This crisis is mostly affecting the fashion segment

Consider the state of retailing in the United States today: a glut of offerings accompanied by the proliferation both of homogeneity and increased specialization.

of the retail business—one fashion store after another offering almost the same merchandise and fighting for each sale! In addition, today's brick-and-mortar retailer competes with online alternatives that operate all hours of the day and keep shop no further than the nearest computer screen. All these facts come down to one thing: *the rules of retailing have changed.* However, a select group of savvy retailers is spearheading a revolution in retailing that will make the art of shopping once again interesting and worthwhile to the American public.

WAL-MART AND TARGET REDO DISCOUNT

Wal-Mart, long condemned for pushing out local businesses and replacing them with one-stop shopping, has made a rapid turnaround in image by building an emotional connection with the communities where it operates. Today's Wal-Mart not only caters to consumers' value-driven buying needs, but also their indulgent shopping escapades and entertainment needs. It has fashioned a convenient and welcoming community-oriented atmosphere that combines diversity, efficiency, and quality. In turn, surveys conducted by WSL Strategic Retail indicate that a whopping 55 percent of respondents shop at a mass merchant once a week, with 39 percent naming Wal-Mart as that merchant.[1] To the surprise of many, respondents rated mass merchants highest not only in their ability to meet basic shopping needs, but also their elusive emotional needs!

But what exactly does Wal-Mart offer to shoppers besides affordable goods? Well, for one, events such as April 2000 bubble-gum blowing contest, which was held across 2,800 stores nationwide and awarded one winner a million-dollar prize while raising money for the Children's Miracle Network. It also provides countless families with an occasion for going out together for an afternoon's fun at Wal-Mart. By tying in with the *Rosie O'Donnell Show*, by offering the winner an appearance on the show, the Wal-Mart bubble blowout gained valuable presence in the homes of loyal viewers for whom Rosie is a trusted morning companion. Wal-Mart was also exclusive home to the "Power Rangers Intergalactic Encounter Tour," which was complete with (at five thousand square feet) the world's largest moonbounce. Although the TV program that inspired it is aimed at young children, the show was geared to entertain teens and adults as well. Other events have included Oreo-stacking contests and Garth Brooks's personal appearances. Combine that with quality merchandise, intelligently laid out stores, excellent prices, and convenient locations, and it is easy to understand why Wal-Mart has become the world's largest retailer. Although the Internet has made leaps and bounds in transforming shopping, it will be years before its entire retail industry can even hope to rival Wal-Mart's revenues. Estimates predict that retail sales online will reach $184 billion by 2004, at which time Wal-Mart can be expected to have $243 billion in revenue–domestically.

Wal-Mart's success is not only a result of business acumen–it is also a reflection of its devotion to aggressively redefining the concept of "discount retail." At a time when stores such as Caldor's faltered, Wal-Mart realized it could dissociate itself from the drawbacks of "discount" without sacrificing value. At the heart of this change is an attention to the emotional state of its customers. Wal-Mart has set out a goal of meeting the needs not of customers but rather of specific shoppers–working mothers, excitable children, cash-strapped college students–both pragmatically and emotionally. Five years ago, discount was about second-rate. Shopping at Wal-Mart today reflects shoppers' intelligence and satisfaction. By tapping into values deep in the American psyche, Wal-Mart has quickly become the standard by which other retailers are measured, and when others cannot measure up (which is frequently), Wal-Mart wins out. Wal-Mart has a real sense of community and an image that spells out all the values in which America believes. Sam Walton himself represented a new success story of integrity that was approachable, sensitive, and populist. The message is clear, the culture unique. Wal-Mart has, in fact, become such a cultural phenomenon that we even see the store as an inspirational setting for the characters in the

Wal-Mart's success is not only a result of business acumen—it is also reflection of its devotion to aggressively redefining the concept of "discount retail."

book *Where the Heart Is* by Billie Letts, which was made into a movie starring Ashley Judd, Stockard Channing, and Joan Cusack, among others. The story is about a pregnant, seventeen-year-old woman who is dumped by her boyfriend, with less than ten dollars in her pocket, in a small Oklahoma town Wal-Mart on their way to California. Because Wal-Mart is the major community gathering place, however, it turns out she's in the right place. She immediately begins to meet some of the eclectic townspeople there who will help her to change her life. The young woman secretly spends the nights in the Wal-Mart for several months, eventually having her baby there. After her creative use of the store as a home is discovered, Sam Walton himself offers her a job, and she is on her way to building a normal life within the fabric of the store and the community surrounding the store.

Wal-Mart may dominate the scene in terms of sheer size, but Target's bulls'-eye trademark has claimed first place in directing retailers toward a retailing future that is both fashionable and affordable. In the past three years Target has revealed itself as the most innovative and interesting mass-market retailer. It positions itself as a culturally attuned discounter, and its merchandise takes the high road with style while preserving the affordability of its discounting competitors. Robert Ulrich, chairman of Target's parent corporation Dayton Hudson, explained to *Fortune*: "People's tastes are not determined by income, obviously. A lot of people want to be 'with it.'"[2] By drawing top-name designers such as Michael Graves and Philippe Starck, Target has produced whole lines of trendy and attractive housewares and furniture that transform kettles and knives into kitchenware-extraordinaire and homes into a stylish metropolitan statement. By working harder to create a unique line of merchandise and drawing attention to that merchandise with flashy, youthful ads completely unlike its conservative competitors', Target has positioned itself as the

hip and creative alternative to discount retail. Sure, Kmart is convenient, but its chief claim to fame is practicality. Target preserves that practicality and links it with "cool," and this allows Target to begin to compete not only with other discounters, but with the likes of Crate & Barrel and Banana Republic as well. Its retail strategy has attracted customers from a broad stratum of economic and social classes, and other discounters are scrambling to decipher and implement Target's formula. Target's average customer is younger, more affluent, and likely to leave the store with a heftier receipt than are the typical patrons of other discounters. Target's success is an illustration of branding at its best. By developing true points of distinction that are valuable and relevant to consumers, it has developed an identity. That identity is propelling its profits and exciting consumers and investors across the country.

While Wal-Mart and Target may be the two largest players shaping retail of today and tomorrow, they are by no means defining it. In fact, their size and broad appeal may limit their ability to creatively challenge the standards of retail, and although they may be leading the way in certain innovations, their stores are still relatively tame. Their efforts at providing better service have been appreciated and boosted sales, but twenty-first-century shoppers are adjusting to these changes quickly. In order to hold consumers' attention and continue inspiring shoppers to shop as opposed to buying, innovation and experience must be more thoroughly integrated into retail. In this realm, specialty retailers are often able to craft more moving and personalized stories to stir the customers' imagination and emotions.

Welcome to the Neighborhood

Kmart: Big K at Astor Place, NYC—when Kmart opened up a store in the East Village a block from NYU, a trendy neighborhood renowned for its bohemian/ artistic past, many community members objected to its presence and executives wondered how they might cater to this funky urban audience. In 2000 artist Paul Richard, a local resident, approached them wanting to display his art in their café. Management quickly secured approval from headquarters, and Mr. Richard's art moved in, including some that subtly pokes fun at the discounter. This was the first art display ever in any of Kmart's 2,000-plus stores, but in a community such as New York City's East Village, it made perfect sense. This is the kind of specific local community-bonding effort that, if done on a larger scale in all of its locations, could really help Kmart to better compete with Wal-Mart and Target.

Remember that effective retailing interweaves social, emotional, and imaginative elements via the portal of an emotional brand. *Retail branding is about storytelling and engaging in a dialogue that connects your brand to a customer's heart.* Here are several examples of retailers doing this in different ways . . .

REI: GREAT MERCHANDISE IN GOOD HANDS

On a recent trip to Seattle I visited REI, a Seattle-based provider of outdoor gear and clothing that understands that retail success is born in a story and led by a passion. In fact, its Web page explicitly tells that story, which goes like this:

It all started with an ice axe . . .

REI (Recreational Equipment Incorporated) began one day in 1938 when Seattle mountaineer Lloyd Anderson sent away for a new ice axe. Upon picking it up, he got an unwelcome surprise: The axe was nearly twice the price advertised, and about half the quality. Vowing not to be fooled again, Lloyd found his own source, buying a top-quality Austrian Academ Pickel ice axe at a lower price! His climbing friends begged him to get this ice axe for them too. He did. Word spread, and here we are many years later, basically doing the same thing.[5]

What an inspiring basis for a brand! Based on that initial experience, founder Lloyd Anderson formed a cooperative venture with friends and acquaintances who pooled money to acquire the highest-caliber outdoors gear. Because all of the contributors were themselves outdoorsmen, they had a personal devotion to securing the best merchandise, and at the end of the first year of operation, eighty-two members of REI received dividends. Although their stores are open to the public, membership now costs $15 and REI has over 1.4 million active members, all of whom receive voting privileges to elect REI's board of directors, as well as a share in company profits through an annual patronage fund. However, it's not simply the membership policies or the history that distinguishes this chain of forty-six retail stores. REI's entire approach to retail embraces unique experiences, distinguished offerings, and personal relationships. Its Seattle flagship epitomizes the REI spirit. Every time someone enters the store, the door handles, fashioned from ice axes, recall the birth of REI. Once on-site, 2.1 acres beckon visitors' adventurous spirit. In addition to a comprehensive selection of gear for biking, hiking, canoeing, skiing, and other sports, REI boasts features like an outdoors mountain bike test trail, the JanSport Kids' Camp, the Gore-Tex rain room for trying out Gore-Tex rain wear, and the Footwear Test Trail featuring various terrain for shoppers trying out hiking boots. As shoppers tramp about on this path in varying pieces of footwear, educational sessions regarding camping and other activities may be ongoing in REI's 250-person meeting room. Most striking, however, is the REI Pinnacle—a sixty-five-foot indoor climbing structure manned by belay experts helping expert and novice alike enjoy rock climbing. However, the richness and quality associated with REI is not a function of the merchandise, the architecture, or the educational seminars. Rather, these are expressions of the REI identity that resides in the men and women associated with the brand. Just as its members are devoted to outdoor activities, so are its five thousand employees that form an in-house test crew. REI turns to them, avid outdoors enthusiasts, for field testing of products. When an employee tells a shopper this is the best tent for a given trip, that employee's advice may well be based on an REI-sponsored camping trip he took with that tent. If employees are dissatisfied with a product, then shoppers will not see it on the REI shelves.

The exemplary outdoors knowledge of REI employees is in stark contrast to many other retailers that are saddled with poorly trained and often inappropriate salespeople. More brands must realize how crucial their employees are. I think of it this way—if a well-written play has excellent publicity, brilliant lighting, divine costumes, mesmerizing scenery, but unprepared actors, is the play a success? No, of course not. Flashy effects and divine atmospherics are great, but in theater, as in retail, it is the people who really define the brand. It's been said that if a play is cast right, 80 percent of the problems have already been solved. It is the same thing if a store is staffed right. I am sometimes shocked at the meticulous effort devoted to articulating brand identity through brand communications when that identity subsequently falls flat in the hands of incompetent salespeople. The importance of employees as the in-store living embodiment of a brand's identity cannot be underestimated. Employees should reflect the brand's intended identity, and also have relevance to the shoppers. Finding a cashier should not be simply an issue of locating a reliable man or woman who will show up for work on time, work cheaply, and not steal from the register. Instead, it needs to be about choosing an individual who, in addition to the former qualities, will send shoppers out of the store not with a fake smile, but a genuine brand experience. Perhaps that means a well-wishing, maybe it implies a sly comment about a cute guy. *From the CEO to janitor, workers should be part of the brand itself, rather than people simply paid to dispassionately tend to its interest.* However, instinctual relevance to the brand needs to be supported with appropriate training. Salespeople need to be trained thoroughly on how to deal with customers in all their endless varieties: happy, hassled and hurried, picky, frustrated, nervous or excited, price conscious, indecisive, depressed, and so on. Ideally, employees of a store will be drawn from the same pool as potential customers. For a little further insight into the state of retail service today and the potential meaning consequence, I would like once again to turn to Peter Levine, the head of d/g* Consulting.

Flashy effects and divine atmospherics are great, but in theater, as in retail, it is the people who really define the brand.

Welcome to the "Service" Millennium   *By Peter L. Levine*

It may be a little lonely, as you are the first to arrive!

Recently I've been traveling the country with a presentation I created, called Timebomb, which deconstructs the three generations—Baby Boomers (35–53), Generation X (23–34), and Generation Y (4–22)—that currently consume over a trillion dollars worth of goods and services each year.

My lecture explains the belief structures, conflicting values, and, more importantly, the shared values of these three dynamic segments of the population. It usually generates spirited discussion, and the same pointed question always rears its curious head: "How is Internet commerce going to affect retail? Will the ability to touch, feel, and try on a real garment or product ever be replaced by the cold, impersonal Internet?" My answer has become a bit stock at this point. "Hell, yes!" I tell the audience. "When Internet commerce figures out how to provide a decent level of service, retailers will have no other choice but to shape up. When apparel makers can send out seasonal books with swatches of their current collection, and when body-scanning for fit is made simple for all family members, who wouldn't want to shop for apparel online with the same ease consumers enjoy when buying books and CDs?"

Especially since we have all stopped counting the myriad of shopping nightmares we encounter, due to the dismal state of service at retail.

A few weeks ago, I was in Florida with Vanessa (my assistant) to conduct a research audit for a new client. I decided to confirm my theory and wrote a "service travelogue": one day of counting the catastrophes.

Vanessa was so excited to combine work and pleasure (that's the Gen X work/play balance) that she had reserved a convertible at Avis. Despite our reservation, we had to wait in a long snaking line of people for over forty minutes. After presenting all of the necessary documents, we were told to wait, as there were no cars available. Waiting another twenty minutes was as good as making us "cry Uncle," and we told the Avis agent that we suddenly didn't care about our reserved convertible and simply wanted our freedom.

However, the angry consultant in me could not help barking (very Boomer— "this shouldn't be this way"): "You're gonna have to try even harder if you want to keep that 'we're number #1' button on your label!"

I believe that any good retail consultant should be able to turn into an everyday consumer and then back into someone who can analyze a situation. In other words, I see myself as a harried war veteran slogging through the trenches and frontlines of the retail landscape.

Stop number two: In search of cash, we stopped by an ATM machine located outside of a local boutique. I slid my card into the machine but nothing happened.

I asked the store owner: "Does this ATM work?" A shrug and a shirk is what I got. After a few minutes I realized that the machine was placed directly in the sunlight and that the screen was blinded.

Here comes the angry consultant again: "Don't you think that this machine would be better placed inside, where the sun is not a problem? People might even be encouraged to buy something!" The sales clerk's blank face faced me—the usual response to a good idea that will never happen.

Once in the mall, our final destination, we were greeted by the Gap's introduction of their new 1969 jeans. When the Gap launches a new product, they usually deliver. Seduced by the jeans, I decided to try them on.

I unsuccessfully looked for my size on the table and realized that the stacks were a mess and ran the fit gamut. "Are these organized by size, or in any way?" I asked. The saleswoman assured me that they were in order. She tried to make some sense of the stacks but realized that it would take one of us twenty minutes of digging to find my size.

I said: "Since this is such a big launch for the Gap, don't you think it would be wise to organize those jeans by size, and try to entice the consumer a little more?"

"They only just came in today," she replied. "I'll go look in the back." But my impulse was gone and so was I.

Next stop: Speedo. I was looking for Lycra swimming briefs. Two women were in. One was loudly chatting on the phone with a friend about her evening plans, while the other was helping some customers try on some sandals.

The phone lady would not be bothered and there was no signage system in the store, so I asked the busy one if they had what I was looking for. She began to direct me but almost immediately started a conversation with another customer.

By then, I was getting really wound up and went back to the original phone lady to practically scream: "Can I please get some service here?!!" She simply turned her back to me and continued her phone conversation. We were outta there.

On to Hallmark. I needed a few Valentine's Day cards for my nieces and nephews. I asked: "Where are the kids' Valentines?" The teen behind the counter simply replied, "In back," with a huge sweeping motion of her hand.

Okay, I admit it—I was a little weary at this point and demonstrated to her that there was a lot of "in back" back there. She helped me by saying "In the middle," which narrowed my search down to about a thousand choices.

We headed to check out a great-looking New Balance store and were greeted by the "new breed" of super-service practitioners who boomed:

"Welcome to New Balance, where 90 percent of shoes are made in the U.S.A."
"Here," he said, drawing us in. "Look at this." He picked up a shoe and displayed it. "Can you read that, folks? I don't have my glasses with me," he feigned. "Made in the U.S.A.," we flatly chimed out, like kids appeasing their crazy uncle.

Soon we were muttering: "Let's get out of here; this place is creepy!"

Time to head for the airport. We grabbed some pure-fat dinner at the cafeteria and noticed that there were no recycling bins for our cans and bottles. I told Vanessa that Generation Y (the "we care" generation) would not stand for that as they got older.

As we passed by a newsstand, I wanted a Butterfinger. Alas, nothing of the sort. And the sales clerk had never even heard of the candy bar. On line to board the plane, there was a vending machine, and a Butterfinger hanged, awaiting me for only 75¢. I ate it happily, enjoying my only positive shopping experience of the day.

My conclusion after such a day? Online commerce will win out in the end if retail doesn't wake up. Blue Jeans, a swimsuit, sneakers, greeting cards, and a rental car should not be so difficult to deliver.

The burning question is: Will retailers shoot themselves in the foot by eventually giving consumers a better e–tail experience? Or will a host of new e-commerce storefronts emerge and eclipse established brands?

Retailers are too slow to realize that their employees are "brand ambassadors." Helpful, genuine service is perhaps the most critical part of building long-lasting relationships with customers. And that is a desire that all three generations share. So where will we find great service in the future? Coming soon to the computer screen in your living room!

THE SHAPE OF ANN TAYLOR

While service is of the utmost importance, atmospherics certainly still play a vital role as well in enhancing a brand's identity and elaborating the communications made through other mediums. Retail designers have the opportunity to impact society by bringing a renewed sense of beauty to all channels of distribution. People are looking for experiences of newness and excitement within stores. Furthermore, retail environments should be inspired by the products they sell in a way that brings total consistency to the brand image. Nike has delivered on this promise, particularly in its Chicago store, but car dealerships are still quite mundane.

Our goal in designing the Ann Taylor store was to create on Madison Avenue and Sixtieth Street in New York City a forty-thousand-square-foot store that presented a feminine, sophisticated retail environment reflective of the Ann Taylor woman's dynamic lifestyle. Through our SENSE® process, we realized that the Ann Taylor woman is real, unpretentious, elegant, and practical minded. To reflect her taste, the store we designed is warm, sophisticated, and refined. The townhouse-inspired façade clad in limestone was inspired by what the fictitious personage Ann Taylor's home would be like. The natural and relaxed interior is comprised of clean, refined spaces enriched by warm,

Ann Taylor Madison Avenue Flagship store.

tactile materials. The centerpiece, a staircase of glass and limestone, the vertical form spiraling up five floors, welcomes visitors with its connotations not of selling products, but rather of an attractive and inviting home. Natural, monochromatic colors communicate the overall identity palette of the brand in a modern, unpretentious, comfortable manner, which plays off the navy blue of the brand's signature color. Sensual shapes rendered in a mix of warm and cool materials like bronze, stone, frosted green glass, and auburn wood create textural contrasts. Sculpted details on fixtures, door handles, and railings are unexpected additions that personalize the store design. We also created a "comfort zone," a sitting area for guests with a view of Madison Avenue as well as personal shopping area with a built-in desk that includes a place to plug in a laptop. The latter is part of Ann Taylor's commitment to service and a reflection of the multiple roles its customer fulfills in her daily life. If more brands undertake such pertinent design, our commercial landscape could become unimaginably uplifting and enriching. Until that happens, though, brands such as Ann Taylor will stand out and above their competitors.

THE FACES OF MACYSPORT

One of the hallmarks of shopping is that it's easy to not even realize you are doing it. You sometimes show up in a store without even the intention of buying, and before you realize it you're leaving the store with shopping bags in your hands. Events are an ideal way to do this. For example, Macysport in New York City hosted a panel discussion sponsored by *Women's Sport & Fitness* magazine that featured pro volleyball player Gabrielle Reece, world champion surfer Lisa Anderson, nutritionist Heidi Skolnick, and other renowned figures in women's sports. Monica Bella-Bragg, vice president of special events at Macy's East, said: "It's hard to quantify an event like this, but we'll see some results in the next few months. Even if customers don't shop that night, when they need sports apparel, they will know they can find it here. It also makes women think differently about Macy's as a place where they can get really good information and, in this case, inspiration."[4] These events not only positively reinforce Macysport's identity among consumers, but elaborate the identity far beyond that of a traditional retailer. For consumers in attendance, Macysport is no longer defined only by its products and price, but also by these speakers who have aligned themselves with the brand. Because working women and men have little in the way of free time, increasing stress, and never enough time for themselves, these efforts are doubly valuable. Any retailer that offers not only quality products but also rewarding experiences can expect to be rewarded in turn by consumers willing to pay a premium for that service.

DOMSEY'S DISCOUNTS FOR DEDICATED AND DEFT BROOKLYN DENIZENS

This vendor of secondhand clothing in a four-floor warehouse in Williamsburg, Brooklyn, is an interesting example of successful retailing to the Gen Y crowd that could be modified and expanded to other retail concepts. This inexpensive store has become a hot spot for the young and hip. What really distinguishes the store is its annex. An outlet on the side of the store, this space is where visitors find barrel after barrel, each some twenty-seven cubic feet in size, filled with unsorted clothes. Customers come with their friends and make a sociable afternoon of rooting through the piles of clothing in search of that one perfect item. But the real gimmick is that upon finding their items, the clothes are paid for by the pound! This store proves that creating a memorable and exciting retail experience does not necessarily require massive investment. Domsey's has turned bargain-basement discounting into an alluring point of difference for treasure hunting hipsters otherwise suffering from thrift store malaise.

GLIMPSING THE ASCENT OF THE TOMORROW'S MALLS

For all the changes inherent in the Emotional Economy, malls remain the most underrated vehicles by retailers and marketers alike. Taken for granted by the first group and misunderstood by the second, they are sadly underused, yet they remain one of America's favorite places to shop. Brands like Godiva, Aveda, Disney, or Warner Brothers have revealed that retail branding, particularly through malls, is a compelling way to bring a brand to life and the most thrilling way to allow a customer to enter the brand experience directly.

Tomorrow's mall will be a place where reality and virtual reality merge. Palm-held computers will scan the prices of items and, via cellular connections, quickly inform us if the product can be found cheaper nearby. Computer consoles and places to link into store networks will allow us to browse showrooms in the real word and order products immediately in the digital world. Most importantly, we will not live in a world of technology so much as technology will live around us. Shaped to the needs and well-being of consumers, technology will serve our needs and emotions in subtle and unnoticed ways with the same ubiquity as electricity. We will neither notice nor think much of this environment–it will simply be natural. In a world where technology and its applications seem limitless, the decisive role will be played less by programmers with computer know-how than artists and visionaries with imaginative know-how. These women and men will develop the most touching and emotionally relevant implementa-

Tomorrow's mall will be a place where reality and virtual reality merge.

tions of technology, merging the worlds of art, storytelling, and psychology within technologically enhanced design. Consumers tomorrow will be likely to demand very sophisticated experiences. One place attempting to deliver this today is the Sony's Metreon mall in San Francisco. This mall (if you can even fairly call it that) offers a cursory glance at what future malls may offer consumers; a fresh and innovative view of shopping. The Metreon mall is a perfectly suited platform for marketing Sony. After struggling with varying concepts for the mall, executives concluded it was technology that united their disparate ventures, from CDs to DVD players to the PlayStation. In the place of department stores, the Metreon has a dozen movie theaters and an IMAX. Attractions such "Where the Wild Things Are," based on the Maurice Sendak classic of the same title, provide entertainment and a reason for whole families to come. While kids play in a field peopled by six-foot moving, mechanical, hairy monsters, parents can eat at one of the exclusive restaurants nearby that replace food-court fare with fine dining. "Wild Things" is one of two carefully designed indoor attractions, and kids can have access to both and play interactive video games in the super high-tech Sony-designed archives for one fee of $20—not too shabby, particularly for parents eager to escape the demands of childcare for a few hours. Carefully selected stores, such as the Discovery Channel Store and MicrosoftSF, mesh with the interactive and technology-oriented theme of the mall, supplementing the Sony-designed stores. Most impressive is the architecture that unites elements such as soaring, suspended arches, and video screens dangling from the ceiling to create a seamless and coherent structure. In the place of walls and doors dividing attractions are large open spaces that rely on more subtle atmospherics to guide the transition from one store to the next.

What's worth noting is that Sony and the other stores within the malls are not traditionally considered retailers. The San Francisco store is Microsoft's first, and the Discovery Channel Stores are offshoots of the cable channel. However, retail has proved to be an innovative and profitable way to market these brands. The mall of the future is going to be just the kind of place to do this. I predict that it will be a place where we come to experience brands, not just to buy products. Brands such as Lancôme and Microsoft will have boutiques alongside Coca-Cola, General Motors, and Canyon Ranch. Brands not traditionally considered retailers will make steps toward retailing as the future continues to blur the distinctions between branding, marketing, supplier/distributor, and entertainment. Marketers will have unprecedented opportunities to make a lasting impact on consumers by "three-dimensionalizing" their brands. Companies like Procter & Gamble and Unilever in the consumer brands category and IBM and Apple in the computer industry will finally be able to free themselves from the restrictions of their traditional distribution systems to reach their consumers in markedly new ways. They will have the opportunity to bring to the consumer powerful sensory experiences of what their brand stands for through exciting interactive environments.

We will see more paid-admission "brand amusement parks," such as the LEGOLAND parks that feature a myriad of exciting hands-on interactive LEGO attractions, like the Imagination Zone, with its emphasis on exploration and creation through LEGO, and Miniland, with its astonishingly precise reproductions of such famous landmarks as the Empire State Building—made from LEGO. It also has water and roller coaster rides; puppet and magic shows and restaurants; and, of course, an enormous LEGO shop. I foresee that stores will become part of advertising budgets and will be used as the best consumer-testing ground, perfect for new product launches or as a way of connecting the retail environment to the Internet for direct selling. Already innovative malls such as Bluewater in England are considering charging an entrance fee to their leisure/amusement parklike atmosphere in order to lift the burden of rents for retailers who will begin to evolve their brand spaces into showrooms where visitors merely view the goods they buy via the Internet. Bluewater is an incredibly well-designed, innovative, and entertaining mall with three thematic sections of the mall that include a section designed around a pathway on the Thames River, and I would bet that Bluewater, if it chooses to charge admittance, will meet with success.

We will see more paid-admission "brand amusement parks."

Several other groups have also aggressively challenged the definition of the mall, such as the Mall of America and the Forum Shops at Caesars, creating enormous "amusement park malls" that are successful in drawing huge numbers in traffic. The Forum Shops at Caesars have made an innovative use of lighting techniques with mechanisms that modulate the lighting and simulate sky on the ceiling to give shoppers the impression of being outside and passing through the changes of lighting in a day. Caesars also has a fabulous electronics show with animated robotics.

Easton Town Center mall in Columbus, Ohio, has found some very interesting ways to respond with greater sophistication and creativity than ever before to

Easton Town Center mall.

complex human needs that have little to do with checking off a shopping list. According to Barry Rosenberg at Steiner & Associates, the codeveloper for Easton Town Center project, the aim of Easton is to become a real community "city center" to replace an increasingly missing urban fabric.[5] The Easton Town Center model is perhaps even a sort of antithesis to our plugged-in culture, and as such just as important to the future of retailing, if not more so, than malls that make abundant use of technology. Easton has become a place to see and be seen in Columbus; it is a place for social gatherings where one might also pick up a pair of jeans at the Gap on the way to one of the restaurants, thirty movie screens, or a concert. It has, in fact, become such a communal gathering place that the local baseball team comes to Easton to celebrate after winning a game, and the new hockey team picked the center as a place to unveil their jersey logo. Easton has a weekly farmers' market and paid jugglers, mimes, and artists, all of which contribute to the sense of a real, bustling, multifaceted downtown community. Therein lies the real power of retail–great products in an environment that enhances the buying experience by reaching out to our emotions.

Some Ideas . . .

As we approach changes in retail, the question becomes *What is a retailer? What can a retailer be?* In my mind, everything. For example, I think it would be interesting if a place like Home Depot had live theater inside its stores. Maybe a sitcom-inspired program based around a handyman's trips to kooky households. Of course, all the sets would be built exclusively with Home Depot merchandise, and the set designers would be available to advise shoppers on incorporating these looks into their own home. For that matter, why use commercials to introduce new product lines? Good street theater, I think, would distinguish a retail brand much better than good but ubiquitous advertising. Although the expenses may be higher in going the street-theater route, I would bet the news coverage and word-of-mouth publicity would compensate for these costs. Performers could even be put in front of the stores, as a way of guiding passersby into the store, where the performances continue.

As we've seen, technology offers a great deal of potential for reinventing retail as well. Earlier in this book I mentioned the Acoustiguides, headsets that provide personal tours of the Museum of Modern Art in New York City. As I've said, I think megastores should consider emulating the MoMA Acoustiguides with headsets of their own. It would be fantastic for consumers to enter a large department store, such as Macy's, and pick up at the door a headset that would guide them through the store. The potential of such devices is immense. On arriving at the store, I could run my Macy's credit card through a scanner

While the Internet craze is offering new ways of "buying," it still has not reached the status of "shopping."

that would analyze my history of purchases and note my age and demographic data. Based on this information, it could draw from an existing database of customer profiles, accessing the one in tune with my own tastes, and immediately upload a tour tailored to my tastes and needs. Alternatively, customers could enter their own data to target their store search more specifically. This would be an excellent device for gift shopping as well–enter in mom's info as well as a price range, and let the store lead you through a tour of possible gift items.

Shopping as an art and a passionate pastime is most definitely here to stay. While the Internet craze is offering new ways of "buying," it still has not reached the status of "shopping," so popular with not only computer-savvy Gen Yers, but most segments of our population! Consumers will continue looking for off-line fun in the shape of great experiential retail concepts.

I'd like to take you now on a quick tour of two of my own favorite stores; stores that, I believe, are great retailers because they don't just exhibit strength in one particular area, but score high in every important aspect necessary to create the kind of unforgettable retail environment consumers love, from imaginative retail architecture to high-quality service to imagination in creating vivid sensory experiences.

STEW LEONARD'S

Rule No. 1: The Customer is always right!
Rule No 2: If the customer is ever wrong, read Rule No. 1!
—Stew Leonard, Jr.

A consumer-oriented retail environment is a style of environment that always puts the customer first in the most fervent way. Stew Leonard's famous store (of the same name) in Connecticut is the ultimate retail experience both in terms of the unique level of customer service provided and the unbelievably enjoyable and innovative atmosphere.

Stew Leonard's is not just about groceries at the right price. It is about the physical experience of shopping: what you see, hear, smell, and taste. It is exciting and memorable. The more of this kind of sensory experience you create for your customers, the more you will be able to reach their hearts and make their shopping a pleasure. And why—unless it is a pleasure—should anyone today want to go through the trouble of shopping for commodities such as food, if they can buy all they need with a few convenient clicks on the Internet?

The service at Stew Leonard's is the friendliest you can hope to experience anywhere. Stew Leonard's really has an understanding of how to treat its customers right. As a matter of fact, it gives seminars on customer service to many of America's top Fortune 500 companies, such as Citibank, IBM, and PepsiCo!

The store caters to suburban Connecticut families. These are, for the most part, hard-core commuters (to New York City) who want to enjoy their weekend time with their families. Stew Leonard's takes the burden of shopping and turns it into a family event.

You have to go there to believe it. It is very difficult to leave with an empty cart because the merchandise is so enticing and different every time.

At first sight, the look of Stew's store is reminiscent of a Connecticut country farm. This brings tremendous credibility to the overall concept of freshness. A small animal farm with cows, pigs, goats, ducks, chickens, and other domestic animals is located at the entrance to the parking lot–a thrill for children and parents alike. At the store entrance you are welcomed by a large stone engraved with Rules No. 1 and 2. As soon as you pass through the doors, your senses are immediately assailed by the delicious and relaxing aroma of freshly baked bread. Stew is a master at making his customers feel good via different olfactory experiences as they tour the store. The tour of the store is guided and follows a well-established traffic pattern that exposes the customer to the total product offering, but it also offers several shortcuts to those who arc in a hurry. Fresh coffee is brewed on the premises and offered to shoppers, and a kitchen prepares take-out food, keeping all those aromas we like so much in specific zones to keep our taste buds awake. A miniature milk factory

You have to go there to believe it. It is very difficult to leave with an empty cart because the merchandise is so enticing and different every time.

with a sign saying "we churn our own butter" shows customers exactly how the milk ends up in those familiar cartons. This mini dairy factory, replete with a conveyor belt that carries the containers, brings authenticity to the concept of entertainment that is so much a part of Stew's.

The store executes many other amazing ideas with similar fanfare and fun. A miniature train runs around the store, as if to deliver the country's best brands and farm products coming in on a daily basis. In the dairy section, you swing to the tunes of the three singing hens–Emma, Blake, and Sarah–or the Farm Fresh Five band (that is, a nice little group of singing milk cartons and chicks just hatched and still sitting in their eggshells). In the produce section, the Cindy Celery and Larry Lettuce Show makes you sing along with their "We're fresh vegetables and good for you" song, whether you want to or not! And let's not forget the Calypso monkey puppet show trio that is located on top of the fresh bananas. One of Stew's employees confessed to me that after a while it can get a bit overwhelming. "Every time the music is on, people buy so many bananas, I can't keep up refilling the shelves! People really do go bananas!"

The Cindy Celery and Larry Lettuce Show makes you sing along with their "We're fresh vegetables and good for you" song.

"Homemade freshness from the source" is the message, and you are tempted to believe that a real farm supplying all that produce is right in back of the store. The original cartons are used for display, and you can read the address of the farm providing the products. You don't feel that any middlemen are controlling the product quality and prices.

Stew's is a retailer constantly focused on providing all that we could possibly wish for in a grocery store: quality, freshness, abundance, and a friendly atmosphere. The customer is always encouraged to participate in the life of the store, even when at home. As you leave, you can purchase Stew's easy-does-it cookbook *You Can Do It* or win a Stew's gift certificate by submitting a photo of yourself with a Stew Leonard's shopping bag taken at any of the great landmarks of the world (the photos are then displayed in a special area of the store). But the last touch in this store relationship is the questionnaire offered as you leave, entitled "What do you like? What don't you like? I'd love to know. Stew Leonard."

ABC CARPET

ABC Carpet & Home is another retailer that has created a special world of its own and clearly understands the consumer's desire to have a good time while shopping. Although it houses one of the most extensive collections of carpets from all over the world, ABC Carpet is about a whole lot more than carpets. It is a shopping adventure . . . exploring Ali Baba's hidden treasure cavern!

Situated in downtown New York, this six-story neo-Greco brick building circa 1881 offers on each of its floors one of the most comprehensive collections of furniture and home-furnishing accessories–from traditional to eclectic–you can find anywhere. The products are arranged to become part of the décor–a wonderful kaleidoscope of interlocking rooms or "sets" with a lifestyle presentation that creates a string of original fantasy worlds in which customers can envision their furnishing dreams. The product display encourages customers to touch, play with, and even rearrange the products. This store also engages all of your senses. Scents are prevalent in many areas and interwoven throughout the décor. Shoppers can take a break and eat in the charming, intimate Parlour Café decorated in an eclectic Victorian style (all the furnishings and decorations are for sale, too, so you can shop while eating!), or stop by the fabulous gourmet Food Hall for a snack.

Shopping at ABC Carpet nurtures socializing, visualizing, and discovering new and exciting products that smartly reflect many different price ranges in an extremely pleasant environment. In this store the customer is the hero. Everything is done for his or her enjoyment; the store helps you to shop at your own pace, invites you for a rest if needed (on the furniture itself or in one of their restaurants), and constantly challenges you with new arrivals from all around the world. The unique offerings and imaginative displays allow you to travel in spirit, something that is very much valued today.

Shopping at ABC Carpet nurtures socializing, visualizing, and discovering.

Both of these models have successfully created the kind of retail spirit that used to make department stores so exciting. These retailers have a special sensitivity that allows them to reach customers in the most sincere and helpful way–by making them happy and transforming an otherwise demanding experience of shopping into a delightful walk in a "wondershop" that truly conveys the "art of shopping" at its best.

ABC Carpets.

184

13

Brand Presence with Presence: A Fresh, New Approach

"The brand is the amusement park, and the product is the souvenir!"
–Nick Graham, President and Chief Underpants Officer, Joe Boxer

What is brand presence?

Presence is the science of creating or leveraging identities by connecting with different national and international audiences through the use of the appropriate visual/emotional stimuli at different points of experience. The Coca-Cola trademark, for instance, conveys different meanings depending upon whether it is used on the Atlanta headquarters building, on a can, at the Olympics, or in signage in the United States, in China, or in Venezuela. However, it is always consistent with Coca-Cola's core brand values.

From Ubiquity to Presence

Presence, unlike ubiquity, is an image-management process that transcends rigorous systems of applications to focus on communication that is targeted, personal, and relevant always, without compromising the integrity of the overall identity. *Presence expresses the emotional and sensory atmosphere that surrounds a brand.*

Brands are not static; they have many facets to their personality. In order to build up and retain equity as a preferred brand in the mind of the consumer, a brand must evolve to stay connected to its target audience in its day-to-day, moment-to-moment existence. Brand presence at its best connects intimately to the consumer's lifestyle. *The challenge is to move a brand forward by understanding the consumer's level of receptivity and sensitivity to a message at a given time and point of contact.* In this regard, brands need to transcend a lin-

Brands are not static; they have many facets to their personality.

ear, primarily ubiquity-oriented mode of expression to connect with consumers emotionally in different ways at different times during the brand experience. My company has created a tool to do just this called the Brand Presence® Management system (BPM), which enables a brand to deliver the right emotional message to the right customer at the right time and place. BPM diagnoses a brand *from the consumer's experience perspective* and helps

Presence that is *felt*, as well as seen, is needed.

companies to assess and audit a brand's total identity in the marketplace, providing solutions on how to manage and optimize the brand's expression emotionally. For more about BPM and an example of how we used this tool to develop the presence program for Coca-Cola for the 1996 Atlanta Olympics, please see chapter 17 in Section IV, which describes d/g*'s most powerful brand design tools.

While it is true that "to be recognized, you must first be seen," a crucial part of a strong brand-presence program must also be to build the relevant emotional experience the brand provides at different points of contact with consumers. Sending your logo up into space, as Pizza Hut did when they put a thirty-foot-tall Pizza Hut logo on the world's largest proton rocket, is not necessarily for everyone! A brand has many opportunities to reach consumers on a much more profound, personal level. Presence that is *felt*, as well as seen, is needed. It is necessary to manage a program that connects with and *engages the consumer with modular messages at different times, in different places in the consumer's lifestyle.*

Advertising is often a masterful way of speaking directly to consumers at different points of contact, but it is only one aspect of a strategy that includes a thorough understanding of all the possible places where a brand-consumer dialogue can take place, such as outdoor presence, Web presence, events, retail branding, or portable communication devices. A brand's outdoor-presence messages are generally very similar, sometimes for years and years. Advertising can (and should) change rapidly to adapt to new opportunities, but for some reason outdoor signage is not usually managed in the same way. This is sort of like having an ongoing conversation with someone who says the same thing again and again. We tend to eventually tune them out! The key is to think like a consumer and attempt to view your brand's presence from their perspective.

JCDecaux SA, the world's largest street furniture company, which partners with advertisers, is entirely based on the principle of understanding and responding to the needs of the public in creative and visually pleasing ways.

The company's kiosks, bus shelters, bathrooms, telephone booths, and so on, reflect an aesthetically appealing design with innovative solutions to daily city life. Their "street furniture"—present in thirty-one countries and eleven thousand cities—is designed by some of the world's best architects and designers, who seek to be sensitive to the particular cultural nuances of their native countries in their designs. JCDecaux transportation shelters and kiosks attempt to help build a city's contemporary image with flair, without detracting from its unique historic character. They have developed helpful devices for the public such as online bus information available at bus shelters. This is the best of all possible worlds; a brand-presence vehicle that is visually attractive and highly useful to people in their everyday lives!

The element of surprise can also be very powerful in creating a bond with consumers through brand presence. Brand-presence initiatives that exceed or play with our expectations can attain more emotional resonance. The first time I saw the "Absolut New York" billboard in Manhattan, I had that great jaw-dropping feeling of surprise, as did half a dozen or so other pedestrians who stood with me pointing and staring in amazement at the incredible life-size reproduction of a studio apartment (furnished by IKEA) stuck sideways up on a billboard! The billboard is replete with lots of real, fun details such as

cartons of Chinese take-out food on the kitchen counter, toiletries on shelves, shoes on the "floor," and glasses set out on the coffee table (martini glasses with Absolut vodka nearby, of course), and so on, so that looking at it becomes a sort of a game and you can see something entirely new each time. This billboard is one of six super billboards Seagram launched for Absolut in 2000. The others included such literally "off-the-wall" outdoor efforts as a fourteen-foot Absolut bottle on Sunset Boulevard in Los Angeles, where performance artists daily layer a thousand coats of paint onto the bottle, and letters spelling out A-B-S-O-L-U-T with a placard let passersby know which coat number the painters are working on. A field of flowers has been planted in Chile in the shape of an Absolut bottle (this outdoor display is called "Absolut Summer"). Richard Lewis, worldwide account director for the brand for TBWA/Chiat/Day has said that Absolut is extending its efforts beyond magazine ads because these kind of outdoor billboards can reach consumers in ways that magazines cannot. When he says of their efforts, "We're trying to create some kind of emotional connection to [a] market,"[1] he clearly has got the right idea about the potential of brand presence!

Although certainly less groundbreaking, the Yahoo! sign on the corner of Lafayette and Houston streets in New York City also succeeds in creating an innovative point of difference in an ad-intensive environment through the ele-

ments of surprise and clever, aesthetically interesting design. At first glance, the sign appears to be a classic retro fifties, Route 66–style motel sign, replete with revolving neon-lit features and a flashing "Vacancy/No Vacancy" light. The sign reads, "Yahoo! A nice place to stay on the Internet," conveying Yahoo!'s brand identity as a fun, accessible home base from which to explore the vast world of the Internet. Through the use of fifties nostalgia the sign evokes at once both a sense of comfort and the excitement, adventure, and freedom of traveling the American open road. In this same way, the role of each of a brand's communication vehicles needs to be modulated and engineered effectively and with creativity to reach consumers in an emotionally relevant way.

Of course it also couldn't hurt to invent an entirely new kind of communication vehicle as well! Joe Boxer has created the Undo-Vendo machine; talking vending machines for its boxer shorts that cannot help but amuse and perhaps even intercept you as you walk by them and they call out, "Hey you, do you need some new underwear?" These vending machines also

Joe Boxer has created the Undo-Vendo machine; talking vending machines for its boxer shorts.

tell jokes and are a perfect way to convey the fun and humor of the Joe Boxer brand positioning. There are currently about seventy of these machines in the United States and they are being tied to the company's Web site in a clever way.

A customer can purchase a gift certificate for a friend online and e-mail them a gift-certificate code that they can enter into any Joe Boxer Undo-Vendo machine. These are just one of many great examples of highly creative and effective brand-presence initiatives by Nick Graham, the founder of Joe Boxer, and king of brand presence if there ever was one! Nick Graham, the real personality behind the brand, is a fabulous communicator whose cross-dressing stunts have made him into an icon personifying the wacky humor of Joe Boxer. His official corporate title is Chief Underpants Officer, and now he has bought an English title that makes him "Lord of the Balls" as well.

Nick Graham has, in fact, achieved a brand recognition of 77 percent on a shoestring budget (in a recent conversation he confided in me that he spends only $500,000 a year on advertising for a company with an annual revenue of $100 million!). He accomplishes this feat through unique brand-presence efforts and highly creative guerrilla stunts. At Joe Boxer, everything and everybody communicates the brand. Just visit their showroom in New York and you will see what I mean. Joe Boxer is very serious about humor. After all, if sex sells, what about humor in sex as a change? The reception area at Joe Boxer's office has chairs with wigs attached to them, so that when you sit down you instantly have a humorous experience of yourself (of course for many men this is even funnier–instant drag queen). The table in their conference room is shaped like a surfboard with "BLAH! BLAH! BLAH!" written all over it.

Can Less Be More?

In the world of emotionally branded presence, it is not quantity that counts but quality. Consumers are so barraged by communications that finding a unique venue for a brand message can sometimes be more powerful than logos plastered everywhere. This is particularly true in New York City and other large urban areas where modern computer technology has made the cost of oversized vinyl panels negligible and, therefore, 120-foot Gap models staring down at pedestrians from buildings are a commonplace sight, and advertising clutter from bus stop ads to passing trucks is abundant. But really, there is every indication that in the future, no matter where you live, ads will be everywhere, including in your hands every time you take a look at your PDA, and in your local grocery-store shopping carts. Companies such as Hardwear International Corp. are developing wearable video and, apparently, soon we will have designer clothing with inlaid intelligent, changeable screens for ads! Many restaurants now even have ads that stare at you in the restroom stall (and, I might add, the tone of these annoying ads usually conveys such a "let-me-grab-your-attention-in-this-private moment in an off-the-wall-clever-way" smug humor that I doubt they are very successful!). Altoids has found an unusual and effective brand presence venue in New York City in the form of pedicabs or bicycle-powered rickshaws.[2] Their brand-presence campaign for the "curiously strong" mints cleverly plays off the concept of the robust strength of the pedicab driver, featuring a giant illuminated Altoids tin suspended on a wrap ad covering the rear and sides of each pedicab. Jeff Grace at Leo Burnett USA, who produced the campaign, explains the choice of pedicabs as a brand-presence platform by saying, "Because of their novelty and friendliness, they are frequent head-turners of even the most jaded New Yorkers." In addition, pedicabs often operate in the most trendy sections of the city, the drivers acting as guides to take people to the most hip spots and fun restaurants, and they lend the Altoids brand a ground-level cachet of "coolness" that has inestimable value! How much more effective is an intimate, unique brand contact such as this, where the ad is linked up with a service and unusual, fun encounter involving another person (the driver), than one of the

Altoid's pedicab campaign in New York City.

many "in-your-face" ads plastered on a building? From the perspective of Emotional Branding, I would say the difference is an important one to consider!

Guerrilla Marketing

Long, long ago, in an economy far, far away, corporate empires and advertising oligarchs relied on big budgets to drive dominating advertising campaigns across the consumer landscape. As these behemoths gobbled up one medium after another, believing "bigger is better," small bands of rebel operations learned to make do with what they had. Using the weapons of creativity and resourcefulness, they succeeded in stretching their limited budgets far into unknown territory. And so guerrilla marketing was born. Frugality was its hallmark and integrity was its trademark. Guerrilla marketing revealed a capacity to attract loyal niche markets that were inaccessible by mainstream ad campaigns, as well as crucial trendsetters turned off by the gloss and plasticity that characterize ad campaigns directed at the masses.

Guerrilla marketing provides the personal encounter that is so vital in the Emotional Economy—the consumer can see the face of a brand. It makes sense to distribute sample goods or advertising for the brand at places where the target audience congregates, such as concerts or a spring-break destination. Fashion brands are more and more frequently giving away their hottest season's designs to stylish editors, stylists, artists, and socialites as a way of subtly influencing the market. Prada sent its bowling bags to a slew of key fashion editors attending the Milan shows in February 2000 and scored a coup when the *New York Times* ran a half-page photo-essay of women on the streets "coincidentally" (or so the *Times* thought) carrying this same Prada bag! Guerrilla marketing also frequently relics on street teams consisting of young, hip, and extroverted recruits who rove urban areas, pouncing on marketing opportunities as they arise. The distribution of free samples, spontaneous street theater, posturing, or just talking about the alleged

For some brands, what works best is to use guerrilla marketing as a way of exploring the creative possibilities for brand contact.

"new" thing—all these are viable and fruitful tactics for savvy street teams. Maximillion Pick of Mosaic Communications, which specializes in guerrilla marketing, says in a November 1999 issue of *Advertising Age*: "We went directly into the clubs and watched to see who was talked to the most, who got in [the club] easiest, who talked to the disc jockey." These are the people they hire to compose the street teams.

Now, this weapon of smaller corporations has become popular to varying degrees with commerce at all levels and for all market segments, particularly as consumers become more adept than ever at tuning out bothersome ads vying for their attention.

Sometimes it's a simple question of personal touch. Food.com, an Internet start-up, decided to go the guerrilla-marketing route after little results from their $2 million ad campaign. One of the several successful guerrilla-marketing stunts they did was to hire uniformed "chefs" to visit offices (posing as delivery people to sneak past receptionists!) to hand out rebates and T-shirts. In order to entice the college crowd, they executed a tie-in benefit program for the hungry and homeless, where the young people were able to get free CDs, rebates, and so on, in exchange for donated cans of food at concerts.

In their book *Under the Radar*, Jonathan Bond and Richard Kirshenbaum[3] showcase novelty in advertising and the crucial need to reach consumers through innovative and relevant channels. They devote an entire chapter to analyzing and suggesting means of stirring and managing positive word-of-mouth reputations for their clients, which is what guerrilla marketing is all about: creating a buzz! There are many, many ways to do this. When managing a campaign for Iron City Beer, a microbrewery based in Pittsburgh, they visited the hottest local bars with video cameras, soliciting new slogans for the beer. This generated quite a buzz, and in time generated the slogan "It's a 'Burgh thing." This phrase, used to characterize anything quintessentially Pittsburgh, was soon picked up by local media and DJs. Every time a casual conversation or morning DJ described something as a "'Burgh thing," Iron City received a little bit of free publicity. Furthermore, the integrity of such endorsements is incomparable to any other medium. The authors of the book relate one anecdote illustrating the success of their campaign slogan to generate spontaneous discussions and brand loyalty, writing "One memorable example took place at Three Rivers Stadium during a Pirates baseball game. Two beer vendors, one selling Budweiser and the other selling Iron City, got into a competition. The banter went back and forth with scores of fans looking on in amusement. The Bud salesman said, 'We have the Clydesdales!' The Iron City vendor countered, 'We have the historic brewery—a city landmark!' The Bud salesman said, 'It's the world's number-one beer!' The Iron City seller responded right off the ads, 'What's that got to do with Pittsburgh?!' The crowd cheered the Iron City vendor. Clearly the tide was turning. The final blow was set up when the Bud guy said, 'It's got 120 years of history!' to which the Iron City guy responded, 'It's a 'Burgh thing!' More cheers erupted from the crowd and the contest was over."[4] Although almost any industry can benefit from intelligent guerrilla marketing, it seems to work particularly well with somewhat specialized markets, because a large element of its appeal is intimacy. In the Iron City example, tapping into the qualities of regional culture created that specialty.

And for some brands, what works best is to use guerrilla marketing as a way of exploring the creative possibilities for brand contact. In other words, to venture into the realm of the outrageous! Just about everyone knows something about Joe Boxer's outrageous promotional stunts, such as launching a rocket into the stratosphere with a pair of underwear in it, or its famous fashion show in Iceland. In 1997 Graham flew two hundred fashion editors to Iceland where for forty-eight hours they were treated to a variety of events such as introduction to the president of Iceland, cocktail parties with sheep, a visit to a Viking village, and an underwear fashion show featuring Viking-helmeted models. The total cost of the well-organized event was only around two hundred thousand dollars. Nick Graham says: "It helped create buzz for Iceland, and the press definitely helped their business. And I know it helped ours when I go somewhere like Little Rock and someone tells me, 'I saw that Iceland thing on TV.'"[5]

That kind of press is of course one of the desired goals and best outcomes for creative ventures into guerilla marketing. PlanetOutdoors had wonderful results with this when instead of going the billboard route the online outdoor retailer set up a complete outdoor expedition in Manhattan, complete with skyscrapers being climbed like mountains.

Another example of clever guerrilla marketing is the recent film *The Omega Code*, which was recognized by *Brandweek* as a "Guerrilla Marketer of the Year."[6] Taking inspiration from *The Blair Witch Project*, this film owed its giant success much less to quality product than brilliantly executed marketing. This Christian-oriented film, based on the Book of Revelation and filmed on a paltry $7.2 million budget, opened in October 1999 in the box office's Top Ten and earned the highest dollars-per-screen of its competitors. How? By enlisting the aid of Christian bookstores, ministers, media, and activists across the country. Congregation outings were planned, volunteers distributed flyers, and activists were encouraged by the prospect of speaking up not through boycotting but rather sponsoring a film that was in accord with their values. Producer Matthew Crouch told *Brandweek*: "It's not the best film in the world, but that's not the point. We've coalesced a consumer group that Hollywood and Madison Avenue didn't seem to know existed."[7]

However, the term "Guerrilla Marketing" remains elusive. Its strategies and success stories are based not on formulaic executions but rather on savvy and intelligent improvisation. In chapter 1, in the section on Generation Y, I mentioned some effective campaigns targeted at that group, which included using trendsetters, clubs, and DJs to inexpensively spread the word. Other products may want to target urban basketball players or college age art majors. Shows like MTV's *Fashionably Loud Spring Break 2000* is a great venue for fashion brands to get huge exposure to Gen X and Y markets. But whatever the target, guerrilla marketing will determine the medium that draws the audience's attention and interests their passions. Tommy Hilfiger tried a new brand presence initiative in spring 2000 with a two-month promotion that offered Tommy-designed Motorola cellular phones as top prizes. This promotion, aimed mostly at Gen X and Y, brought about the first-ever fashion-designer cellular phone. Only two thousand of the Tommy Hilfiger phones were manufactured for this promotion, but there are sure to be more designer phones to come in the future. *Others will surely come up with new and offbeat ways to target particular audiences. Maybe a new magazine for mature women wants to distribute flyers to elementary-age children's soccer games . . . or perhaps Barnard's twenty-year reunion . . . or maybe it wants to secure the genuine support of someone like Rosie O'Donnell, whose belief in the product will cause it to be mentioned on-air without even the cost of sponsorship.*

Conclusion

Well-thought-out, emotionally charged presence makes the customer want to join you in the brand story you have created. It is obvious that branded presence allows a product to rise above the competition by bringing a visual and experiential realm of the brand to life. We do not know yet what marvels the future may bring in terms of new venues and techniques to help us to achieve this goal, but as interactive ads become more prevalent daily, and the technology behind them is quickly being refined, we will obviously soon have new creative outlets to challenge us in our quest for emotionalized brand expression.

The Nasdaq in Times Square, New York City, was one of the very first interactive billboards.

14

Emotional Packaging:
The Half-Second Commercial

The bond between Heinz ketchup and our customers is essentially emotional and personality-based. The Heinz bottle is intrinsic to the brand personality.
—Bill Johnson, CEO of Heinz[1]

Packaging is a half-second commercial. It has to work instantly to catch your attention or establish your familiarity with a product. A package has half a second to be acknowledged and another half a second to be loved. The message needs to be instantaneous and direct—highly intrusive yet emotionally connected. For a package to work you need to have the following ingredients:

1. Clarity of proposition as a product definition
2. Proprietary visual expression
3. Emotional connectivity—through an integrated sensory message and an element of surprise

From Impact to Contact: Packaging Is Concentrated Branding

Packaging has many practical objectives, not the least of which is that consumers don't want to waste time finding a product. Consumers are more comfortable with packaging that is easy to identify. But beyond the practical considerations it is incredibly important to keep in sight the added value of engaging the consumers' senses to bring them into a different relationship with the product. *Packaging has to compete based on impact in order to be seen, but it must also create an emotional contact with consumers in order to be loved.* This alone can create product preference. Once the product is purchased, this experience of discovery can and should continue. The opening of a container or a shipping carton influences our brand experience; even the impact of the shape of a key holder for a car needs to build on the brand promise. Packaging is the ultimate communication tool, and the most imaginative ideas have emerged from the strict confines of the challenge of packaging products. To humanize, emotionalize, and tap into the senses a product needs to make the connection between perception and aspiration by translating the packaging forms and product graphics into a presentation that connects immediately to the end user.

Absolut Vodka is a great example. Absolut positioned itself as a unique proposition by initially targeting Gen X consumers with an alternative, more cerebral and contemporary packaging design that has become a badge for this generation. Absolut Mandarin, for instance, strengthens the flavor concept through an innovative proprietary visual expression that connects powerfully to our senses. By raising the bottom of the bottle in a half-mandarin shape sprayed with the color orange, Absolut

Packaging has to compete based on impact in order to be seen, but it must also create an emotional contact with consumers in order to be loved.

is able to pull the mandarin color up into transparent vodka. The color glows softly in a diffused manner as we perceive it through the frosted bottle that also enhances the refreshing aspect of the drink. Bold orange letters in the Absolut typeface create a vivid impression. The proposition is clear, relevant. The visual expression enhances the overall theme (refreshing mandarin). The frosted and colorful treatment appeals to our senses connecting with our need for beauty. And last but not least, the smooth, silky touch of the frosted bottle adds to the overall refreshing cue. These uses of glass are unusual in liquor bottles, but they have been used in the fragrance industry in some very innovative ways, giving a new dimension to the possibilities of glass packaging.

The physical realm of a package is generally small, offering little space or volume for brand-design expressions. Great packaging needs to work hard to stand out on the overcrowded shelves of stores and supermarkets and claim our attention. It is precisely because of these constraints that we see some of the most interesting innovations in this area; innovations that attempt to bring out sensorial elements, to enhance our relationship with a product. Branded products are close to our heart, and this allows them to have many functions and purposes in our lives. They can be used to simply fulfill our needs or become instead a badge that expresses our personality, style, or status. All kinds of products are part of our home décor and therefore play a very intimate role in our lives. The Givenchy Rouge Miroir lipstick packaging is one of the most innovative lipstick packaging concepts I have found in the marketplace. It incorporates a mirror into the packaging, a perceptive and elegantly executed solution to the problem of searching for a mirror when applying lipstick.

Givenchy Rouge mirror lipstick.

Packaging can also raise our expectations of a product and make us reevaluate an entire category. We expect superior presentation from any wine packaging regardless of price, and an element of surprise and sensuality from a fragrance package. We feel that liquors should embellish our bar cabinet. Soft drinks strike our senses in the moment. Ice cream is about indulgence and fun, whether it is exclusive like Godiva or more accessible like Ben & Jerry. Food packaging needs to have appetite appeal, and home products convey lifestyle cues. Packaging, like music, needs to tune in with precision to the consumer's desires. A wrong note can mean an immediate expulsion from the shelves.

Packaging can raise our expectations of a product and make us reevaluate an entire category.

PACKAGING IS SOMETIMES THE ONLY THING THAT MAKES A BRAND SING

Products with little support in advertising rely on the strength of their packaging to attract consumer attention and the favor of retailers, sometimes with great success. But packaging can also be the most powerful element of large-scale brand communication programs. As I mentioned previously, I am convinced that it is the iMac product design itself that has given strength to the Apple advertising campaign. In the same way the Evian ad campaign relies heavily on the beauty of the product and its packaging to convey the message of purity and healthy lifestyle. *The Absolut Vodka packaging is the advertising super model that never ages. Packaging is the essence of a brand crystallized in a small space.* This is why some marketers will go to great lengths to invest in packaging and why packaging agencies are, generally speaking, such great brand specialists.

PACKAGING IS EVERYBODY'S BUSINESS

Everyone has an opinion about packaging, and a packaging redesign never goes unnoticed. For certain products we have a very strong perception of what

An example of Evian's recent advertising.

the packaging should be like and will not forgive a marketer who makes the mistake of downgrading or even upgrading a familiar product's packaging. In fact, the emotional attachment people exhibit toward a particular design or element of design for a product demonstrates the tremendous and sometimes surprising equity packaging holds in the consumer psyche.

Nineteen-ninety-nine was the year for Campbell's Soup to finally change its packaging. After 102 years! This event made the cover of the business section of the *New York Times*. Why such an interest from the press and public? The changes in the overall look of the famous can are actually minimal, more of a "tweaking" than a redefinition. An evolution, but certainly not a revolution! But because of the emotional attachment people have toward certain brand "icons," we are interested–very interested–in what happens to that red-and-white can. Since Andy Warhol exalted the role of the Campbell's Soup can as a part of American pop culture, this commercial product has come to "belong" to us, and its fate concerns us all. It is truly an art to evolve a packaging design with this kind of heritage, to attract a new generation of consumers without alienating the loyal customer base. To boost their business, which was in need of some help, Campbell's Soup decided to show a new kind of responsiveness through their packaging redesign. The five new color labels are designed to showcase their newer products and help customers choose their favorite soup more easily from the selection of "classic," "fun favorites," "special selections," "great for cooking," and "98% fat free."

A lot of sophisticated research techniques have been developed around the impact of packaging on consumers' lives. While changing a TV campaign is accepted easily by an audience, a change of packaging could be unsettling, uplifting, troubling, or reassuring–but never neutral in the consumer's mind. Focus groups prove time and again that the emotional attachment to packaging is profound and powerful enough to puzzle any psychologist, even in the case of something as mundane as the design of a beer-bottle label or a soft-drink image. Given the impact of such communication, I am mystified by how little attention it sometimes receives from the top management of a corporation and how it is rarely integrated from the very beginning of a major communications program. If packaging is "everybody's business," it should certainly be the business of corporate CEOs. Heinz is a brand that has recently realized that one of its greatest brand-identity assets is the familiar, squat, octagonal glass bottle design which over the past few years has often been replaced in some of their markets by other, more practical bottle designs. Heinz is now spending a great deal of money to achieve a global standardized presentation of their ketchup in the iconoclastic bottle. Plastic imitations of the glass bottle are now being explored as well, thanks to innovations in plastic manufacturing technology that allows lower weight and higher durability and squeezability. Bill Johnson, CEO of Heinz, explains this renewed commitment to consistency in their packaging by saying, "If it keeps changing, if you can't rely on it, what kind of relationship can you build?"[2]

PACKAGING IS A MESSAGE . . . AND A CONTAINER

The primary functions of packaging are to protect stock shipped from the factory to the distribution centers and retailers, as well as to display and market a product on a shelf in a retail space by giving important product information and an overall sense of the brand's emotional attributes. Packaging as a container needs to respect quite rigid criteria, such as shelf space and the size of visual merchandising units in the distribution sector. Product packaging also needs to fit well into refrigerators or other storage spaces in the home. A product must be packaged for consumer use in ways that facilitate our daily usage.

Packaging informs us about product function and features and must often also carry legal information, weight, nutrition facts, and the bar coding system as well. Packaging that is destined to be international needs to allocate space for the translation of several languages and must be sensitive to the cultural values endorsed by different populations. It is crucial to keep in mind that over-packaging is often negatively perceived in markets where ecological sensitivity is very high. I have always worked closely with our clients on minimizing packaging waste and on the impact our work has on the environment. When you are working within all these constraints, there is little room to communicate your product's overall brand image and distinct advantage to the consumer, but this is what makes the art of packaging such a challenging and rewarding task. Despite all these practical considerations, it must also sell the product. It has a very big job!

Packaging defines cultures and periods of time and it is fascinating to see how a brand can evolve through packaging to stay relevant.

I have always been a fan of packaging design and graphics from different countries because it is a very interesting indication of specific cultures and tastes. Here I will share with you some of the packaging innovations that I have found around the world and that have sometimes been used as inspiration for our work. *Packaging defines cultures and periods of time and it is fascinating to see how a brand can evolve through packaging to stay relevant.* Recently, packaging has reached a new level of expression as technologies in printing and the treatment of materials have evolved to enable marketers and designers to explore new opportunities. The competitive pressure of today's marketplace has also challenged marketers to innovate by bringing a new level of communication into their packaging—one that is based on emotions.

Packaging Innovations in the Liquor, Fragrance, Beverage, and Food Industries

THE LIQUOR INDUSTRY

The success of Absolut Vodka has awakened a new set of competitors to the power of packaging, and these brands have begun to push the limits of innovation in glass packaging. The Polish vodka Belvedere has managed to achieve a stunning three-dimensional graphic presentation of their brand through an unusual bottle shape and by using the fact that the back of the bottle is visible through the front. What you see through the snow-covered tree branches design on the front of the bottle is Poland's presidential palace, magnified through the liquid. This tall, slender bottle is frosted all over except in the spot

where the palace is viewed, which allows you to see the palace as if you were walking through the palace garden on a cold winter morning. This is a most compelling, refreshing brand expression that engages our imagination.

The Japanese liquor industry is obviously a great example of how to emotionalize packaging, since culturally the Japanese have always been highly artistic and have carried this sensibility over into the world of product enhancement. Each time I travel to Japan, I visit the food section of department stores for inspiration. The sake bottles are always packaged to invite the consumers to discover what is inside in a subtle yet dramatic manner that engages the senses and heightens our expectations. There are lovely, unique combinations of materials such as in the Tenzan sake packaging, which uses bamboo leaves and coarse rope ties to wrap the outer layer of the bottle, and covers the layer closest to the bottle with rice paper. The Mutsu Hassen brand covers the bottle in a transparent rice paper–type sheath, enfolding the cap in black paper tied with a burgundy rope. These colors and materials beautifully enhance the overall product presentation and express in a celebratory style the special moment of consumption. The Sho Chiku Bai, precious Giyo sake, uses a very interesting technique to package a collection of products using different colors. Liquors are bound by the legal restriction of a warning back label

with long mandatory copy, and Sho Chiku Bai has found a clever added use for this label by printing the back of the labels in colors to bring a diffused coloring to the entire frosted bottle. This is a great usage of labels to enhance an overall package design.

Packaging can tell stories and inspire us to make up our own stories.

Packaging can also tell stories and, most importantly, can inspire us to make up our own stories. Robert Mondavi's innovation of a clear wine bottle top that allows the cork and its information to be seen was a breakthrough concept in the wine category. The sensory elements are also well played out in the overall look of the Robert Mondavi bottles, such as the frosted 1997 Fumé Blanc wine bottle or the exquisite label of the 1996 Stags Leap Sauvignon Blanc that communicates the rich heritage of the brand and the pleasure of the drinking experience. Mystic Cliffs, another winery brand, has a 1997 Chardonnay label that symbolizes the steep coast of California and takes us to a place associated with world-class wine. Through the use of a clear label, the design is so well integrated with the bottle that you feel that the spirit of California wines is embodied in that very bottle. An emphasis on heritage does not have to mean boring! Traditional packaging from the thirties and forties was centered around storytelling, with a wonderfully enchanting use of color and style, such as the tin cases for Velvet tobacco that conveyed a

romance and sensuality I sometimes miss. This kind of imaginative aesthetic could be translated into today's packaging beautifully.

THE FRAGRANCE INDUSTRY

Packaging is everything in the world of fragrance, where image is the only means to convey the subtleties of the fragrance and differentiate one fragrance from another. The outer packaging, the bottle, and the name are often the only tools for conveying to the consumer the invisible "genie" of promise inside. Fragrances need to deliver on an emotional promise to the buyer immediately. Fragrances are a fashion item that touches our most intimate romantic and sensual cords; they are strictly about emotions and sensations–not many real, "practical" benefits here. *The benefit is clearly in the psychological realm. So fragrance packaging needs to express an idea in the most emotionally potent way possible!* Textures, shapes, and materials have a critical role to play, and innovation is more than a rule, it is a necessity. The fragrance industry is a great source of inspiration for mass marketers since this industry constantly pushes the limit of the "doable" in packaging. Fragrance packaging designers are known for challenging manufacturers to live up to their visions, which sets off new trends all around.

The most successful fragrances have always been about telling stories or sending messages, such as the tale of exoticism from Yves St. Laurent's Opium, the very personal message from Christian Dior's Remember Me, the Snow White/

Left: Yves Rocher's Neblina.
Below: Dior's Remember Me.

Eve story told by Christian Dior's Poison, or the tale of eternal passion told by Calvin Klein's Eternity . . . I love the way the story behind the Yves Rocher's fragrance Neblina is transmitted through the packaging copy that reads, "Between heaven and earth, in a sea of clouds high above the Amazonian forest, a shimmering mist releases a rare, delicate fragrance of nature. This is the essence of Neblina." Every year there are hundreds of new fragrances, but only a few survive to become fragrance stars. These are the ones that strike a profound emotional chord.

Most fragrances are still designed for women, but the men's fragrance business is growing, and unisex fragrances such as cK One continue to have remarkable success. I have seen fragrances test well in focus groups but fail miserably on the market because of weak packaging and poor communication. In my experience with fragrances, the packaging and the communication are the product. This wonderful, modern puzzlelike bottle design for the Issey Miyake's eau de toilette and aftershave lotion for men is so mechanically clever and compelling that you have to reach out and test the smooth slide of the way the bottles fit into one another; a beautiful solution to a practical problem of using two products in sync.

The need for innovation in fragrance packaging is also driven by the limited distribution channels available for fragrances. Most distribution takes place through department stores, very challenging and static environments for the sales of fragrances. Specialty stores such as Sephora are raising the emotional bar for fragrance presentation, but this weak link in creating the right envi-

PHOTO BY PAUL TILLINGHAST.

Issey Miyake's eau de toilette and aftershave lotion.

ronment for fragrance distribution is, I believe, what has allowed specialty fashion retailers such as the Gap to enter the fragrance business so successfully with unique packaging and retail environments that enhance the sensual experience consumers can have with the brand. What about MAC's fragrance in a necklace? Is MAC selling a fragrance product, a piece of jewelry, or just the attitude of a hip brand that makes you hip by sharing its values? The answer is in our heart–where we will also make the decision to buy or not to buy. I certainly like the idea of packaging that you wear; a new level of intimacy with the brand.

In the fragrance and beauty industry everything needs to communicate.

In the fragrance and beauty industry everything needs to communicate–the container, the closure/application systems, the secondary packaging, and the visual merchandising systems. All these elements need to work together to heighten the emotional experience a customer will have with the product and provide a sensorial discovery. The Kenzo fragrance for men, Zebra, for which my partner Joël Desgrippes designed the bottle, has simulated zebra hair on the cap to make the concept more vivid. Another of Joël's famous designs, the Boucheron Jaïpur bottle, is modeled as a bracelet and has transcended its category to become a decorative item. In one case I even heard of it being used as a home accessory! A Bloomingdale's salesperson once told me that a customer bought sixteen of them to use as napkin rings and gifts for a special dinner.

The Armani A/X DUO bottles, designed by Fabien Baron, clearly express the sexual nature of the product, and the outer packaging challenges standard

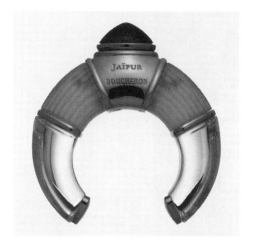

Boucheron's Jaïpur.   Kenzo's Zebra.

approaches by presenting the product in metallic-finished sealed envelopes. The Ann Taylor fragrance bottle for Destination, which I designed, is meant to convey an invitation to travel. The mysterious name and jewel-like shape of the bottle for Victoria's Secret fragrance Encounter, another of my creations, tells the story of romantic anticipation. Jean-Paul Gaultier's first fragrance, which is in a bottle shaped as a woman's torso, has a can as an outer packaging, which communicates the concept in a very antichic, antistatus hip manner—one of the first expressions of the class-meets-mass trend. Another Gaultier's fragrance, Fragile, is also a groundbreaking take on fragrance packaging design. The concept and the story behind this brand is the most important thing (and the more interesting the story, the better the fragrance). Taking inspiration from some of the fun, cheap tourist souvenirs one can find in Paris, Gaultier created a fantasy world of "snowflake globe" with a figurine of a woman inside immersed in the perfume with gold flakes floating around her. The outer packaging of an old-fashioned shipping crate used to pack fragile and valuable items that opens like a flower to reveal the perfume inside adds to the sense of discovery and wonder. This packaging breaks some of the traditional fragrance marketing rules, reclaiming the territory of fragrance that is about escape and fantasy. In this category, packaging moves product through emotions. It's as simple as that.

THE BEVERAGE EXPERIENCE

Beverages, from soft drinks to wines, are moving from an impact-only strategy to one that relies heavily on emotions and sensory experiences. A good example is Snapple, a once successful, then flailing brand under Quaker Oats,

which is now a successful brand again. Snapple has reconnected powerfully to consumers through new product concepts and new primary containers supported by fresh and imaginative naming and graphics. Through its new product concepts and new primary containers with fresh and imaginative naming and graphics, *Snapple has challenged everything in the soft-drink arena. Something fundamental has changed when a ginseng black tea is called "Lightning," normal teas are called "Sun Teas," and fruit juices "Whipper Snapple."* Such innovations require a forceful packaging expression to work, and Snapple has integrated the emotional lifestyle core elements of these brands into its packaging well.

Snapple has challenged everything in the soft-drink arena.

The new labeling and packaging system we designed for Coca-Cola in 2003 provided a new look for the world's number-one brand. In reintroducing the historical but abandoned Coca-Cola "Dynamic Ribbon" Desgrippes Gobé elevated the brand perception from its functional image of refreshment characterized by

PHOTOS BY KEIFER CHEN.

the contour bottle to a new emotional language. Research told us that the new abstract graphics were perceived as an expression of energy, fun, and optimism without losing the traditional values of the brand as being genuine, authentic, and real. But the best discovery in what turned out to be a two-year-long process was how an emotional strategy can bring a richer and deeper personality to a brand beyond its ubiquitous, rigorous expression. Emotional feelings toward a brand are indeed different if you are a mom or a teenager, if you are at the Olympic Games or in a supermarket. In the qualitative research that we did worldwide, we tested youth-driven, innovative designs to see if we could bring "cool" into the perception of the brand and connect with teenagers. We named those the "slim cans" in reference to their shapes. The cans were tested minus the famous Coca-Cola script to reduce its commercial look, relying only on the brand's historic icons. The result was beyond our expectations. The "slim cans" are now distributed in a very narrow and tightly targeted marketplace to create buzz around the brand and build an emotional connection with youth world-wide. Indeed, brands are not static entities with rigorous expressions but lively personalities capable of appealing to different audiences at once. One of the club cans was even auctioned off for $36 on eBay!

Gatorade, the sports drink par excellence and another one of our clients, has gone to great lengths to cater to its demographic population segment of seri-ous athletes. The lightning bolt of the Gatorade logo is one of the most dynamic and compelling logos in the category and can fuel great impact in any pres-ence program. The shapes of the containers are athletic and functional, and give the feeling of control when held in the hand. We recently repositioned the Gatorade brand image and evolved the packaging image to move the brand from the original refreshment concept graphics with a neutral green back-

PHOTOS BY PAUL TILLINGHAST.

ground and water drops to a variety of extreme sports graphics. These visual expressions bring the brand back to its core territory of "liquid fuel" for athletes. This new approach allowed Gatorade to expand more easily into new flavors. Gatorade Fierce Melon is an example of how far you can extend a core brand identity consistently through emotionally driven language and innovative packaging graphics.

FOOD PACKAGING

Food has always been the most conservative area in packaging expression. Most graphics are based on product description, historical or heritage cues, appetite appeal, and, except for youth-driven products such as cereals, do not engage in lifestyle, generational, or experience-oriented graphics. This is slowly beginning to change and there are, of course, some exceptions. In Japan, for instance, the packaging of noodles is very appealing and creative, showing the product as a work of art. There is also a Japanese yogurt container that I love, with a miniature plastic spoon encased in the lid for convenience. In France, an Amora ketchup dispenser in the shape of a cartoon-style icon with arms, legs, and a head represents a character they have named "ketchoupy." A brilliant idea. *Suddenly this packaging can really come alive outside of the shelves—as a plaything, an animation on a Web site, a character in a children's book, and so on—and become a desired mascot that sells the product.* Packaging that is designed with this kind of cleverness turns an otherwise commodity product into a communications symbol.

Certain food categories are entrenched in a morass of "sameness." The cereal aisle could be a lot less silly in its effort to captivate kids.

Pepperidge Farm also knows well how to balance quality and expectation. The packaging is reminiscent of an old deli bag, and this brings a homemade feel to the brand. The name supports this concept, and the cookie collection, made up of famous city names such as Brussels, Milano, Bordeaux, and so on, takes it all a step further to the world of international delicacies, inciting our imaginations and taste buds.

The Lea and Perrins Worcestershire Sauce packaging has always been one of my favorites; it communicates an added value to me in terms of taste expectation and special recipes just by the overall look of the packaging graphics.

Certain food categories are entrenched in a morass of "sameness." The cereal aisle, for example, could be a lot less silly in its effort to captivate kids and

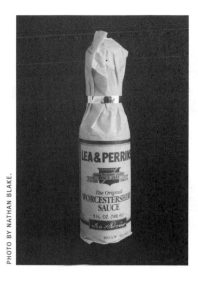

instead reach for deeper aesthetic emotions. Why are almost all the cereals sold in the same printed cardboard boxes? Imagine the experience of actually picking a differently shaped box or container in the morning, such as the new Kellogg's Special K Plus. Cereal brands could develop new unique shapes that integrate sound and toys into their packaging in this way and attract new customers. New concepts can be challenging for corporations—it certainly means risk—but surprising and delighting consumers with newness means desire . . . and market shares!

Borrowed Cues for Packaging Inspiration

I have always used other categories as inspiration for packaging projects because it brings an element of surprise and discovery to consumers. Some brands have done this very successfully. For example, the deodorant brand Fa Body Splash has developed a package that looks like a soft drink can . . . a refreshing symbol! When I designed the Gingham fragrance bottle for Bath & Body Works, which is based on the concept of honesty and quality from the Heartland, I was inspired by the shape of an old-fashioned glass yogurt jar to communicate the integrity one expects in the milk products industry. The bath line called Cottage gives us a delightful new take on bath salts that are packaged in a sugar dispenser. In the Gillette Series primary packaging, the grip inspiration came from tools, sports equipment, motorcycles, golf clubs, and other "grip" situations with which men are familiar. The Joyful Garden packaging we designed for Bath & Body Works was mean to reflect the shapes of

PHOTOS BY PAUL TILLINGHAST.

the antique glass bottles that I collect. These bottles were used for medicine or drinks sold in rural general stores and we found them to be a great inspiration for conveying the authentic and natural style of the line. The "down home," country style of this packaging gave it a charm that made the product line very successful in the stores.

When we designed the logo and packaging for Leap batteries, a Toronto-based start-up aiming for the specialty batteries market share (such as the lithium,

PHOTO BY PAUL TILLINGHAST.

The Joyful Garden packaging and the bottles that inspired their design.

nickel-metal hydride, and so on, batteries used in mobile communications devices and laptops), we were seeking to express the company's commitment to product innovation and design aesthetic, which sets it apart from such monolithic competitors as Duracell and Energizer. To achieve this goal, we leveraged our expertise in the beauty and fragrance categories by creating a logo and label with a decidedly distinctive, sophisticated, premium feel. The red triangular brand mark (the line across the A) is meant to become a design element which eventually can be used alone to convey the brand in a more shorthand, dynamic fashion. The packaging is futuristic and daring, with gradations of lines that are meant to convey a vibrating energy. We designed an outer packaging of clear tubes ... very different from the "expected" cardboard tube in this category! To further emphasize the brand's emotional territory of surprise, discovery, and innovation, the merchandise display systems are reminiscent of cosmetics or lipstick displays.

CULTURAL INSPIRATION

Some products gain enormous credibility if they are associated with a specific culture. Russian vodka is still the authentic one, and we would have a hard time buying Irish pasta–even if it were the best in the world! Hershey's Ronzoni pasta brand communicates with its graphics and packaging the authenticity of an Italian product. The old-world typography and décor pictured is clearly European, and the name Ronzoni places the brand in the geographic area of the known specialists. Häagen-Dazs has a Scandinavian name even though it is made in New Jersey. Godiva, owned by Campbell's Soup, still trades on its original European aspirational image with stores and packaging styles that reflect the elitist nature of European gourmet foods. Most mustard presentations reflect a French heritage. *Some might say that marketing is manipulative in this way, making false promises, but I doubt that anybody is really duped by these marketing efforts.* Instead we are enticed by and want to participate in these aspirational stories which are more fun than a generic, utilitarian product experience because they help us to dream. Most people are quite willing to let Ronzoni pasta be "Italian" in their minds!

We are no longer eating food or drinking drinks; we practice "body management" and are buying convenience, escape, energy . . .

Lifestyle Expectations

Each generation has different expectations and desires. New trends are constantly evolving, such as concern for the environment, the treatment of animals, a better planet, a healthier lifestyle, and our ever-growing need to explore new experiences in products. These trends encourage marketers and retailers to create alternative products that deliver to new expectations. The Body Shop came up with "dressed-down" packaging as a response to the fanciful packaging used in the beauty industry at that time and to strengthen its point about environmental responsibility. Instead of expensive, glamorous-looking packaging, The Body Shop introduced us to the concept of simple, "undesigned" containers that were an antimarketing statement for a new group of young consumers looking for products with a cause and without all the hype. Many brands have been successful in communicating honesty and a sense of specialness through "dressed-down" packaging. This is part of the cultlike enthusiasm for the small "mom & pop" hair-and-skin-care line Kiehl's, which became so successful solely through word of mouth that it was just bought by L'Oréal, which plans to distribute the brand globally.

The current trends associated with health, vitamins, and natural and healing ingredients for mind and body have triggered a whole gamut of innovative products in the fruit- and tea-based drink categories, such as the Arizona line and the "New Age" Snapple line named after natural elements that I mentioned previously. Fresh Samantha, a juice company from Maine, manufactures real (not from concentrate) fruit drinks and smoothies blended with protein, vitamins, and plant extracts such as echinacea, the modern urban cure-all plant that builds up our energy and immune systems. *Clearly we are no longer eating food or drinking drinks; we practice "body management" and are buying convenience, escape, energy* . . . anything that conveys pleasurable, life-enhancing experiences. Gatorade is about winning, not thirst. Coca-Cola is about refreshment, not a cola drink, and Snapple is about elevating experi-

PHOTO BY PAUL TILLINGHAST.

ences having to do with the natural elements, not juice. The shift in the paradigm which makes products evolve from a commodity/need state to an emotional and sensory experience is the result of consumer demand for new, surprising ideas to nourish not only the body but also very human, emotional desires.

Whether the aspirational aspect of a product is primarily anchored in borrowed cues, based on culture or on a lifestyle concept, being relevant to a consumer is what is important, and many concepts can help you reach that relevancy. I have used all of these approaches for inspiration in packaging design, and they have helped me to have a creative platform for new product development or rebranding programs as well. The final goal is to build a unique and proprietary "dress" for your brand, a design voice that makes a tangible difference vis-à-vis your competitors and communicates powerfully to your consumer target. Packaging that has great emotional and sensorial messages creates an instant connection based on contact, not impact, with the consumer in . . . half a second!

15

Emotional Advertising: Not Gratuitous, but Relevant Emotions

If you say it with a degree of sincerity and honesty and with a great love of the craft, it will come through.

–John McNeil, Art Director at Ogilvy & Mather (twenty-eight years old)

I still remember my first job with Botsford Ketchum, a great creative ad shop in San Francisco in the seventies, and how proud I was to work there with people who wowed me everyday with their breakthrough ideas and brilliant creative vision. It was a golden age in the business, when real artistry in advertising was highly valued. Concepts in those days were created on storyboards, and print ads were not swiped out of a photographer's book but were born first entirely from the creator's imagination as drawn visuals that were then photographed or filmed. Art directors and copywriters were heroes in the business. We were supposed to (and very often did) have a very direct and singular insider's connection to the heart and soul of the marketplace. We were valued for our creativity and controlled brand imageries; living and loving the business day and night! Our only goal was to share this passion for our brands with consumers.

As a twenty-three-year-old Frenchman "just off the boat," I was given the art direction responsibility for the French airline account, UTA, which specialized primarily in trips to Africa and Tahiti. Although I had never been to these places, I had gone (almost) around the world once already and I wanted to convey first and foremost a love of travel to exciting destinations such as these. But I wanted to do it in an unusual and compelling way. I remember waking up at night racking my brains over how to break through the clutter of the overused, stereotypical "beautiful photos" favored by the travel industry. I finally came up with the idea of using hand-drawn illustrations, which I felt would communicate more deeply the true soul of those places than would the usual, cliché scenic photographs. My dream was to create a visual vocabulary that would explode with sincerity and transcend commercialism, and . . . it worked! I am still proud of that campaign, which ran in most U.S. magazines. It was also the last campaign I did as an ad man. I began to feel a pull to use my design skills to support my entrepreneurial spirit, and I started my own company a year later. But I never lost my love and respect for the world of advertising, keeping a constant eye on the trends and evolutions in the business from the neighboring and very similar perspective of a design-oriented, brand-image consultant. And what I have observed recently are some very exciting and promising changes; changes that can take advertising in the direction of building powerful Emotional Branding strategies.

From Push Communication to Push/Pull

Until very recently, advertising has been a "push" form of communication; meaning the sending of commercial messages without the benefit of any major interaction with the receiver. Now, with the help of the Internet, it is on the verge of a complete reinvention, perhaps even a renaissance. With this new media, advertising is becoming the multidimensional "push and pull" communication tool everyone in the business was looking for all along. Advertising can now instantaneously convey a brand message and actually help build a real dialogue (that will, in turn, affect the brand message) with people!

Who else can bring a brand to life, if not the advertising and brand-identity professionals?

Advertisers have been limited by the vehicles at their disposal to reach an audience; for the most part, the media of radio, TV, print advertising, and billboards. These "push" media were primarily used to target passive consumer groups. Today, the Internet is just beginning to reveal the tip of the iceberg of the vast opportunity for engaging people in a dialogue. "Pull" messages, or messages that encourage a response from people, are helping connect brands with the public in a very dynamic way. As this "push/pull" communications trend strongly influences advertising in both old and new media, it will be, I believe, an all-around very good thing for advertising!

On the whole, excluding the stellar work of a few, advertising over the past fifteen years has become stale, and consumers, overloaded with a barrage of unexciting commercial messages, have become more and more impervious to these messages. When some of the old-world economy brands squeezed ad agency fees, organizing some of the most cutthroat competitions that were often being handled through third-party consultants, it only encouraged short-term vision and compromise. To make things worse, advertising decisions were often being made by people in corporations who, for safety's sake, preferred, above all, to remain unchallenged. When we first worked with Sergio Zyman, the former chief marketing officer of Coca-Cola, around six years ago, he demanded that his ad agencies be only one thing: kick-ass creative! This was not a terribly popular practice at the time when some of the major ad groups wanted to become "marketing consultants," envying the successful evolution of some of the "big seven" accounting firms into lucrative consulting practices. But he was, of course, absolutely right in making creativity the top priority with the agencies, because *who else can bring a brand to life, if not the advertising and brand-identity professionals?* He was an exceptional client for the times. Most clients remained in the "risk-free" zone, and the result of this was that, overall, the creative life went out of the business and audiences disengaged from watching what had become cookie-cutter ads. Formula communication became the norm; a way to avoid presenting innovative ideas by showing snippets of other people's work . . . remember the overuse of rip-o-matics, the practice of recycling and splicing pieces of images from commercials to create a "new" concept? Fortunately some firms such as Wieden & Kennedy, Fallon McElligott, and TBWA/Chiat/Day continued raising the creative bar by avoiding compromise and became sources of inspiration for others. But for the most part, ad agencies became as bureaucratic as the people they were supposed to inspire with creativity, and executives from the top down started to speak, think, act, and look like their clients, offering none of the provocative ideas a brand needs to really stand out.

Now, however, as advertisers are forced to strive to meet the demands of a new economy and a newly empowered consumer, the paradigm is changing. I believe that the result of this will be a new infusion of creativity in the business. Innovation and breakthrough thinking will once again become the primary assets of an ad agency. As we have seen, in the new economy, entrepreneurship and innovation are accepted as the norm, and so now we have an influx of new (and some old-new) companies who want . . . guess what? To take creative risk! Usher in a new breed of young communicators who are bringing a fresh outlook to the business and a new set of values! Ad agencies are once again taking control of a brand's communication strategy and are jumping on the creative bandwagon by empowering this new generation of fresh talent who are having a blast setting the tone for a renewed approach to brand messages. The stage is set to build a communications paradigm only available in and around a new medium: the Internet.

But first of all, let's take a look at Emotional Branding in traditional advertising and then move from there into the world of new media. Regardless of the medium, from the perspective of Emotional Branding *it is essential to start any advertising endeavor with the acknowledgment that there is a new ad-savvy and marketing-Tefloned consumer out there* who is ready to act as a tough interlocutor. In-your-face visibility and brand dominance was a very nineties idea, but consumers in the new millennium expect more sensitivity and honesty from the brands they like and will appreciate those that will respect their spiritual and physical environment. The McCann Erickson motto, "The truth well told," takes us back to the root of advertising and is clearly relevant in the current market environment. The old communications tricks will not work; a new approach and a large dose of responsibility need to be developed around brand communications. Cynicism is huge among the public, and certain generations (especially Gen Y, the first generation to be marketed to "from the crib") just hate advertising with all its excesses. Statistics tells us that we are, after all, barraged by close to three thousand messages per day. This is why we see the advent of magazines such as *Adbusters* and *Brill's Content* that play the role of watchdogs for what is being communicated by the media. These magazines cater to people's desire to know the truth. Poised to respond to these consumer needs, but not yet highly visible, is a new generation of younger ad professionals, which has definite ideas about their personal impact on the world with the work they do. I believe that they will bring about a new sincerity reflected by the way they communicate. They know that only culturally relevant messages about great products will break the clutter of our overwhelming visual environment.

OGILVY & MATHER AND IBM: WHEN OLD BECOMES NEW AGAIN

Ogilvy & Mather, which was groundbreaking at its inception but had become kind of stodgy in the late eighties and early nineties when its brilliant founder retired once and for all to his castle in Toufou, is a great example of a successful turnaround for an agency, as well as one of its major clients, IBM. This was a unique situation where both parties' desire to succeed culminated in one of the strongest agency/client relationships in the business. Ogilvy & Mather is now offering some examples of campaigns that break all the rules in the best possible way. Their campaign for IBM has completely changed the way people perceive the brand. IBM has transformed its image of an old tech, out-of-touch company, to one of the most exciting companies in the world today.

IBM had been struggling awhile against its Big-Blue image of a cold, high-tech machine that lacked a dose of humanity. This brand perception was, of course, made even worse by Apple, which had managed to communicate a very warm, consumer-friendly image and, most importantly, a culture of innovation that came through powerfully in its ad campaigns. Its now famous "1984" commercial created by Chiat/Day for the launch of the Macintosh line, showed a woman breaking through the drab, freakishly uniform world of computerized big business (meant to symbolize IBM, of course) with a rebel toss of a hammer, shattering a huge computer screen. This was the expression of a company that seemed to own the future! The situation is obviously very different today as IBM, under the leadership of Lou Gerstner, has changed from "Big-Blue Brother" into a brand that spells humanity.

I met with Steve Hayden, president of worldwide brand services at Olgivy & Mather, in the course of writing this book, and I was certainly pleased to talk with one of the people who created the "1984" Macintosh commercial. Meeting with one of the few true creative visionaries in this business is always fascinating, and it reminded me again that advertising is about committed people. "You can contribute to the ugliness of the world or you can contribute to its charm," Steve told me, and he has made this motto a reality in his work. In his previous position at Chiat/Day on the Apple account, he mentioned to me how advanced he found the Apple internal culture. Steve Jobs and his people were committed to the democratization of technology, believing that sharing information would empower people and change society. With a corporate philosophy as strong as this, the emotional component of the brand can only come powerfully forward and become a great platform for branding strategies.

The idea for the "1984" commercial came from a headline in a newspaper lying around at Chiat/Day, "Why 1984 Won't Be Like 1984." Steve Hayden and Brent Thomas came up with the idea that the future was not about fear but hope, because the power would be in the hands of the people. The Cold War was real then, and the commercial that was aired during the Super Bowl resonated beyond its original intent.

Steve eventually came to Ogilvy & Mather to work on the IBM account, because the challenge was great, "kind of like putting the Soviet Union back together," he says. On the trail of Bill Hamilton and Rick Boyko, Steve started to challenge the agency itself with the support of Shelly Lazarus, CEO of Ogilvy & Mather. They knew that history was in the making if they could turn IBM around, a challenge for both of these "formerly great" companies, which were now afflicted by bureaucracy. The return to greatness could only happen if people on both sides committed to changing the future. They did, and it worked.

The story is actually quite astounding, starting with the "Solutions for a small planet" concept for e-business, the idea that launched IBM and Ogilvy & Mather into the next century. The first letterbox e-business campaign commercials were shot by Joe Pytka as a trial concept, at the same time as the Lotus spots (a new IBM acquisition) with Denis Leary were being created. Both campaigns got thumbs-down from IBM management and would have been relegated to the lost archives of brilliant commercials were it not for Lou Gersner's son, back home from college, raving about the Lotus campaign as being really cool. This saved the Leary spots and eventually created an opening to present the Blue Letterbox spots some weeks later.

Steve Hayden calls this attitude "the California style," which is, "getting the work done and running before the bureaucracy could kill it." Steve Hayden calls this attitude "the California style," which is, according to his words, "getting the work done and running before the bureaucracy could kill it." This is the signature of confidence. The success of these campaigns transcended the realm of "good advertising"; they succeeded in positioning IBM as a new economy force and a major player in the future of technology. Wall Street noticed, and business began moving, and Ogilvy was able to attract the best talent to work on an account that had in previous years been a nightmare for creative teams!

Ogilvy & Mather has rightly steered IBM toward communication strategies that show how great the people of IBM and their clients are, establishing a visual vocabulary that resonates with a new level of sensitivity. The IBM print campaign shows real IBM customers and employees photographed in a way that feels "real." The photographs are unpretentious and do not reflect any commercial setup. They are simple, amusing little vignettes about people striving and succeeding to do business on the Internet. They ring true to the audience and are successful in creating the kind of intimacy that is so important to Emotional Branding. This has gone over well with consumers; according to John Bukovinsky, IBM's director of corporate communications, public awareness for IBM as the place to go for e-business solutions has climbed to a current 42 percent from the 20-percent level at the beginning of the campaign in 1997.[1] IBM's TV commercials hit the same humanity note. One com-

mercial shows a typical family on Christmas Eve with the parents struggling to put together a bike for their eight-year-old daughter without the lost instructions. The daughter, watching in hiding from upstairs, races to her computer, pulls up the company's Web site, prints out the assembly instructions and sends them floating down to her parents when they are not looking. "Oh, here they are," says the relieved father to his wife. Then the tag line: "Self-service Web sites from IBM serve customers better."

Today Apple owns the emotional territory of innovation demonstrated by its innovative and friendly product design, but IBM has cornered an emotional territory around the strength of its people and a deep understanding of the concerns peo-

ple have in a new economy. The message created by Ogilvy & Mather is powerful, taking the company from the message of "technology matters" to "man matters" and giving a new face to a brand that was previously unable to express its emotional character.

Ogilvy & Mather has successfully pulled off another amazing feat, which is to promote an antibrand brand; the new magazine *Brill's Content.* How do you advertise and establish credibility when you are promoting yourself as the voice of reason in a media-crazed world, encouraging people to regard anything presented to them in the media with skepticism through the motto "Skepticism Is a Virtue" . . . when you are a medium? Ogilvy & Mather answered this challenge in the most imaginative way. Their solution was to take the message to the street, where advertising often hits us on the most visceral level. They located hip neighborhoods where opinion makers are most likely to live and welcome the message, such as SoHo, NoHo, and Tribeca in New York City. But they did not merely put up traditional billboards, which would have appeared too commercial for a magazine that wanted to be grassroots and controversial. *Brill's Content* started posting their name letter by letter on construction walls covering the existing posters along the way. Every day a new letter of the *Brill's Content* logotype was glued on the board leading the passerby to wonder what this campaign was all about. In this quasi-interactive day-to-day campaign the magazine that "covers all media" did exactly that, proving that they were on top of the media, literally!

Good brands are generally perceived as the "good guys," and this emotional perception is sometimes overlooked for concepts that focus too much on product benefits and market dominance. In advertising and brand communication there is always a dose of intuition, a dose of magic, and passion for the business; a passion that is once again becoming part of the language with most professionals. Ogilvy is now going even farther in changing its culture, with a new identity program around the signature of David Ogilvy printed on a red background–very striking and elegant. Peter Wood, creative guru at the agency, has started a "young gurus group" by hiring fresh, just-out-of-school creative stars and training them in the communication business in order to bring more novel ideas to the agency. Great work is always the privilege of great clients, and I believe that IBM has allowed its agency to be a terrific partner. Some people at IBM must have gone the distance to get the work through the system and give the benefit of the doubt to creative brilliance. Steve Hayden told me that he made a personal effort to hire people that the clients would think of as "different" (meaning "creative types") and never hire people the client themselves would hire. These kind of initiatives in advertising are exactly what makes brands be noticed in the marketplace. Ogilvy & Mather today is a phenomenal idea incubator and a brand that has successfully understood the mission given to it by its founder; a mission based solely on "a great love for the brands."

McCANN ERICKSON AND MASTERCARD: A PRICELESS PARTNERSHIP

Another fabulous campaign that very effectively transcends the doldrums of nineties advertising is the MasterCard "Priceless" campaign by McCann Erickson. Everyone has noticed how effective this campaign has been, but what exactly is it that makes it so special? Caught between the very "Members Only" American Express brand positioning and Visa's global services approach, MasterCard didn't have much of a vantage point and came to represent a mere commodity. Then MasterCard began to champion a new message that connected the card to a personal experience and began to put value not only on the service that the card could provide, but also on the type of experiences one could have with a purchase. "Greens fees: $116. Lunch at the turn: $13.50. Balls, tees: $36. Hole in one, and a witness, priceless! There are some things money can't buy . . ." This astute portrayal of a consumer's aspirations creates an instant link between the offering and the consumer. It also shows that the dream connected to objects or products is sometimes as powerful, if not more so, than actual material objects themselves. What is really priceless in this advertising is the company's understanding of the consumer! I believe that communications programs that trade on the powerful elements of fear and insecurity such as American Express's "Don't leave home without it" campaign of yesteryear ultimately miss the mark because they do not provide the kind of aspirational perspective of the MasterCard campaign. Remember, Moses did not take the Jews out of Egypt so much to escape from the unbearable living conditions as to attain the promise of a new life in their own land. In this age of emphasis on emotional needs, moving people with brand initiatives that allow customers to enter into the "promised brand" is a lot more powerful!

VIRGIN AND THE SPY WHO SHAGGED ME: BRITISH HUMOR AT ITS BEST

Another example of consistent, emotionally powerful advertising from a total branding perspective is the Virgin Atlantic Airlines campaign based on the popular movie *The Spy Who Shagged Me*. Virgin, perceived as a people-friendly airline, cleverly capitalized on Mike Myer's quirky British character. Given this airline's unique British character and positioning as an entertainment airline, the connection was particularly relevant and strong. The line, "There is only one virgin on this billboard, baby," was very funny and arresting, and the "Five times a day, yeah baby!" tag line to describe the five daily New York/London flights was consistent with the movie's retro-fun production and the airline's desire to make traveling an enjoyable experience. The emotional component of these ads was powerful, I believe, because through humor they emphasized Virgin's brand image as an "entertainment airline." They give a new perspective to transatlantic air travel which is, let's face it, mostly viewed as a chore for frequent travelers: to give up a good night's sleep and deal with the plight of being jet-lagged . . . and not jet-shagged (sorry, I couldn't resist)!

The Spy Who Shagged Me was one of those movies that unleashed a forceful promotional activity months before the release of the picture, as everyone knew it would be a great success. Many of the brands that tried to associate themselves with this runaway success did not consider enough the relevance of their brand to the picture. Those brands were simply looking for visibility, presence, and awareness. Virgin, to the contrary, moved smartly to reinforce its brand image with the ad campaign, which pushed far beyond the immediate hype of the movie to convey to people that Virgin is first and foremost a service-driven, entertainment airline, while others are still in the "transportation business."

What these IBM, *Brill's Content*, MasterCard, and Virgin campaigns have in common is a powerful emotional message that is consistent with their overall brand strategy. This consistency is what makes them memorable beyond a great ad, forging the connection to the brand in a more permanent way. But since emotions are so potent, it is important to handle them carefully when trying to create an emotionalized brand strategy. Emotions can make or break a brand, and once a mistake is made and you have an explosion, it can be very difficult to put the pieces back together. The stronger the emotional territory, the longer the brand impact will live—for better or for worse.

Real Issues = Volatile Emotions: Navigating Choppy Waters

In this vein I will describe several examples of powerful Emotional Branding strategies that have had different success stories. Marlboro's communications program has helped the company sustain its power, even in light of the government war on the tobacco industry and people's negative perception of smoking. Benetton's strong communications program, however, is an example of an ad campaign evoking negative emotions in a manner that got completely out of control, seriously damaging the company's image in the U.S. market. On the other hand, as we will see, Kenneth Cole takes on the exact same issues in his ad campaign with success.

Whatever you may feel about the tobacco industry, it is hard not to admit that the ever-enduring Marlboro campaign has been incredibly successful. This is because it is all about emotions conveyed through powerful visuals that make smokers and nonsmokers alike believe in the positive brand imagery. Marlboro's message of open spaces, freedom, and adventure is clear, consistent, and gives everyone the ability to make their own interpretation.

Benetton, the Italian retailer, has been taking the stance of provocation since the late eighties and in the end it seems to have alienated a lot of people from the brand. Provocation is not a brand strategy, just a short-term tactic to claim the spotlight. Brands are not in the business of changing society. Brands need to clearly express humanistic solutions messages in line with their consumer's concerns and demonstrate that they are sensitive and supportive of their values. Benetton's visual of a black horse mounting a white horse to sensitize the world to racial issues is not necessarily the most effective expression of the message of hope that was originally at the core of the Benetton brand identity. Benetton did it again in 1999 with their incendiary advertising portraying death-row inmates, another exploitation of a very touchy social topic for commercial purposes. These moralistic ads, steeped in pedagogy, seem more of a ploy to get their brand attention than a sincere attempt to either make a statement or build brand awareness. There are no facts given about the death penalty or the people on death row we are being confronted with visually through intense close-

UNITED COLORS
OF BENETTON.

www.benetton.com/deathrow

SENTENCED TO DEATH

JAMES EDWARD THOMAS
BORN: 1/20/1956, PROVIDENCE,
RHODE ISLAND
CRIME: FIRST DEGREE MURDER
SENTENCE: DEATH BY LETHAL INJECTION

ups and, as usual with the Benetton's advertising, no connection is made to the products or the people of Benetton. Unfortunately, the failure of these advertising campaigns has been reflected in a serious underperformance in the world's biggest market, the United States,[2] and Sears recently dropped the brand from its four hundred stores in the United States after having been picketed by victim's families. And now Oliviero Toscani, the creative director for the Benetton ads, has made a quick exit from Benetton, ushering in perhaps a new era of more intelligent and emotionally sensitive advertising.

This is not to say that a brand cannot successfully make strong statements about the world. Kenneth Cole has made his mark in adopting causes as marketing tools, but with a different sensibility. The Kenneth Cole ad campaigns were conceived as a way of giving the brand that sense of being current, so important to fashion brands, by talking to consumers about current events. Their 1999 campaign takes on the same issue of the death penalty, among others, in a way that, I believe, works. Let's take a look at the difference. The Kenneth Cole ads, which certainly do have an edge, handle this and other social issues in a more sensitive way by challenging people's beliefs through questions and facts and through the use of gentle, wry humor. By posing provocative questions, such as "If every year people are found innocent prior to their execution, how many aren't found in time?" and giving facts through the sardonic use of the "cc," the ads remain conversational in tone and attempt to create a dialogue. Rather than use a heavy, moralistic tone, the ads bring a fresh perspective that encourages an open-ended debate. Kenneth Cole is positioning himself as being on the same side as his customers; the side of the truth. Another important difference here is that the Kenneth Cole ads show product and people wearing the product. It's as if the note, which is printed on a translucent overlay cutout, was written by the young person shown in the ad (and not necessarily by Kenneth Cole himself) wearing the Kenneth Cole fashions, and in this way the ads create a rich and complete world of a brand image with a fully fleshed out personality. On his Web site, Kenneth Cole expresses his values by stating that "To be aware is more important than what you wear" and lists the different causes his company supports. Best of all, though, he has a terrific chat section on this site which allows visitors to speak freely on topics such as "Violence in the media: Killer entertainment or killer influence?," "The Confederate Flag: Pride or prejudice?" or "Selling Supermodel Eggs? Model society or ugly idea?" This is great because it gives a feeling of an open conduit of expression between the brand and consumer. Kenneth Cole is finding out, unfiltered, what his customers really think and feel!

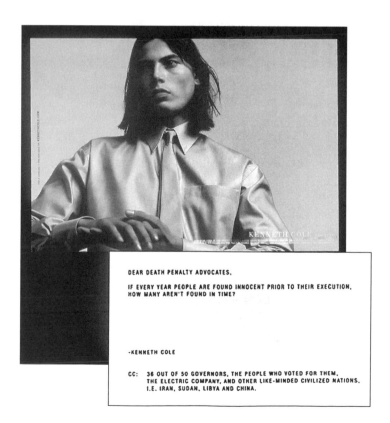

DEAR DEATH PENALTY ADVOCATES,

IF EVERY YEAR PEOPLE ARE FOUND INNOCENT PRIOR TO THEIR EXECUTION,
HOW MANY AREN'T FOUND IN TIME?

-KENNETH COLE

CC: 36 OUT OF 50 GOVERNORS, THE PEOPLE WHO VOTED FOR THEM,
       THE ELECTRIC COMPANY, AND OTHER LIKE-MINDED CIVILIZED NATIONS.
       I.E. IRAN, SUDAN, LIBYA AND CHINA.

One of the best things about the Kenneth Cole ads is their clever use of tongue-in-cheek humor. Humor should not be forgotten as a way to sell products! It is a bonding element between human beings: if you can make someone laugh, he will feel friendlier toward you and perhaps even remember you! As a recent *USA Today* article put it, "Perhaps the biggest trend in the ad industry in recent years has been the absolute triumph of humor as a way to keep consumers interested in watching TV commercials."[5] Humor is effective when product-centric and relevant to a sale message. The silly little sock puppet from Pets.com is absolutely hilarious, for example. He seems to represent for a pet owner an agglomeration of the lovable characteristics of their pet. This campaign, created by TBWA/Chiat/Day brings the Pets.com brand to life through the zany, adorable, wise-cracking "mutt/sock" character who tries so hard to be your friend and is summed up quite well by the tag line "Because pets can't drive." This simple but clever idea is what I would call buzzworthy. It has succeeded in charming both consumers and the media, so much so that the now-famous puppet has even been featured on *Good Morning America*. The puppet sang "Three Times a Lady" to Diane Sawyer who responded by flirtatiously asking if it had a girlfriend. Now that's creating emotions around a brand!

Old and New Media

Now let's venture into the world of the Internet, where the results of the challenge of the successful promotion of a brand are immediate. As I said before, this is a medium that requires bold thinking. The Internet, which today exists as an extension of media strategies, will soon become the primary media. The war between the old media and the new media is already settled before the fight. They are complementary; allies in bringing better, more truthful information and awareness to people.

Emotions can be exposed and shared in cyberspace in a personal way with people, and that is the most important element offered by this new medium. It is an opportunity to build an intelligent path to winning a person's trust and belief. Good-bye "push" communication, hello heart-to-heart, "pull" dialogue with people in cyberland. This is where a brand can become a true friend and ally to people.

Emotions can be exposed and shared in cyberspace in a personal way with people.

Babycenters.com, for example, sends weekly updates to its customers, tips targeted to new parents in search of much-needed answers for raising a young child. A traditional retailer would be hard-pressed to provide this service with such speed and regularity. The enormous potential of this kind of highly targeted, voluntary e-mail marketing remains largely untapped as yet. The Strategis Group's 1999 "Advertising on the Internet" study showed that only 20 percent of the consumers questioned were on an automated commercial e-mail list.[4]

How does a brand impact people in cyberspace? In this new media the big question today is how can we quantify and qualify the type of data that would give us clear answers about the impact of advertising messages on Web surfers. Many tools now exist that monitor traffic and experience, but finding the impact of a banner ad on specific sales or overall brand awareness, for instance, still needs to be further developed and refined. Extremely valuable tools that identify purchase per visit and return visit, as well as the amount of time spent on the site are just now becoming available. But it is also important to remember that click-through and even purchase or intent to buy are not the only important things to measure. There is also the immensely important realm of the intangible but very real positive (or, as the case may be, negative) feelings that are created by the online interaction with a brand. After all, even an immediate purchase does not guarantee return visit and brand loyalty!

The development of these tools will give advertisers and marketers the information they have been longing for all these years; what do consumers really want? Measurements are beginning to be provided within days of an ad campaign launch, giving advertisers the opportunity to adjust a message almost instantly according to the consumer response! The biggest drawback of the metrics research is, of course, how much the visitors want to be probed. I believe that what people really want from the Internet is both personalized marketing *and* privacy. Beware of getting unwanted data on unwilling customers.

Despite ongoing questions and confusion, it is very clear that a new, effective media is born, one that will eventually serve to reinforce the other media models. We know that, for starters, the Internet's power to build brand awareness is enormous. A study conducted by MSN showed that online advertising increased brand awareness by as much as 300 percent.[5] And intent to buy a brand after seeing an online ad has also been proven to be significantly higher; 72 percent versus 62 percent for users of a brand and 28 percent versus 19 percent for nonusers of a brand.[6] A study by Anderson Consulting in November 1999 showed that 25 percent of 1,500 Internet users surveyed went shopping on a Web site after viewing a banner ad, as opposed to 14 percent who clicked onto a site after viewing a TV or print ad and 4 percent after listening to a radio commercial.[7] In fact, according to Datamonitor, global online advertising revenues have been doubling since 1998 and are expected to reach around $36.5 billion by 2003![8]

Despite the current confusion and debate about the future of advertising on the Internet, every day there are more companies beginning to smartly use the emotional power of the Web to promote their brands. In order to look forward to what can be done in the future, we can start with examining recent branding efforts that lead us in the direction of Emotional Branding in advertising on the Internet.

BANNER ADVERTISING

Banner ads are still far from fulfilling their true potential. After an initial period of large advertising budget investments, there is much talk today about disappointment in the effectiveness of banner ads. While it is true that recall of online advertising is declining due to the clutter of sometimes dozens of ads that pop up on one site on the Internet,[9] the truth is that many of the banner ads today are not done right; they are boring, intrusive, and unimaginative. Banners really do work when done right, and are such a cool way to access a brand message! Cathy Olvany Riordan, director of e-marketing at Kraft Foods, found a terrific way of using banner ads. Kraft created a Web ad campaign with banner ads that offered to show consumers how to make a meal with whatever ingredients they were able to find in their fridge at the moment. This Web effort was so phenomenally successful that an off-line campaign was developed to trade on the success. This is the kind of one-to-one initiative that makes the Web such a great branding tool and personal experience.

Banner ads are still far from fulfilling their true potential.

IBM's award-winning Internet effort with banner ads is also truly unique.[10] They are one of the first to use rich media technology for interactive banner ads. IBM's banner campaign, also created by Ogilvy & Mather, is well integrated with the TV commercials and print campaign I mentioned earlier and is incredibly innovative. It gives a glimpse of the potential of banner ads to surprise and delight. One of my favorites is the banner ad for the online store REI Corp., the Seattle-based outdoor equipment co-op. The banner starts out all black, and as you move your mouse across the ad, a flashlight illuminates a campsite at night, with a campfire next to a tent and forest creatures such as a deer whose eyes shine in the beam of the flashlight. A sign then appears with the words: "e-outdoors. When REI wanted to find its way on the Web, it called some experts to shed some light on the subject. *www.REI.com* is an IBM e-business. Discover why." Other great IBM banner ads with Java script allow viewers to participate in the ads, such as the banner for eSeeds, an online vendor of plant seeds. This banner allows viewers to sow online seeds that grow and flower when watered by holding the mouse button down, which turns the cursor into a watering can!

Procter & Gamble have also been successfully using the Web in creative ways, with banner ad units with games or music (with no click-through required) to convey the fun of eating Pringles chips.[11] PepsiCo, in its quest to reach teenagers, has made a marketing deal with Yahoo! to use its site to promote brands such as Pepsi and Mountain Dew. The promotion will allow teens to collect points that can be redeemed on Yahoo! Web sites for merchandise like video games.[12] This is a great idea as long as it also finds an imaginative way to expand beyond an initial resemblance to the traditional brick-and-mortar coupon promotion approach to include the larger context of establishing a real emotional bond with teens. While it's true that teens do have a finger permanently glued to their mice, they also seem to have boundaries in terms of how much commerce they are willing to accept in this universe. From this perspective, what is important to keep in mind is the entirety of the "user experience," meaning how the cyberclicker experiences a banner from sequential moment to moment. Instead of looking for a one-shot impression, a banner ad can be divided into an entertaining storyboard-type adventure that revolves around the brand equity. This adventure need not last a long time or involve time-consuming detours, it can quite simply be a moment of pleasure that leads to a potential purchase encounter with the brand.

Sometimes though, the innovation needed to make an impression on consumers is relatively simple. For example, a banner ad for Loctite Super Bonder glue, created by DM9 DDB, doesn't contain links, but instead, when a viewer touches the Super Bonder ad with the computer mouse, a little tube of glue sticks to the arrow and goes wherever it goes. The company, Comet Systems, has created a program that enables Web surfers to change their cursor arrow into a fanciful image and this is being used to reinforce awareness of banner ads. For example, in a study conducted by Millward Brown, Web surfers who explored a page with a cursor shaped like a cartoon tooth were far more likely to notice a banner ad from Crest toothpaste than those who had only a plain cursor.[13] A new alternative to banner ads is to amuse consumers first with thirty-second animated cartoons and games, which are then followed by an ad. The Dutch company BitMagic is developing this angle in online advertising and has signed up Heineken and Mitsubishi Motors.[14] This may work well since one surefire way of getting an emotional response from consumers is through the use of humor. Catharine Devlin of Devlin Applied Design, a Web design firm, says that from its research with consumers on effective banners it discovered that, "There are two factors that stand out: humor and color. People need a laugh these days. You are inundated, and anything that is pleasant to look at . . . gets an emotional response."[15]

BROADBAND BRANDING: THE BIG BANG

General Motors was enormously successful in using broadband advertising to promote Concept: Cure, a copartnership between GM and the Council of Fashion Designers of America to fight breast cancer. In 1999 five fashion designers, Nick Graham of Joe Boxer, Max Azria, Joseph Abboud, Dana Buchman, and Vivienne Tam, were asked to design a GM car to be auctioned off as a fund-raising effort. Terry Beltran-Miller, GM's interactive director, organized this rich-media online promotion to allow consumers, mostly women between the ages eighteen and fifty-four, to obtain a vast amount of information about GM cars and the Concept: Cure campaign which would not have been possible to access via traditional media such as television. The interactive ad ran for twenty-four minutes, had a full-bodied digital "narrator" named Bonnie, and was a mix of video, audio, and interactive elements. Ms. Beltran-Miller says that the recall average of the ad was greater than narrowband by about 34 percent, and Joshua Greer of Digital Domain, the creators of the ad, says that during the campaign consumers returned again and again to the site. This program helped GM to raise $2.6 million for breast cancer research.[16] Jupiter Research has claimed that by 2002, 60 percent of online ads will be rich-media enabled,[17] and as broadband expands, we will undoubtedly be seeing many more ads in the vein of the GM example.

Over the next few years the opportunities will surely migrate into the territory of broadband, strategic sponsorships, and . . . who knows what else?!

Over the next few years the opportunities will surely migrate more into the territory of broadband, strategic sponsorships, and . . . who knows what else?! Internet radio, for instance, is at its early beginnings and shows all signs of becoming another great opportunity to reach people and provide them with information. Advertising on old media is mostly about creating awareness and desire for a brand. *If old-media advertising is the invitation to the party, then the Web must be the party*, the place where people meet, share information and tips, and generally have fun! We have to think of the Web as the village square. It's all about connections.

Today some of the brightest creative minds in the communications business have not yet fully understood how interesting and effective this new medium can be . . . well, TV commercials *are* fun, too! Agencies are still shy of a full commitment in bringing groundbreaking innovation in this area, but the advertising of the future is going to be cross-branding, cross-channel, and based on cross-marketing!

Tommy Hilfiger has taken an interesting initiative in testing the power of convergence in communication, on- and off-line, by creating a miniseries-type program for the brand on his Web site called "House Party." This program, which started on Valentine's Day 2000, was conceived and produced by Kirshenbaum & Bond as a six-episode streaming video production about hip young kids and their adventures of love and friendship, all decked out in Tommy wear. The Tommy Hilfiger Web site is also conducting a talent search called "Unreleased Cuts" for DJs and bands with the grand-prize winner receiving a $10,000 demo deal from Qwest Records. Of course his site has been flooded with responses![18] Through these kinds of promotions, Tommy Hilfiger is not only promoting his brand but also building a direct pipeline to street trends that are of an inestimable value in the fashion business where every season is a new challenge. For the visitors to the site, access to this cultural musical melting pot allows them to be privy to the potential emergence of new music and feel ahead of the times . . . no need to rely on MTV to get the latest. This kind of cultural connection is exactly what can make a brand hip and relevant to people; adding a dimension that traditional ads cannot convey. What this means for traditional ads remains to be seen. But as interactive TV emerges in the near future, we are sure to see more of a mix of branded content, such as the Tommy Hilfiger Web site, and highly entertaining infomercials that last for thirty minutes or more. And banner ads for television will surely be an important part of the future advertising landscape as well.

WHERE IS EVERYBODY?

Nobody is glued to a TV set or listening to radio at home anymore. People now take the electronic equipment that used to be nailed to a wall or plugged into some outlet with them everywhere. Our cell phones and portable computers are always with us, and we are definitely on the go. Soccer moms are in a car most of the time, shuttling kids to different places, and businesspeople are always flying to destinations far away from home. As people spend less and less time in their living rooms in front of a TV set, computers are attracting more eyeballs than ever. Of course we all want to know how this will change the world of advertising, because there is no question that it will!

The chase for reaching an audience is becoming more complex, and getting people to sit down to hear a message is, well . . . challenging! We have to adapt and, fortunately, the rapid progress of technology, particularly in the wireless area, offers potential opportunities in reaching people wherever they are at a myriad of different points of contacts.

The "push/pull" perspective is a helpful one, given this wide array of communications choices. This is a new, friendly way of speaking to people, based on the give-and-take principle. Yes, you're asking for something–the consumer's precious attention–but if your ad can also be helpful and receptive to the response, then you are giving something in return! Go to any open-air market in France and watch how the vendors are selling foie gras, wine, cheese, fish, or poultry. It's one of the most delightful, amusing experiences you can have! Vendors talk, flatter, and jest with you in the most clever ways to lure you over to their stalls. They are entirely themselves; full of personality, with the rural clothing, mannerisms, and accents that give total authority and credibility to the origin of the goods and their quality. The products in these markets are presented in a way that tantalizes your taste buds, and even the brown paper bag in which they are handed to you adds to the charm of the buying experience. Has anything really changed? As the creators of myths and stories, we are only as good as the impact we can have on our audience, and only our passion, sincerity, and love of the brand will be able to create a dialogue and, eventually, a brand based on trust.

> **The chase for reaching an audience is becoming more complex, and getting people to sit down to hear a message is challenging.**

section IV:
vision

inspiration for change:
how to get there from here

E-motions

How will Emotional Branding best be put to use in the future and what will be the new challenges to creating branding in our fast-changing world? This section investigates the huge potential for creating a more emotionalized brand expression on the Web, describes the process behind d/g*'s most successful branding tools, and explores the cultural fabric of our new millennium via five social trends that will have far-reaching effect and in turn spur other important trends.

Predicting the future is tricky business—it is much more accurate and interesting to approach it as a question. After all, the future is what we make it! The true answer to this question lies in a continual, passionate dialogue with the market—in other words, in simply asking the question over and over again!

We must all fine-tune our creative capacity for insight to connect intuitively with the ideas or events of the world around us. At d/g* we have always felt that visionary ideas could be disciplined and channeled to shape the future of corporations and affect their products. The purpose of our proprietary tools is to help us understand people's lifestyles and emotions. They are what allow us to discover and identify unfiltered, raw, and powerful ideas. Our process means to challenge the past to create the future.

Very few decisions are made based on logic alone; at some point, instinct supersedes facts and data—what *feels* right becomes the dominant driver of our choices. This emotional component of our reasoning helps us unconsciously comprehend the future and the trends that will affect it.

Here's my motto in a nutshell: Think out of the box, be a keen observer, and follow your gut—become a natural magnet for new ideas. And as the magnet attracts new ideas, begin to work by association and foresee trends.

16

Branding Emotions on the Web: The (Real) Future of Cyberspace

Much ink has been used to analyze the impact of the Internet on our planet, and specifically on the retail world. The race for e-tailing is clearly on in a quest to capture the ever more numerous mousers worldwide. The Forrester Research Group has predicted that the Web, which accounted for less than 1 percent of retail sales in 1998, will account for 6 percent in 2003, and Jupiter Communications, a New York market research firm, has estimated that interactive home shopping will expand to $82.35 billion by the year 2003.[1] In addition, the amount of time people spend online over the past two years is at a growth rate of 31.5 percent.

The successful strategy thus far has been to get into the game as fast as possible in order to benefit from the migration of millions of people into cybercommerce in order to begin to build pockets of loyalty

The ultimate winners in this extremely competitive game will be the ones who have not only a great business plan but also a brand-driven consumer plan.

within this population. The market potential and a well–laid out business plan seem to be convincing enough to impress a venture capitalist. Going public has become a goal in and of itself; to sell before getting started seems to make more sense than building a clear corporate vision and unique consumer proposition. The good news: lots of money! The bad news: in this gold rush for quick returns, one fundamental element to commercial success has often been forgotten . . . branding!

From High Tech to High Touch

The ultimate winners in this extremely competitive game will be the ones who have not only a great business plan but also a brand-driven consumer plan, based on a clear process and an emotional relationship with the consumer. This emotional relationship is the basic tenet of any powerful branding strategy and the core foundation for success. To build a leading business in e-commerce is to understand that the customer (not you!) will decide if you will win or lose.

This new world of e-tailing is divided as usual between the innovators, the early adapters, and the followers. The resounding approval from consumers and the success of some operations has encouraged many to jump on the bandwagon fearing that missing it would be a fatal mistake. Others are taking the more traditional stance of "wait and see" to determine who will survive and then coming in full force. Old-economy brands with their great recognition will surely have their day as long as they are willing to reinvent themselves according to the culture of this new medium. What is certain is that this new model will revolutionize forever our traditional channels of distribution. Already in 1994 research was observing a saturation phenomenon in conventional retailing. Sales per square foot had gone down from $195 in 1978 to $160 in 1994 as an average while the square footage built had gone up from eleven to nineteen square feet per capita during the same period of time; clearly a situation where fewer people were buying goods in stores that kept on expanding for a consumer who was not interested. A new model clearly needed to appear and replace this tired, unprofitable formula. The "cybermall of the future" may very well be anchored by brands such as Amazon.com that could replace the role of department stores as the main traffic draw. Amazon.com is becoming landlord and retailer at the same time, using its consumer base of 17 million, its recognition by 118 million U.S. adults, and new-age technology to attract other e-tailers.

There are inherent opportunities on the Web for expressing the emotional component of a brand.

For Web pioneers like Amazon.com, who have planted their brand flag first in the Web wilderness, *branding obviously will be the tool for keeping their advantage,* and for the unstoppable waves of other new ventures it will be the only real way to challenge leading and established players or create dominance in new areas. Branding nevertheless works *differently* on the Web. While it still is the key to conveying the quality, value, and image to the buyer that results in brand uniqueness and differentiation, *there are inherent opportunities on the Web for expressing the emotional component of a brand.* Because of the openness and flexibility of the format, including of course the extraordinary multimedia capabilities, the potential for the visitor to enjoy a new experience is almost limitless in this medium. Along these lines, one of the most effective concepts on the Web is the idea of unhindered communication between the brand and the consumer and among consumers themselves. Brand communities can be fostered around the fact that buyers can communicate with each other, learn from each other, and help each other.

Barter.com and eBay, sites for people to swap goods and services online, are based on this highly popular and successful Web concept. So, as always is the case, understanding people and how to provide them with what they want is the single most important element of success in this new retail format.

People are looking for answers, not only goods. The book *Blown to Bits: How the New Economics of Information Transforms Strategy* suggests that, "The response is to offer a navigation service that solves consumer problems instead of merely pushing products."[2] 1-800-Flowers offers a good example of this on the Web. It maintains a customer information file with clients' anniversaries and birthdays, and alerts them when an important date is approaching. We can learn a lot by looking at how companies like Marriott set up their business models around this concept. Marriott, long an industry leader in using technology to pamper customers, has purchased from Siebel Systems Inc. software that tracks guests' preferences in great detail. Thanks to this new technology, Marriott has expanded its brand from the business of hospitality to the business of event planning and lifestyle consulting. Marriott does a surprising amount of legwork for its guests: setting up golf tee-times, restaurant and sight-seeing reservations, travel itineraries, even flowers for a loved one . . . all the while keeping careful track of all this information for the next time around.

Understanding the varied and relevant emotional needs of Web users will require this kind of constant contact and connection. *We must use our imagination in this new, still largely uncharted territory to achieve a real connection in unique ways that will enhance the browsers' shopping experience–make them buy, barter, and come back for more.*

The Web "gold rush" introduces a new set of questions about the future of these new business channels, such as who will be using the Web and how. An understanding of the generational dynamics and major lifestyle trends is essential to deciphering exactly who are and will be the Web users and what brings consumers into the cyber arena. At present, the percentage of both e-shoppers and Internet users is divided evenly between the Generation X and Baby Boomer users, with Generation Y falling slightly behind in both categories. But the crucial differences we've been talking about between what attracts these different generations to a brand are certain to be at play. In addition, there are also sure to be gender and ethnic differences. With close to 60 million people connected to cyberspace in the United States now, men are still a strong majority. But as we saw in chapter 3, women, currently at 48 percent of the online population, are closing in fast and are sure to catch up and bring enormous numbers to the Web. Researchers predict that women will outnumber men online by 2002. In Japan, already 60 percent of the people buying online are women.

Most importantly, this medium is global in nature. It is connecting people everywhere in new and innovative ways. The small-planet concept is key here as the power of information transcends cultural boundaries and even political systems. Louis Vuitton Moët Hennessy (LVMH), the French conglomerate that invests in prestige brands such as Dior and Vuitton and original distribution systems such as Sephora and DutyFree Shops, has understood the power of eBay and Sotheby's.com in trading luxury goods and is pouncing full force on this new opportunity. It is currently investing in at least twelve international luxury dot-com companies, with the thinking that consumers are frustrated by not being able to find the latest styles if they are foreign brands or because the local stores aren't carrying them. *And that's the point. Shopping on the Web empowers consumers to achieve the ultimate shopper's quest (which is often nearly impossible in traditional retail settings): find what they want, at the price they want, when they want it . . . and that is NOW!*

Shopping from the comfort of your own home! Gone are the cashier's lines, the physical tiredness, and pain of lost time spent searching for products or services in different locations. What store could ever have the unlimited inventory of the Web? E-commerce can be a very exciting shopping experience. It brings power to the buyers with the ease of shopping 24/7 with great time savings since all locations are just a mouse-click away. Customers are expecting greater choice and value from this more efficient business model and, as we all know, the choices *are* numerous!

As time becomes a rare and coveted thing, the Web brings a new set of answers. Life has become so compressed that people are willing to pay extra for ordinary services to come to them in their homes, such as car washers, cooks, grocers, or anything Kozmo.com can bring to the doorstep. People today feel that personal time or time with family and friends is more important than money! It is no surprise that we are seeing a recent revival of doctor's house calls, and success with online grocery shopping with brands such as Webvan, Netgrocer, or even Streamline.com, the company that installs refrigerators that keep track of and reorder perishable goods without the owner even being there!

So how can branding be a tool of difference and distinction to attract people, sell products, and deliver a personalized service in this new virtual world? And how important is brand image and personality? Furthermore, how can the shopping experience be enhanced by using communication concepts that will make e-browsing a positive and memorable experience? These are some of the crucial Web-related questions I want to answer in this chapter.

Building a branded store into the medium of cyberspace without the disadvantages inherent in a physical location opens opportunities to explore concepts that would not be feasible in a brick-and-mortar store. You are connecting with a different mind-set and attitude, replete with a fresh set of expectations. Cyberspace is about imagination, fun, and discovery and it is redefining our culture to form a new virtual community. Web surfers still view themselves as "cyber-rebels" of sorts; there is a pronounced sense of self-decision, exploration, and discovery. The attitude of nonconformity and empowerment is fostered with pride through the use of this futuristic medium. As management guru Tom Peters likes to say, "We are the CEOs of our own life." To be a brand in cyberspace, it is essential to understand this culture and work within the realm of the mind-set of this very demanding and savvy consumer. You need to bring a big idea!

In light of the great business opportunities, the proliferation of businesses on the Web seems justified, but there are also difficulties to overcome. The main handicap and challenge is the lack of any human presence and the absence of many of the visual and sensory elements that add drama to any good retail venture. Cyberclickers are removed from the sensory experience of holding a product in their hands or speaking with someone about a service. There are also still in most cases short-term issues with the quality of the images limited by an evolving but not yet quite ready technology and bandwidth capacity. In addition, the myriad of new companies and offerings on the Web is huge and sometimes very confusing.

Most Web sites today are still very linear and are, above all, engineered for smart links and access. The emotional zones are still not defined or expressed. The Web today, in reality, is operating within only a narrowly defined territory, when the expression of its branding potential is limitless through use of truly multisensorial elements such as sound, color, and animation, and even, eventually, scent (see chapter 9), which will lead to enhanced entertainment and connectivity. In a nutshell, I believe that Emotional Branding can be at its best on the Web–a driving force to help attract, connect with, and retain consumers.

These are the questions to start with in order to create that essential emotional bond with consumers on the Web:

1. How to ATTRACT people to sites? Through an understanding of their expectations and desires, *by Creating Brand Awareness*
2. How to best SELL my brands and keep a visiting customer in cyberspace? *by Creating a Unique Brand Identity*
3. How to DELIVER the kind of personal touch and service in this new medium that will assure user loyalty? *by Customer Dialogue and Service,* and *by Packaging (the "Back End" of Service)*

ATTRACT The Web Consumer through Creating Brand Awareness

In order to coax visitors across the threshold of a cyberstore, the relevance and clarity of the brand proposition, the promise of an exciting experience, and the overall emotional benefit to the consumer needs to be well articulated and communicated.

It is difficult to attract people and compete for a share of voice in this very busy marketplace! In the mad search for recognition, some e-commerce companies have, with varying degrees of success, created relationships with celebrities hoping that their popularity will carry the brand visibility through their endorsement, such as Priceline.com's William Shatner ads. The desperation is so high among some of these dot-com companies that don't yet have a recognizable brand that they are willing to "pay up" a stiff price in communications to achieve the awareness that will provide the necessary traffic and eventual dominance. The year 2000 Super Bowl was a pricey venue that was squatted by seventeen dot-coms, all scrambling to reach this most concentrated of audiences, hoping to get the "motherload" of hits Monster.com had the day after the run of its commercial in the 1999 Super Bowl. But the investment made by some of them (up to $3 million for a thirty-second spot) did not necessarily leave a very lasting impact. What was needed here was a clear definition of a brand image for these companies and the kind of emotional connectivity that draws people to commercials.

The Super Bowl opportunity, a hundred million people watching your commercial, is difficult to pass up when your survival depends on the notoriety of your company . . . but why not use an Emotional Branding strategy to achieve the objective? An investment in the Super Bowl needs to be well prepared and planned out in order to succeed. Traditional marketers such as Anheuser-Busch are major winners in the Super Bowl ad saga because they prepare pre- and postpromotions in stores that culminate in the Super Bowl ad investment. The action is on and off the screen at the same time. E-commerce companies, interestingly, have even more opportunities than traditional marketers to sell themselves through connectivity, dialogue, and instant discovery. Pre- and postshows could be orchestrated on these sites, for instance, with commentaries by players, fans, and sports or entertainment stars. Tickets could be pledged to the event through contests or links with other sites. These sites could even have a live Web cam to observe some of the most interesting postgame parties attended by the rich and famous.

What's missing from most of the dot-com communications and marketing programs is exactly what can make them so great: innovation, daring, and a clear understanding of the consumer. With regard to the consumer, there is a lot to learn in this area, but one thing is for sure; different generations interface differently with the Internet. Is anyone really addressing the intimidation factor that some generations feel when entering this world? Women, who handle 75 percent of family finances and 80 percent of all purchase decisions, are increasingly going online to save valuable time. But they are not yet really being spoken to from this angle by most Web communications efforts. We know that teenagers have a perception of the medium that is totally different from other market segments. As we saw in chapter 1, teens have said in studies that the number-one thing they want from the Internet is social interaction! It seems logical to presume that Generation Y will redefine the Web to conform to its own cultural aspirations.

When it comes to men on the Internet, it is clear that the shopping adverse male consumer finally feels empowered to enjoy, explore, and shop in a territory in which he is immensely comfortable and savvy. There are none of the lines, hassles, confusion, intimidation, or sometimes downright embarrassment of stores . . . and it's fast. Let's face it, men on the whole have never loved the extensive shopping "excursions" that many

When it comes to the Internet, the shopping adverse male feels empowered to enjoy, explore, and shop in a territory in which he is immensely comfortable.

women consider special, pleasurable occasions. Victoria's Secret is a great example of this phenomenon. While 90 percent of their store customers are women, 60 percent of their Internet customers are men![5] Of course, Victoria's Secret may be the quintessential opportunity for male e-tailing (what man wouldn't want to spend time checking out a plethora of sexy lingerie viewed on supermodels on streaming video in total privacy and at his leisure?). The Web is a great way for traditional retailers to expand their business and win over men. Both Jean Mombert from Brooks Brothers and Barbara Geiben from Bloomingdale's agreed in a 1999 *Women's Wear Daily* article that the Web is attracting new clients to their brands; an answer for those who may be afraid of cannibalization. Bill Bass, VP of e-commerce at the highly successful Lands' End site, has an answer to the cannibalism question, "At the end of the day–this has become my mantra at Lands' End–you ask, 'What do customers want?' and give it to them. Then, discussions about cannibalization and channel conflict go away–because customers don't care." In his view, worrying about cannibalization is to mire oneself in an "internal, company-centric point of view."[4] And that about says it all!

As the name of the game in the new cybereconomy is speed and urgency; a quick-business pace of fast financing and then a rush to a successful IPO, the need for awareness is fundamental to attracting traffic. But awareness moves at a different pace. It demands investments of time and money. Existing old- or new-economy brands with strong recognition but declining financial results could be great bargains for cyberstrategists and a base from which to operate, because with very little capital they could acquire the necessary brand recognition. LVMH, one company to watch in the twenty-first century, has never been shy in articulating its strategy, which is first to own all the great luxury brands in the world and then own the distribution channels in which those brands are sold. Although it can't buy all the department stores in the world, LVMH has understood that it could be a great player in the new distribution paradigm and it has invested heavily in e-commerce. But, of course, you need brands to fill the pipeline, and creating new ones demands a greater investment than reinvigorating dormant ones, such as Pucci, that have a great history and awareness. Pucci is more than a business, it is a real brand with enormous emotional content based on a great fashion heritage with very little distribution. And, of course, that is the true value that LVMH is buying. In the future, the smart dot-coms will realize that it is money well spent to buy, in whatever form, what they are missing in the beginning—the emotional content that links people to brands.

By simply focusing on conveying the brand identity to Web consumers in a creative and emotionalized way, however, a company can achieve remarkable results. Life Savers leveraged the Internet in a clever and emotionally compelling way to create a buzz around its brand by announcing that it would discontinue its pineapple flavor unless people voted on its Web site to keep it. Four hundred thousand Life Savers lovers went online to save their favorite flavor from extinction. e*Trade did a great job pulling people into its Web site with its Tina Turner promotion, which gave out free CD-ROMs included in a complimentary seat cushion to the 1999 Super Bowl attendees and offered two free premium tickets to Tina's concert for opening an e*Trade account. Allherb, a cyber herbal shop, had great success with its campaign that tied in with the last *Seinfeld* episode when it advertised that it would give away sixty-five thousand free bottles of St. John's Wort for those who were depressed to see the show going off the air! Its business increased significantly.

One terrific way to create awareness of a cyberbrand is to leverage what makes the site unique by building links between the site and other forms of marketing communication. There is an opportunity to connect people through a multimedia extravaganza that dazzles the senses, and through content that is relevant to users. Why do so few of the commercials for dot-coms on television recreate or show the actual look of the site? Think about how much success a sitcom promotion would have if it never presented the actors or the look of the show. This is such an important element of the brand identity, and if the site (hopefully) has an intriguing or cool look, then people will want to log on. The ad for Altoids site promoting its new cinnamon flavor, Toohot.com, works from this angle. It shows the campy, retro cool look of the site that is unmistakably Altoid's without saying explicitly that it is an Altoid's site, with a sexy she-devil, "Sinful Cindy" the brand icon, asking the question "Curious?" The ads for Bluefly.com also recreate the look and feel of its site with its overwash of blue tones.

An important advantage of a Web store is the flexibility in its visual appearance and the opportunity to manage the site's visuals in an innovative, constantly evolving fashion. The Empire State Building changes color depending

Altoid's Toohot.com ad.

on occasion: red, white, and blue for the Fourth of July, a pumpkin-orange for Thanksgiving, and red and green for Christmas. Why not do the same on Web sites? People might log on regularly, just to see the latest lighting or graphics "show" and . . . tell their friends about it!

As I mentioned in chapter 11, the highly successful Victoria's Secret 1999 Super Bowl commercial, which tempted a tidal wave of viewers to go online to watch its supermodel fashion show, was the first in making this kind of brilliant connection between the Web site and the commercial. Ed Razek, president and chief marketing officer for Limited brands and creative services of The Limited, Inc., has said that the main goal of this ad was not to create awareness for the Victoria's Secret brand, but to encourage people to log on to their site.[5] Why then, if it was so successful, have very few cyberbrands tried this same dramatic formula? Nike has recognized the potential of this "cross-referencing" strategy with its "Whatever.Nike.Com" commercials, where viewers must log onto the Nike Web site to see the dramatic ending to a compelling story begun in its "teaser commercials." On the Web site surfers are even allowed to pick and choose from various potential endings. This is a smart and truly interactive communications strategy!

SELL through Creating a Unique Brand Identity

A strong visual and sensory identity is the most important element of brand differentiation. It can truly manifest the personality of the brand and set it apart from the crowd, and it is the only place to start. Designing a Web site for visual clarity and uniqueness will enhance the experience, increase buying intent, and create memorability. Besides content, you can often recognize a magazine simply by its cover and typographic style. *Vogue* has a photographic attitude that's different from *Elle*, and Martha Stewart's personal touch is all over her magazine. The point of view in the J. Crew and Brooks Brothers catalogs are totally different and relevant to each brand and the target group each wants to capture. The way Target uses its logo identity to communicate fashion and innovation is consistent with its strategy and demarcates it completely from competing stores such as Kmart.

But in the Web landscape the uniqueness of the brand design identities are, on the whole, not yet well defined. The brand differentiation between one site and another is very weak. Such companies as eToys, CDNOW, and Amazon.com use similar typography for most of their sites, a sans serif typeface. Almost all of the leading sites use blue as a dominant color for headlines and it seems almost as if a great concern exists in not looking too different. You could even replace the logo of some with the logos of others and it would not stand out immediately as a mistake. *Let's not forget that market shares are always supported by a strong share of brand voice!*

In many of the most popular e-commerce sites, the point of entry with the brands is through a table of contents, no introduction, no brand message . . . no foreplay! Could you imagine a magazine with no cover? Or a store with no windows? Or a catalog with just product lists and bad visuals? The convenience aspect and the "hipness" associated with shopping on the **A cyberbrand's visual identity is probably one of the most underestimated tasks in any e-commerce business place.** Web could end up being less attractive after a while if it remains in this "unemotionalized" realm. People buy dreams, not product sheets.

A cyberbrand's visual identity is probably one of the most underestimated tasks in any e-commerce business place. Corporations like Gap, Brooks Brothers, Macy's, Victoria's Secret, IBM, Crate & Barrel, or others have clearly translated their existing proprietary looks onto the Web, as we naturally recognize when we go to their sites. These brands are carrying their notoriety and dependability over into the digital world. But many other Web sites have adapted too much to the constraints of efficient commerce strategies, losing in the translation some of the aesthetic style that is so relevant to a brand identity. Sephora.com's site, for example, does not feel like the store and is now very similar to other fragrance and beauty sites. I am also surprised that a brand like Target does not (yet) really capitalize on the dynamic, fashion-forward visual identity built around the innovative use of its bull's-eye logo on its Web site. Based on my perception of the brand, I had envisioned a fun, well-designed, Flash-enabled "logofest" when I logged on to its site, only to be greeted by a dull, cataloglike, product-listing site with the famous logo relegated to a tiny place in the upper right-hand corner. Amazon.com has, at this point, cornered its business territory but not yet a proprietary visual territory. This will be the next step for it and others who will be struggling if they lack a clear brand strategy and vision to support a much-needed continued awareness and recognition.

Most sites have been designed by people who come from an engineering or programming background. Web designers have had to balance the opportunity of unleashing the true multimedia experience of exploring those new worlds with the need to create easy navigation in a graphic-intensive environment. *For some companies direct and simple may be better, especially when it comes to the issue of slow downloadability. But simple does not mean generic.* Designers will tell you that there are tons of solutions for creating great graphic imagery without compromising the technical parameters of a site. The fashion retail site Bluefly.com has created a very recognizable look simply through the consistent use of the color blue, although its home page remains somewhat uninspiring and cataloglike.

Compromising the unique identity of your brand is a big mistake. What is important is to express your brand in a voice that is unequivocally yours through a visual identity like no other; an identity that demarcates your brand territory powerfully.

Such sites as Swatch.com have a vibrant unmistakable look with colorful motion, Flash-technology home pages. The home page shows an animated

outline of a man walking, morphing into different color patterns as he moves. This works well in conveying the brand's "Time to Change your Colors" message and the overall identity of cool, fresh, dynamic (and colorful) design.

The retail site Girlshop.com has a fun, well-designed cartoon-style home page with vibrant colors (above). Their cartoon girl mascot/logo appears undressed on the home page, wearing only shoes and clutching a bag, ready to go shopping . . . and she subsequently appears on every following page in varied attire. The entire layout of the site, which, by the way, always shows miniature visual icons of the products as opposed to text, is consistent with the cartoon graphics of this first image, giving a quirky and hip feel to the site that sits well with their Gen Y girl target consumer.

A few other sites to look at for a unique branded experience are:

• The Virgin Atlantic site (*www.virgin.com*); it has that unmistakable "Virgin" look and feel in absolutely every aspect!

• The very popular Stolychinaya site (*www.stoli.com*); it reflects on every page the colorful, modernistic look of the brand. This site offers great games and lifestyle content with video clips of bartenders that teach consumers how to make a variety of drinks.

• The ultra-cool snowboarding site M-Three (*www.m-three.com*); it has a great use of music, consistent color, and fun Flash motion graphics.

nourish your senses
indulge.com

Through their advertising we see that this brand clearly understands the importance of appealing to the Web surfer's ultimate sensory experience of its products.

- The Web design firm, Balthaser (*www.balthaser.com*); it will show you, as it promises, that there is no limit to your imagination on the Web!
- Reflect (*www.reflect.com*), the site for customized beauty products; it has a beautiful fresh look to its home page that is consistent throughout the site.
- The Web site for Everest gum (*www.everestgum.com*); it is particularly compelling from a sensory point of view. To convey the concept of the frozen freshness of Mount Everest, the site gives cohesive and dynamic display of imagery (mountains, snow) and Flash text (words like "icy, cold, frigid, pure, invigorating") and sounds (high-energy music, intense winter winds blowing).
- Joe Boxer (*www.joeboxer.com*); it has built a terrific, entertaining, perfectly branded site which has been very successful (at launch the site was selling approximately two thousand dollars worth of underwear a day . . . without any advertising at all!)

THE SENSORY EXPRESSION OF THE BRAND ON THE WEB

Beyond the visual elements, any and all sensory expressions of the brand will reinforce the brand's overall identity. As we have seen, branding, as in any brick-and-mortar store, has an emotional and sensorial component that creates brand preference. To do away with this side of the equation is taking the risk of being put out of business by the next, cheaper, competitor with aggressive promotional programs. And on the Web the emotional and sensory elements can be very well integrated into the brand message.

Sound, which addresses hearing, the most "Web-accessible" of the five senses after sight, is one of the best ways to strengthen your image and integrate sensory elements onto the Web. There is no store that I know that does not have its own music style and many sell the music that you listen to as you shop. Music is identity. Music is mood enhancing and sensorial. One of the challenges of brick-and-mortar stores is to keep customers in the store longer. Music, as we see in chapter 5, is a powerful mood affecter, and it does just that. It has been proven to positively affect the amount of time customers shop, and it conjures positive associations with the brand and products and, overall, creates the kind of memorable experience that spells "return visit." The Volkswagen Turbonium Web site (*www.turbonium.com*) is visually very simple even though imaginative, but it is the "sound design" that is sophisticated and makes the experience so exciting. The site is set with a constant pulsating beat in the background, and as your cursor touches on the different elements of the site, a "technomelody" of musical notes and sounds jump out at you to draw you into exploring the various site pages. This energizing mix of sound and music matches the dynamic graphics and redefines the browsing experience of a Web site all together. The VW Turbonium site sound design, including the "whoosh!" sound the Beetle makes as it flashes across the screen, besides being very compelling in and of itself, also of course strengthens the VW Beetle brand identity as a fun, cool, and fast car. The experience is distinctive and memorable!

Another, different but equally imaginative, use of sound was explored at one point on the Gap Web site where they used different sounds to represent one of the five senses that is not (yet) accessible via the Web: scent. In order to create a buzz around their new fragrance line, Gap showed the different products with attached sounds and musical notes that were meant to convey the essence and overall note composition of the fragrance!

Sound itself, including music, can make the experience of shopping more interesting and truly enjoyable. Precisely because the taste, touch, and smell senses are not accessible on the Web, it is an element of experience and identity that is clearly fit for the Web format.

E-commerce brand identities must be multidimensional, multisensorial, and engage consumers in an emotionally compelling brand story in order to stand out from the crowd and attract visitors. Web sites have many communication opportunities at their disposal, particularly for telling a dramatic story that will add dimension and emotion to the brand. Tommy Hilfiger has done an excellent job of this on his site, Tommy.com, which has the proprietary look of his brand, in terms of the red, white, and blue flag-shaped border in every Flash-motion-filled window. On the home page, Tommy Hilfiger himself (photo + voice) invites you to be a part of the "cool Tommy world" with tons of entertaining lifestyle features such as Tommy Radio, Clubtommy, Tommy News and Events, Music tour information, and video clips of the ongoing serial "minisitcom" called *Houseparty* that I talked about in the last chapter.

E-commerce brand identities must be multidimensional, multisensorial, and engage consumers in an emotionally compelling brand story.

Web sites certainly have many communication opportunities at their disposal to do what traditional businesses are not able to do. Creating a relevant brand identity that communicates a proprietary emotional message is the first step in building uniqueness of vision and recognition. It is the first strategy for attracting and increasing traffic!

WON'T YOU STAY A LITTLE LONGER?

Once you have attracted a customer, the objective of course is to keep this potential customer from leaving and transform the visitor into a buyer, or a "brand fan." Everyone in the Web business knows that retaining that customer at your site is a very essential aspect of branding strategy. But how do you do this? Give them a memorable experience based on great navigation systems, clarity of offering, and service and you will make them stay . . . and come back for more.

DESIGN FOR NAVIGATION AND SPEED = SALE

As we have just seen, most leading sites are still about function, not emotion. Most sites do not yet have a clear, brandcentric hierarchy of information and content to help orient a consumer and provide him with a branded experience. Everything is thrown at the visitor at once, from inventory to information, and there is often no real, definite indication of what the brand stands for outside of being a Web-based commercial venture. Identity graphics and color, sound experiments, and interactive programs are not being used enough to make site navigation a pleasant, easy, and emotional experience.

What is different about Gap is the smooth translation and recreation of its retail experience, based on clarity of offering, onto its e-commerce site. As in the Gap's other consumer communications, a key-item-driven, seasonal promotion, reflective of the fashion attitude of the moment, is presented. This organized, conceptual approach, combined with very clear pricing information, is enticing. Time-limited promotional offers and sales are easy to find. This retail marketing approach is tested and proven in stores and it will also work on the Web. The recent move of Jeanne Jackson–previously CEO of Banana Republic and head of the Gap online business, among others–to Wal-Mart to head its flailing Web business means that Wal-Mart has finally caught on to this fact: retail branding genius is necessary for a successful e-commerce!

The Amazon.com home page is not about the brand but about products. It is about efficiency and directness. Amazon.com's expansion strategy into music, video, auctions, kitchenware, electronics, toys and games, free e-cards, and more is one way of becoming the only Web site you will ever need, the first Internet department store, but it is not the branded experience one might expect. It is clear that a "follow the leader" (i.e., Amazon.com) attitude exists among many sites that have weak, undifferentiated visual personalities. Web architects and designers have their work cut out for them! Thirty years ago the only look you could find in any American mall was "white and cheap." This remained true until The Limited brought a new attitude to building branded stores that stood out in ways that made them an instant success.

As an example of the kind of smart (and often simple!) differentiation that's needed, let's study a common but powerful shopping symbol: the shopping cart. This symbol has a reassuring psychological connection to physical, hardcore shopping. But there is a great opportunity here to define a different shopping cart expression on the Web, a more imaginative digital version. This could be done with symbols, typography, colors, language, or even animation. What if the shopping cart became a 3 D animated character of sorts, replete with a personality? The shopping cart could become a shopper's "friend," which would help customers make choices, answer questions, make fun suggestions, and so on, introducing some sense of the missing social element of "shopping buddies" into the cybershopping experience. Or it could be a graphic representation that shows items as they are added and becomes a game that would reward customers with surprise gifts or discounts when their cart reaches a certain, undetermined, point of fullness. As it stands now, most shopping carts are pretty much the same; boring, with the possible exception of the "tic-tac-toe" symbol found on the Blair Witch store site, which is animated to open and close with the firebrand witch's seal when a product is added. In all of the big Web retailers we find only small, one-dimensional icons of carts or bags that list the products inventory-style when you click on them. The shopping cart at Target at least has a more definitive style that reflects somewhat the Target identity; it is a photograph of an actual oversized, red Target shopping cart. Not very imaginative, but at least a bit more inviting.

As the competition heats up and more businesses are established on the Web, brand design initiatives will need to be integrated to create fidelity and memorability with a consumer who has no patience and is always looking for "what's next." Technology now opens new avenues and the highly innovative possibilities for building loyalty with the customer through constant dialogue and a more thorough knowledge of the visitors. This technology needs to be dressed up from a design perspective to feel more friendly, approachable, and compelling. Design that incorporates an understanding of the aesthetic, sensory, and social elements that engage people emotionally can be the bridge between pure technology and humanity. Brand design offers the tools for creating a shopping experience that is memorable and positive; a challenge already important for the most successful brick-and-mortar companies and even more critical for the new Web start-ups.

As the competition heats up, brand design initiatives will need to be integrated to create fidelity and memorability with consumers.

THE EXPERIENCE OPPORTUNITY

Web commerce is very similar to brick-and-mortar retail/branding; there is a shop, even if virtual, there is a product offering, a cart or a shopping bag. As in a store, people want the following: speed, service, and experience. Speed through clarity of offering and quick payment in order to get in and out with a purchase in the minimal amount of time. Professional-quality service to help you with your purchase and make you feel special. And, last but not least, the experience of indulging in the brand offering.

Each store in the street or in a mall competes with other nearby stores, not unlike any e-commerce site under scrutiny from new browsers. Brand-identity recognition and experience are critical to helping a potential customer choose a store, to staying in it for a while, and to perceiving that store as a destination. First, it is the look of the windows and the entrance, and then the feel ing when inside, the style of the other people shopping, the music, the coolness of the architecture, the clarity of offering, and courteous, professional help and service. These are the elements that will first express how relevant a store is to you and will determine whether you cross or don't cross the threshold.

When first clicking onto Amazon.com, you feel very welcomed. Their home page always displays a customized greeting with your name (wishing you a "Happy New Year," for example). Listed below this are product suggestions based on previous purchases. Amazon.com also encourages a sense of community where you can share your shopping experience with people around the world. Ratings of books and movies are a place for people to connect with others who share the same interests. Amazon.com asks visitors to participate in improving the site—another sign of its desire to please consumers. Barnes & Noble's Web site, on the other hand, does not give the same kind of first impression. I know a young Gen Y person who is put off by the dull, dark, and boring colors of the site, and I would bet that she is not the only one. This is unfortunate, given the easy navigation of the site and features such as a page called "Pick your Passions" that offers consumers the opportunity to get information about their interests in books, music, and other areas. A photograph of a consumer is shown with a brief history about why he is interested in a particular topic, with a link to his e-mail for communicating with other customers. Barnes & Noble's brick-and-mortar stores convey a warm, relaxed, and welcoming atmosphere, and this is somehow not yet fully translated onto its site. A missed opportunity!

Toysrus.com as well as eToys make you feel like a little kid again. The page graphics in both of these sites are colorful, cartoonlike, and fun, although the baby-blue background color of eToys is much more compelling and in sync with the content than the slate gray background of the Toys "R" Us site.

Both sites have found clever and interesting ways to keep children and parents alike coming back, although the eToys site succeeds better in this endeavor with a bit more added-value content. The Toys "R" Us site has a section called the "Toy Guy," which gives advice on toys, and parents have the option to subscribe to a magazine called *The University for Parents*, a very useful collection of information about techniques in child rearing and interests children develop at different ages.

On the other hand, eToys has a toy search option called the "Personal Gift Finder," which gives suggestions based on age, sex, and special interests. The site also has a toy review section called the "Oppenheim's Toy Portfolio," where the famous child-development experts review toys, and "Rosie O'Donnell's Book Club" with recommendations and information about children's books—an example of a smart way to use celebrities for site content. The navigation of eToys is very user-friendly, and great efforts are made to build a relationship with the visitor . . . you are even thanked at the end of your visit.

My favorite site is still eBay, and I feel it is likely to become and remain a powerful brand. People have a truly cultural and passionate connection with this brand, sometimes even in spite of the technological difficulties encountered by eBay, such as breakdowns or sabotage, which did not affect its business in the long-term. In terms of having a very charged brand perception, eBay is more similar to Apple than its founders themselves could have even imagined. What eBay provides in the most profound way is a sense of exploration and community. It is not only about commerce but about being able to open a huge Pandora's box full of products at prices that everyone can afford; the biggest, most exciting attic in the world! One of our interns at d/g* New York can't quite describe the emotion he felt when he found a rare gift on eBay, and that emotion has become a true attachment to the brand. In his case, he wanted to find some items relating to Jack Kerouac as a gift for a dear friend and, indeed, someone, somewhere, fulfilled his quest. The pleasure of discovery excited him, but the pleasure of seeing the joy in his friend's face brought him his best reward. Besides, eBay is supporting new forms of business; some professional antique dealers have found new ways to reach clients but amateurs have also realized that eBay could provide them with a format for making a living. The biggest ongoing garage sale in the world! This is the true spirit of the Web, I feel. Entrepreneurial, social . . . a completely open format where a sense of excitement and discovery is constant.

All of these successful sites have the advantage of leadership in their category but, ultimately, they are all also in competition for the same customer. Amazon.com has started to trade on eBay's turf, and Barnes & Noble.com will fight Amazon.com tooth and nail to keep its own presence on the Web. Not everyone can survive this game, and I would bet that the winner will not necessarily even be the best business models, but the best brands.

In a brick-and-mortar store you really have to create a shopping environment centered around storytelling that is conducive to engendering a positive mood in your consumers and that facilitates their shopping. Graphics, music, visual merchandising techniques, and salespeople help make the difference between one store and another. Most successful stores are destination stores with strong brand identities. Whether you go to Target, Home Depot, Ann Taylor, Saks Fifth Avenue, or FAO Schwarz, you have a very clear idea of what the store stands for. This is something that works, and retailers spend a lot of time and money to get customers into their stores. Once the customer has crossed the threshold, unique product presentations based on well-researched customer traffic patterns ultimately make the sale. In a way, once in, the consumers will work harder to find what they want. Obviously, on the Web patience is a very rare commodity and consumers have the power to click through any location in nanoseconds. In a store, some areas are dedicated for sitting and resting, some stores offer food, others create music or sound zones that change in each department. We all understand the limit of technology today and the importance of fast "downloadability," but some of us are ready and equipped for the big picture, and in a few years everybody will be able to receive great programs as the bandwidth will be empowered.

What exactly are the opportunities on the Web that outweigh challenges such as the patience factor? The first one is the possibility of empowering visitors with instant customization. Customization is the continuous dialogue between retailers and consumers that can define better for the cyber-retailer what his customers want and need. Technology today already allows for custom-fitted clothing. The Levi's store in San Francisco is one of the first retail environments to experiment with this idea and very soon our scanned body measurements will help us shop online with great precision. Customization empowers consumers to design for themselves the products they buy according to their individual tastes and needs. For the brand, the customization of products is the best research a company can get and a source of inspiration unlike any other! (For more about customization, please see chapter 18 on trends.)

If done right, Web sites are as personal and human as can be; they are places where people can feel they are heard and, most importantly, served well.

The second and perhaps most important opportunity is the potential for fostering a branded community atmosphere where people have the chance to engage in a dialogue with one another; recommending and discussing products, sharing their favorite brand. Harley Davidson has capitalized on this by organizing vastly successful rides for groups of its customers on its site. Lastly, you can bring enormous added value by offering information such as cookie recipes and travel tips, and so on, or lifestyle recommendations. On the Web, this kind of content replaces the missing human factor. Most sites are beginning to recognize this very important element of their brand and the fragility of their connection to the customer. The best Web brands are responding by managing the consumer relationship and experience to the highest level.

DELIVER Personalized Service/Touch and Consumer Dialogue

What do people want from the Web? As we've just seen, people using the Web are not simply looking for products at great prices in a quick-response environment, they are also looking for great experiences, and this allows retailers to build a strong bond with consumers. But everything could be destroyed if a promise fails to materialize. On the Web, brands can engage in instant communication with their customers in this self-service mode and build a fruitful, constant dialogue. *If done right, Web sites are as personal and human as can be; they are places where people can feel they are heard and, most importantly, served well.*

CONSUMER DIALOGUE AND SERVICE

In good Web stores, shoppers are getting the personal service that technology can provide easily, which would be impossible to sustain financially in a normal store. Amazon.com upgrades orders from its loyal customers to priority shipping or offers them coupons and recommends products that correspond to their previous buys every time they log on and via e-mail. The *New York Times'* Web site sends you notices about news pieces of particular interest to you. That's personal, and that's great service. The great e-commerce site Lands' End has taken customer service a step further with its "Lands' End Live" feature that allows customers to have a "text chat" with a customer service operator, or to type in their phone number and be called back within minutes. Lands' End's investment in this intensive customer service system is smart when you consider that 37 percent of online consumers use customer service, and a full 90 percent of online shoppers consider good customer service to be critical when choosing a Web merchant!

New software programs are allowing companies to track consumers better and better even while they are shopping, by making pitches to them and anticipating their needs. Everybody is scrambling to grab the customer and hold on tightly through these new software programs. Streamline.com in Massachusetts, a virtual grocery store, has used Oracle and Sap, two software innovators, to help it craft an improved customer-loyalty program that will reduce the risk of picking out-of-stock items.

Vignette, another brainy software company, has a package that allows Web sites to generate targeted, custom-made pages for visitors and Web-site operators, allowing Vignette to pitch products more relevant to the customer's desires. Siebel is also offering Web-site sales and service tools that provide great insight into customers, whether they buy on- or off-line. Companies like Pink.dot in Los Angeles are enormously successful in using this kind of technology to suggest complimentary products to their customers, who invariably fall in line with the statistics for suggestions that would not be so obvious otherwise. It's not about suggesting milk to go along with cereal, but knowing, for example, that 70 percent of your customers who order peanut butter also might need some diapers . . . or in a further (and even less logical) refinement, that 60 percent of men who order peanut butter after 8:00 P.M. are likely to be receptive to a suggestion of beer. You get the idea; these statistics don't always make sense . . . but they work; which is why it is so brilliant to be able to make use of them!

The Internet is an open market where consumers can, among other things, invest their money, prepare their next trip, order groceries, read their favorite newspaper, communicate with anyone in the world, find a job, buy clothes and beauty products . . . the list goes on! It is the ultimate conduit to what the world has to offer.

One new travel agency site, Eurovacation.com, is launching what promises to be a great Web site that will empower consumers to design all aspects of their trip themselves. The wonderful thing about this Web site is not only the all-encompassing links that allow consumers to book everything, from plane, train, hotel, restaurants, and so on, from one site but, above all, the wealth of information that will be available. Consumers will be able to contact people who have already visited the places they want to go and get recommendations and unfiltered feedback from them about their experience with the place and businesses they patron-

The Web is transforming industries, changing business models, and creating a new kind of rapport between consumers and service providers.

ized. Talk about consumer power! For the travel agent, the business model is not one of travel tours, but one that is about relationship. What he gets from his customers is invaluable information about who they are and what they want. This is an easy way to track travel trends so that he can buy bulk space at hotels and on airlines in advance at great savings to himself and his customers. In this business model everyone wins. According to Bernard Frelat, the chairman, president, and CEO of this new venture, sites such as Eurovacation.com will change the paradigm of the travel business from a static, inventory-driven business with little flexibility to a completely consumercentric industry where the site will become the "property" of the clients.[6]

As just mentioned, the trend of mass customization is a perfect example of this business model and it is one that, I believe, will expand rapidly. This trend runs a wide gamut from merchandise selections that are customized to the particular tastes of a Web population, as in the case of Alloy.com, the Gen Y site that bases its merchandise and content on teen commentary (a "dig" or "dis" section) posted on the site, to sites such as Reflect .com, where customers can concoct, design, name, and label their own completely individual lines of cosmetics, skin care, and perfume products. Product customization sites are proliferating, but they are just the beginning of an even bigger idea that is about totally personalized consumer experience. Technology, with its capability of collecting consumer information, is giving us the ability to have completely personalized Web sites where each individual can have an entirely unique, tailored experience and see content that no other user will see. The Web is utterly transforming industries and changing business models in a way that creates a new set of values and new kind of rapport between consumers and manufacturers or service providers.

How the different functions of sites are designed and communicated is very critical here. If Web sites are to become consumer destinations, they will have to provide a memorable, quality experience that will entice people to come back. *This is where branding comes into play; by identifying all of the points of contact between the consumer and the site and defining how to deliver the right emotional experience at each one of those points of contact.* The technology does not limit the emotional and sensorial branded experience a consumer could have; it valorizes and even extends it. Lands' End has virtual models customized to the consumer's measurements and body type that can be dressed with different outfits. There is so much that can be done at this level, given the flexible nature of the medium. Imagine how fun it would be

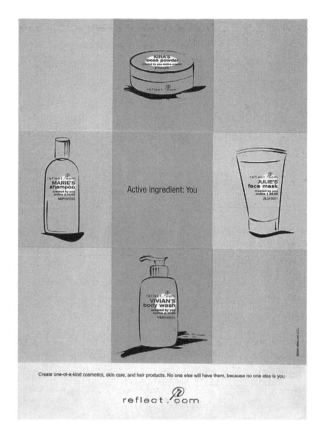

Active ingredient: You

Create one-of-a-kind cosmetics, skin care, and hair products. No one else will have them, because no one else is you.

reflect.com

to see someone packing your order and to be able to follow in a visual manner the transaction until it arrives at your door. At many sites you can choose from and listen to brand-specific music while you shop. Technology actually can deliver a lot more opportunities and ideas, but they have to be relevant to a market, unique to the personality of the brand, and consistent with the objectives of the company. A great idea would be to facilitate even more the possibility for people to shop together. Web sites such as the Lands' End site with its "Shop with a Friend" feature are having great success exploring this possibility. A mother in Seattle can spend time shopping online with her daughter living in New York, exchanging comments in a live chat area while selecting merchandise and sharing the great feeling of being together in a virtual world. This is a concept that will go far and, I am certain, be refined as technology advances. Shoppers' assistants sites like Respond.com, MySimon.com, and Rusure.com, the portals that work as a concierge by sifting through thousands of Web sites for price comparisons and consumer information to find a customer the item they are searching for are also a great idea that will certainly be refined and expanded. Whatever the groundbreaking idea, one thing should be focused on above all: creating a long-lasting and heartfelt connection between the brand and consumers by finding ways to always solve their problems.

And by giving (and getting) instant feedback, the online business can respond better and faster to people's expectations. But it has to be done right. It seems better to offer less on your Web site and do it right than to provide a source of irritation (and potential brand alienation) to consumers. Too many Web sites tend to lean in favor of the high-tech "bells and whistles" approach, leaving out altogether the factor of workability. It's a tease of the worst kind to try to click on some exciting, potentially mind-blowing animated feature of a site only to discover that it's not really up to snuff. *It's even worse to send e-mails into the cyber "black hole" of a brand's customer service that never responds or answers questions only partially, or to wait for a birthday or Christmas gift that never shows up on the all-important date.* One of my partners, very upset about not getting a pair of shoes she ordered for a Christmas gift, decided to endure the wait of connecting finally with someone who could take a complaint. All this effort only to be told by a company representative, "Oh well, things are so disorganized here, I am not surprised . . ."! Obviously my partner will never ever shop at this site again. Why alienate your consumers with half-baked ideas that don't really work? I think that Levi's "original spin" jeans are an example of this. It's a great concept to offer consumers jeans custom-made to their exact body measurements. But on their Web site, all you can do is get some details about the different styles of jeans to choose from and a list of stores you have to visit in person to order the jeans. Wouldn't it be great to just click and order this custom product?

WHEN THE DOORBELL RINGS . . . OR, THE LAST STRAW!

The final but often overlooked element of relationship on the Web is the actual, physical experience that the consumer has when the merchandise is delivered. The packaging in which the product is delivered reflects immediately the care a company takes in pleasing its customers. Often, as is the case with catalog purchases as well, the difference between the photograph that made your heart beat faster and the actual presentation of the goods is so strikingly different that it can seem as if the corporations have no interest in pleasing shoppers once the payment is made. This is a lost opportunity, because *the next sale starts the minute your customer receives the goods* . . . plain old common– or "commerce"–sense!

One of my clients, the president of a major cosmetics company, showed me a gift she had bought for a friend from the catalog of a top department store. The product was a collection of soaps for every month of the year, which came in a corrugated box and was wrapped in an ordinary (and unattractive) paper— a far cry from the magnificent photo in the catalog. Her disappointment was so strong that she will not buy anything from this catalog again. Relationships on the Web need to be carried out to bring satisfaction to the consumer from beginning to end.

A WORD ABOUT WORD OF MOUTH

Before a customer leaves your site, you need to manage this "parting of ways" in a manner that will make the customer a positive ambassador of your brand. One who will tell her friends about your brand, because nothing works better than word of mouth as a promotion when the message is positive. We all know this. But word of mouth can also break the reputation of a brand. *Word of mouth has credibility–is trusted–because it is based on someone's personal experience. It is Emotional Branding at its best.* In today's cyberworld, word of mouth has taken on a different dimension; it has become global and immediate. It can affect millions of people in milliseconds.

Word of mouth has credibility—is trusted—because it is based on someone's personal experience. It is Emotional Branding at its best.

In the course of the research for this book, people of all generations were asked for their impressions of brands they buy, and one of the consistent key reasons teenagers shopped in certain stores was because they had heard about them from friends. Traditional media, advertising, product and packaging design, store design, and corporate branding certainly do their job to create this kind of awareness for consumers. But I believe that nobody has sufficiently tried to understand how emotions are the main factor in the hard-to-control "word of mouth" link to the market. Word of mouth requires a real commitment from the messenger to pass on the brand message. This commitment can only come from strong emotions; the thrill of sharing good news with others; sometimes the desire to gather support for stopping what we feel are injustices and abuses. And, in the last case, that is when word of mouth could become every marketer's nightmare: boycott! And boycotts are a very real threat; there are about 150 full product boycotts put in action per year.

I had a conversation with the communications director of a major French oil company who came to New York to speak with various branding consultants about how to handle the impact of a very public corporate and political scandal that continued to rock the company every time further news of it hit the press, even though the people involved were long gone from the company's ranks. Any new development of the scandal persistently dominated the more important business news the company wanted to convey to the public, its clients, and shareholders. I was surprised to learn that, although many Web sites had been created around the scandal, the company had made only minimal efforts to use the Web to provide its own version of the issues. It was clear to me that this company was not managing the emotional content of its brand and had no control of the digital rumor mill that was seriously damaging its reputation. The company has now been acquired and what was once a major brand has disappeared. Tommy Hilfiger intelligently made use of the Internet for diffusing a potentially damaging rumor about Mr. Hilfiger being racist even before Hilfiger had an official Web site, by posting a notice denying the charges at the company's Web address while it was still under construction.

In cybershopping, customers are increasingly able to speak with one another about the brands they buy online, as evidenced by the growing number of successful consumer critique sites such as Deja.com that are built entirely around this concept. There is also a proliferation of Web sites set up by disgruntled consumers such as *Wal-Martsucks.com*, which have been largely deemed legally viable and are an outlet for consumers to voice their concerns and objections. The Net is proving to be the biggest word-of-mouth forum ever created, and wowing your customers until way after the sale is done is good business and a powerful strategy.

If you are still not convinced of the power of word of mouth, think about the story of Mahir Cagri, a Turkish man whose charming Web site (*www.kiss-mahir.com*) with broken English and quirky personal photos suddenly became so popular through word of mouth that the traffic generated eventually crashed the Turkish telecom system, and Mr. Cagri has become something of a global "cybercelebrity," mobbed by crowds when he visits a foreign country!

Since all good branding is about managing people's emotions and creating positive receptivity to our brands, taking a few extra steps in making customers' sensual interactions special—through memorable packaging of products, or the gracious voices and attentive ears of service representatives—will go far in building a lasting loyalty with consumers. When opening the box, wouldn't it be great to get thank-you gifts, promotions, and discounts? Or what about entry into a contest to win a trip to wherever you want to go? That would certainly make the customers more likely to talk favorably about a brand with others online . . . *the best word of mouse!*

The Digital Economy: How the West Will Be Won

Access to goods and services is quickly transferring to this new distribution system, the digital "Wild West." As a result, products will be designed to meet a new demand for customization. TV, telephone, hi-fi stereo, computer, and cable services are beginning to merge in more and more interesting ways. Sephora.com has entered in a partnership with Ajaxo Inc, a wireless delivery company that will make the site available to people via any Web telephone. The physical products connecting Web users to the information are changing to fit new lifestyles and express a unique image that reflects the future, such as with the miniature handheld electronic organizers that allow people to surf the Web from anywhere. We will see a continuation of this trend of more transportable items and less fixed units. Products will follow people and be at their disposal. All this, 24/7.

But at the same time, the entertainment aspect of the Web, as opposed to the pure convenience of e-commerce, will also continue to expand. And in both of these realms, I believe, content will be the ultimate marketing machine and will eventually separate "technoboring" from "human-touch" sites. Content is what will bring the emotional component that fuels a brand.

This realization is, of course, why AOL has merged with Time Warner. AOL woke up to the fact that its future lies not in the technology behind the Internet revolution, but in content. This is also the reason behind the Ralph Lauren/NBC joint multimedia venture. The resulting lifestyle destination Polo.com site, which will sell its products through video clips, shows, fascinating links to travel and other kinds of information, marks the beginning of the merging of content and commerce. At his site Ralph Lauren will bring to life in unimaginable ways the power of his brand; the dream he has created and the possibility of owning it. When most sites are still only about products and pipelining more goods, Ralph Lauren is once again giving everyone a lesson in the way to brand in cyberspace . . . by letting people be a part of the dream!

By merging the content of shows with shopping, Lauren not only provides the viewer with passive entertainment, but also gives him a chance to interact through purchasing product in the story. I am imagining myself going to Africa on a safari trip organized through the Polo.com site and experiencing firsthand the lifestyle expressed in Mr. Lauren's ads, or watching a sitcom called *Romance* (after the Ralph Lauren perfume) where I could order the sexy jacket the actor is wearing–and maybe his car. Why not even be an assistant producer for the show, jump into the action on my screen, and influence the script, direct the actors, and perhaps even have a cameo role, too!

For NBC this is a new paradigm switch, changing the captive audience they are attracting into a whole new kind of shopper with a simple little click! With the Internet, we are going to see the merging of print, audio, television, film, and stereo into the same medium. With mushrooming bandwidth and technologies such as teleimmersion–the future of virtual reality which will give incredible 3-D visual dimension to anything we choose to view–empowerment will be more than just giving people more control in their choices. They will become actors, designers of sets, content contributors, and creators of movies . . . In short: cultural influencers and opinion leaders. And why not? Our culture of silos, where "professionals only" operate, will become one where people are masters of their own lives.

So while, in my opinion, entertainment and knowledge are very important in the Web arena, content will be the ultimate key. Robert Redford, a very powerful "brand star" in his own right, was quoted on the Yahoo! Web site saying, "The future is going to be with content, not technology. The young directors I meet today are incredibly smart. The ones I started with did not know much about filmmaking when they started . . . but they knew about life." This means that it is crucial to add to the offerings the pleasures of easy navigation, imaginative promotions, chat rooms, a plethora of useful and interesting information, videos and games . . . all in a well-designed, "emotionally charged" environment. This is what will enhance the experience of the user and build preference.

17

d/g*'s Recipes for Emotional Branding Strategies

The Emotional Economy needs new yardsticks for discovering the real, emotional meaning of brands . . . and what is more interesting for this purpose than a sensory and visually driven research tool to bring to light how people feel about brands?

My company has designed three new proprietary research tools to better connect emotionally with the market. The first one is BrandFocus, which helps line up the management of a company behind a heartfelt brand vision; the second, SENSE®, a visualization process that helps pinpoint the core attributes of a brand and build up an imagery around these attributes; and the third, Brand Presence® Management, a tool that helps determine the most powerful places, times, and ways for a brand to express itself in the market. It is essential to define how people feel about a brand in the context of what corporations think their brand is and in what ways there are connections and where the disconnections may exist. Where does the brand hit the consumer the most? Through the head, the heart, or the gut? Maybe the head, like Aveda, or the heart, like Godiva, or the gut, like Prada? By understanding the emotional relevance of a brand, corporations can build an aspirational brand vision.

TOOL #1. BrandFocus: An Interactive Tool to Clarify a Brand's Positioning

BrandFocus is an interactive consulting tool used to clarify a brand's positioning and unlock its potential to communicate beyond its current message. The centerpiece of BrandFocus is an interactive exercise involving senior management and other members of the brand team. The BrandFocus goals are the following:

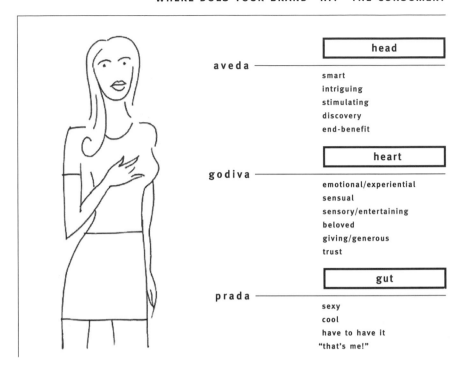

- Team alignment through interactive creativity and collaborative discovery of a strong vision.
- Visual definition of the future brand image.
- Dimensionalization of customer personality and brand emotional connection.
- Construction of key (pillar) attributes that define your brand through concise descriptive images and adjectives that craft your brand's unique DNA

The outcome of the exercise (and the synthesis phase that follows) is a focused brand positioning expression communicated visually and verbally. Implications for brand development and communication programs are outlined by integrating the results of the group's activity with cultural trends and opportunities in the market and beyond. The final presentation is multisensorial and can be used internally, to brief creative agencies and to serve as a foundation for brand image programs in the future.

The following is a description overview of the BrandFocus process divided into phases:

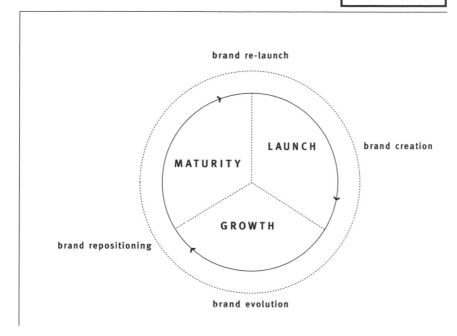

PART I. STRATEGIC FOUNDATION: INFORMATION GATHERING

d/g* worldwide initiates assignments by gathering existing information from our client's management regarding current competitors, consumers, media, and any other relevant data. We meet with our client's management to receive a formal briefing and to discuss specific concerns, considerations, and requirements for the development of a cohesive brand vision. In this phase, through our interviews with key executives and project directors and employees, we explore the internal strategy and concerns of the company as well as initiate our investigative process into the company's overall spirit and culture. The brand's life cycle will be discussed to clarify the challenges ahead of us.

After the initial research and interviewing, we execute BrandFocus sessions in order to accurately assess the range of input from all of our client's audiences. We do this either in one large session, or sometimes in several separate sessions for different corporate contingents. Once the BrandFocus sessions are complete, we analyze all of the results and develop a single, cohesive and relevant brand strategy that is effective and meaningful.

BrandFocus is set up and played as an interactive game. This format encourages a wide range of unfiltered viewpoints to flesh out hidden nuances within the brand that can be expanded upon in creative and strategic ways. Several visual categories for discussion are defined in advance. A series of images representing a range of attitudes and styles, all easily representing the brand, are compiled and placed on a board for the team to assess. Although the images selected by the group are used to craft a brand portrait, it is the words and vocabulary used to rationalize image choices that lead to brand opportunity discussions. The purpose is to find the images and cues that represent the brand's point of view beyond the product. An adjective brainstorm is conducted with the participants in order to explore a variety of meanings associated with the brand. We steer the group away from standard, prototypical brand descriptions. Each BrandFocus is unique, with images and categories chosen to gain insight into a specific brand's equity and opportunity. The first visual exercise is to define "the state of the team"; visuals are shown that immediately connote either positive or negative reactions relevant to clarifying a brand's strengths and weaknesses.

BrandFocus is set up and played as an interactive game. This format encourages a wide range of unfiltered viewpoints to flesh out hidden nuances within the brand.

Because BrandFocus is interactive, and responses are meant to be spontaneous, comments arise, like, "Picture number one is who we are today, but number three feels more like who we want to be." All of the edited selections from the image exercise are collected and placed on the master board. The moderator leads a discussion about what we see emerging. The brand's unique personality comes alive as the visuals give insight into the look, attitude, mood, spirit, and usage of the brand.

Other categories of visuals are presented with questions such as:
- If (Brand) were a ride—what would it feel like?
- If (Brand) were a wedding—what kind would it be?
- If (Brand) were a kiss—what would it look like?
- If (Brand) were a dream vacation—where would it be?

The second part of the exercise focuses on the identification of core brand attributes that will support the visual voice created through the image exercise. Adjectives mentioned during the course of the exercise are recorded. At

under attack

exuberant

sandtrapped

strong spirit

playful

leadership

the end of the image game, each participant is asked to pull the three defining words from the board that speak to the essence of the brand.

Following this session, we synthesize the selected visuals and attributes into a proprietary brand-positioning platform.

CONCLUSION

BrandFocus has proven to be a great motivator and team unifier—with the final result playing a major role in our clients' day-to-day brand development and management. BrandFocus allows teams to consider where a brand has been and where it is. Most importantly, BrandFocus defines where a brand can go. It stimulates creative thinking and motivates teams to break the traditional constructs of brand definition and brand communication.

american
classic
genuine
authentic
heritage
established
original
international
service
quality

AN EXAMPLE OF ONE OF OUR CLIENT'S ADJECTIVE SORT RESULTS

FUN	**DARING**	**THOUGHTFULNESS**	**VISIONARY**
Humor	Radical	Friendly	Curious
Wit	Alternative	Honest	Trail Blazers
Surprise	Guerrilla	Decent	Story Telling
Outrageous	Counterculture	Common Sense	Inventive
Sexy	Brave	Responsible	Alternative
Quirky	Demanding	Care	Innovative
Creativity	Challenging	Heart	Intelligence
Entertaining	Audacious	Integrity	Contemporary
Color	Break the Rules	Compassion	Ideology
Trendy	Controversial	Goodness	Instinctive
Fashionable	Anti-Establishment	Decent	Leadership
Young	Unique	Worthy	Integrity
Hip/Cool	Provocative	Concern	No Hype
Fresh		Compassion	Discovery
A Giggle		Service	Philosophy
		Positive	Solutions
			Bravery
			Values

SPIRITUAL

Mind-Body-Spirit
Holistic
Vibrancy
Energy
Vigorous
Balanced
Whole
Free
Vital
Charisma
Self-Actualization

NATURAL

Organic
Earthy
Quality
Green
From Nature
Environmental
Healthy

SELF-RESPECT

Celebration
Women
Specialness
Esteem
Realness
Beauty
Multicultural
Confidence
Well-Being
Be Yourself
Self-Expression

PARTICIPATION

Community
Solidarity
Sharing
Social
Inclusive
Education
Local
Giftability

PLEASURE

Sensuous
Fun
Love
Passion
Physical
Intimacy
Sensation
Femininity
Indulgence
Sensorial
Luxurious
Pampering

MESSAGE

Campaigning
Respect
Animal/Human
Rights
Recycling
Activism
Awareness
Outspoken
Issues
A Stand
Advocacy
Concern
Anti-Cruelty
Issues
Opposition
Ethical

TOOL #2. SENSE®: A Visual Territory Development Tool

SENSE® is a visual process that helps identify product's equities, profiles the customer, analyzes the competition, and develops a multidimensional, emotionally charged visual and sensual vocabulary that serves as the foundation for the design process. At d/g* New York, our design begins with a unique planning discipline called SENSE®. SENSE® helps our clients establish a strong emotion-based visual platform for the brand that can convey the brand's persona and character. An acronym for Sensory Exploration + Need States Evaluation, SENSE® combines the talents of observation, synthesis, and creativity with disciplined research techniques to assure that the premise for our ideas is grounded in the real-life experience of the target audience.

SENSE® begins with an analysis of a brand's inherent values–its equities–and encompasses the many ways it interacts with the consumer: intellectually, visually, associatively, and sensorially. A carefully illustrated customer profile explores the role the product plays in the consumer's lifestyle and pinpoints visual cues that establish brand preferences. An astute and trend-driven visual assessment of the competition completes the preliminary audits and brings out the strengths and weaknesses of a particular business or product category.

SENSE® begins with an analysis of a brand's inherent values—its equities—and encompasses the many ways it interacts with the consumer.

As the final synthesis, presentation boards consisting of a rich palette of imagery are brought together to achieve a dynamic brand positioning and bring to life the emotional connection of the brand with the consumer.

Once a solid image-based strategy for creativity is established, we move into full-scale creative exploration in any one or a combination of four design disciplines: graphics, industrial design, architecture, and interactive design. This unique proprietary visual methodology ensures that each creative solution is consistent, compelling, and strategically appropriate. The result is powerful, coordinated packaging, graphics, environments, and interactive design programs that generate an emotional response in the consumer and give companies a competitive edge.

SENSE® goes beyond the merely eye-catching to include the tactile, the psychological, and the experiential; all the things that generate excitement among consumers worldwide. SENSE® is a great way to build a powerful emotional brand territory!

CASE HISTORY: GODIVA, 1994

When Godiva management came to see us for an analysis of its retail branding strategy with recommendations for improving the performance of its stores, we proposed that it use our SENSE® process as a way of determining the lifestyle of its existing and potential customers. We wanted most of all to discover more about the sensory experience people have with chocolate, and we had a lot of fun doing just that! Our offices became saturated with the pervasive, delicious smell of chocolate, and one of the most difficult parts of this project was to keep everyone from eating the samples! However, we discovered that the store was not about the sensory experience that we were having in the office, and we became motivated by the desire to recreate a place where the enjoyment of chocolate was paramount.

Above: Godiva's former store design. *Below:* Godiva's new Art Nouveau look.

Baby Boomers, we know, are interested in status and rewards, and Gen X and Y are more attracted by experiences. This insight at the time revealed that the existing Godiva store, with its heavy black and gold packaging and fixtures, with all the chocolates tucked away behind cold, unfriendly glass cases, was communicating a very elitist message. This elitist message had helped establish the credibility of the brand originally, but today was too imposing for a younger customer who just wanted a little indulgence. SENSE® allowed us to visualize the trends in the new potential customer's lifestyle and access the existing visual cues and codes of the store in comparison to that customer's aspirations.

The result of our audits told us that the stores were intimidating and that shoppers came only to visit for special occasions. Most products were out of reach in cases for refrigeration purposes, but we felt that this issue could easily be handled in another way.

The first sensory boards we presented to our no-nonsense client Cathy Green, general manager of global retail for Godiva, were screaming for indulgence, sensuality, the emotional reward of sharing, and just plain old good time! Cathy, who understands better than anyone the importance of emotions in retail, suddenly realized how much her stores lacked the pleasure that one feels with a chocolate experience and that Godiva's relationship with the customer was not focused on wetting their "chocolappetite."

During a trip to Düsseldorf, Germany, a few weeks before the presentation, as I was walking down the street with one of our architects, we stumbled upon a fashion retail store that was designed in the Art Nouveau style, the same style that is so popular in Belgium, Godiva's country of origin.

The style worked beautifully in this store, and we looked at each other thinking the same thought at the same time . . . this would be the perfect style for Godiva. Those luscious curves, which are so typical of the Art Nouveau look, seemed so appropriate for this project that we promised we would come back the next day to take some pictures. We almost didn't make it back to the store—in our excitement we had forgotten to note the address of the place—and it took us a couple of hours before we passed it totally by chance. The style was very well received by our client, and we all knew that this distinctive look would enhance the brand perception. The final design of the store expressed the intimate relationship a store needs to have with consumers; an intimate understanding of their desires in the design folded into an overall framework that suggests a warm welcome, as if you were invited into someone's home. We found refrigerating wall units that limited the necessity of cases and used this opportunity to recommend some visual merchandising concepts that encouraged more browsing in the store. A station placed at the store window allowing the personnel to dip fruits into hot chocolate brought a magical ritual into full view, encouraging more customers to enter.

In dollars and cents, this new concept increased sales by 20 to 30 percent in comparison to the old stores, and we have now rolled the idea out worldwide with great success.

Understanding your customer well and catering to the taste and the aspiration of that customer is the key to building a long-lasting relationship–and for us, the opportunity to keep enjoying those wonderful chocolates.

TOOL #3. Brand Presence® Management (BPM): An Assessment Tool to Explore the Many Facets of a Brand's Personality in the Marketplace

BPM is a brand-presence assessment tool that allows an expanded exploration of the many facets of a brand's personality in all its expressions in the marketplace, from "impact" to emotional "contact." In order to reach a maximum efficiency, each brand-identity expression needs to be modular to reach people where and when they want to be reached. BPM is a tool that helps strategize what I call "proximity communication"; the way to accompany or "escort" a consumer throughout his daily activities. BPM takes into consideration and measures levels of an audience's receptivity to a brand personality in the course of their daily lives. People's receptivity to a brand is obviously not the same at 7:00 A.M., when commuting to work, as it is at a club or a bar at night, or on the weekend at a ballpark, or on vacation. It is therefore critical to match people's acceptance levels and expectations of a brand message through a multidimensional, sensitive brand dialogue. The chart on page 281 suggests the receptivity level of different venues at various points in time in consumers' daily lives.

It is by understanding these different "moments in time" and tailoring brand presence programs to interact with consumers with sensitivity and innovation at a particular moment, that memorable, emotionally relevant contact with consumers can be created. This is when a brand can become like a friend, neither shouting nor interrupting you . . . nor whispering so softly that you cannot hear what she is saying!

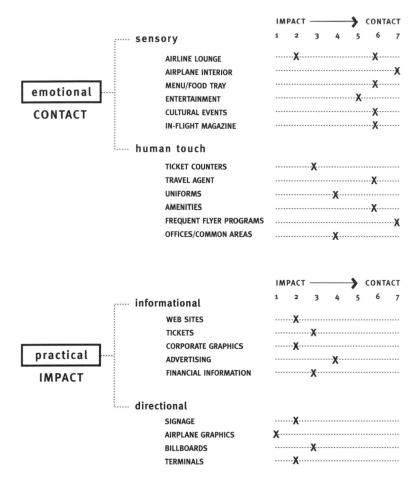

IMPACT ──────▶ CONTACT						
1	2	3	4	5	6	7

sensory

	1	2	3	4	5	6	7
AIRLINE LOUNGE		X				X	
AIRPLANE INTERIOR							X
MENU/FOOD TRAY						X	
ENTERTAINMENT					X		
CULTURAL EVENTS						X	
IN-FLIGHT MAGAZINE						X	

human touch

	1	2	3	4	5	6	7
TICKET COUNTERS			X				
TRAVEL AGENT						X	
UNIFORMS				X			
AMENITIES						X	
FREQUENT FLYER PROGRAMS							X
OFFICES/COMMON AREAS				X			

emotional CONTACT

IMPACT ──────▶ CONTACT						
1	2	3	4	5	6	7

informational

	1	2	3	4	5	6	7
WEB SITES		X					
TICKETS			X				
CORPORATE GRAPHICS		X					
ADVERTISING				X			
FINANCIAL INFORMATION			X				

directional

	1	2	3	4	5	6	7
SIGNAGE		X					
AIRPLANE GRAPHICS	X						
BILLBOARDS		X					
TERMINALS		X					

practical IMPACT

Example of the BPM strategy of an airline company.

In the case of an airline, for example, the exterior of the plane, the logo on the body and tail, need to be highly visible from afar and are an "impact"-oriented mode of brand presence, but the interior of the plane, the menu, the in-flight magazine, and the uniform of the flight attendants should bring a heightened level of emotional comfort and be more "contact"-oriented to put customers at ease, since these visual cues and sensory elements will interface with a passenger before and during the flight. It is important to evaluate the balance between the emotional contact the company will have with a customer and the visual impact a brand needs to convey. The chart above, which uses an airline as an example, helps define balance of the level of emotional contact and impact a brand needs to convey in order to create the most positive experience.

On this numbered scale you can evaluate the level of the emotional expression of the brand in different arenas. This chart helps to audit and modulate the level of emotional communication a brand delivers as well as compare that analysis to the competition. By adding the numbers you have assigned to each area, you can reach an overall indication of where your brand stands in the emotional landscape. If you fall in the lower range, around one and two, it means your brand has an "impact" brand-presence style, while ratings around six or seven are leaning toward a totally emotional and "contact" identity. Since the objective is to achieve a balance of visibility and experience, this tool can help format the emotional territory and identity of the brand.

It is important to evaluate the balance between the emotional contact the company will have with a customer and the visual impact a brand needs to convey.

CASE STUDY: COCA-COLA, 1996 ATLANTA OLYMPICS

One of our first significant brand-presence programs was created for Coca-Cola for the 1996 Atlanta Olympics. Our goal was to create a program that was modular, targeted, and engaging. This brand-presence program attempted to reach consumers through virtually every channel of communication throughout the city of Atlanta: information booths, vending machines, concessions, restaurants, and an Olympic City Theme Park that invited the fans to experience the Olympics from the viewpoint of the athletes through its fifteen-acre interactive amusement park and welcomed visitors for entertainment between the games. The Olympic City logo we designed was the cohesive element for all of these communications. We wanted to expand Coca-Cola's visual vocabulary into entertainment without losing the core character of the brand.

The strategy was to make fans and visitors the heroes of the games instead of focusing solely on the athletes by leveraging the concept of "Refreshment" inherent to Coca-Cola's core identity. This "Refreshment" concept was expanded to include refreshment of the mind, body, and spirit, which was translated into:

- Refreshment of the body: Consumption
- Refreshment of the mind: Information
- Refreshment of the spirit: Entertainment

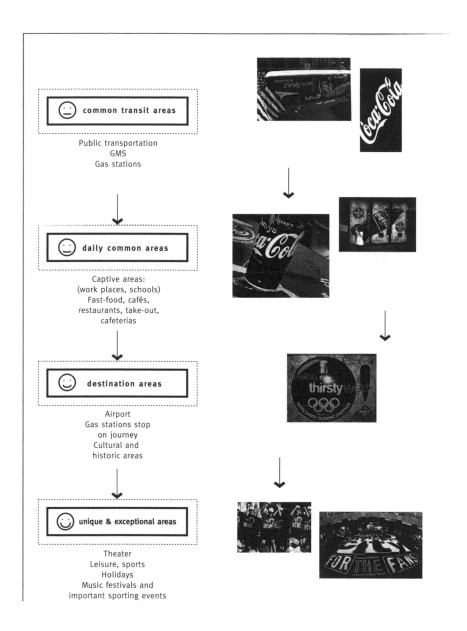

😐 **common transit areas**	
Public transportation GMS Gas stations	
🙂 **daily common areas**	
Captive areas: (work places, schools) Fast-food, cafés, restaurants, take-out, cafeterias	
😊 **destination areas**	
Airport Gas stations stop on journey Cultural and historic areas	
😄 **unique & exceptional areas**	
Theater Leisure, sports Holidays Music festivals and important sporting events	

Expressing brand presence to connect with people at different points of contact. A presence strategy for the 1996 Olympics in Atlanta.

Based on this multifaceted concept of "Refreshment," different messages were created to reach the Olympic visitors at different points in their experience in Atlanta. At the airport, visitors were welcomed by the billboard sign, "Traveling is thirsty work," and at the games and on the streets of the city, on buses and vending machines were brand-presence messages saying "Cheering is thirsty work," to communicate Coca-Cola's passion for the games shared with the public. The paper cup with writing in different languages was part of the experience at the games and a welcoming gesture to all the international visitors by Coca-Cola as a global brand.

BPM helped us develop this complex presence program–which could have been a very homogenous, "Let's throw the logo in everywhere," strategy–as an engaging and emotionally responsive program with the goal of enhancing the positive experience fans would have at the games–thanks to Coca-Cola.

BPM is one of the foundations of an Emotional Branding strategy and can also be used as a creative auditing tool that explores the many opportunities a brand has to engage an audience in the most meaningful way.

18

Key Trends for the New Millennium

The most important commodity and the biggest luxury of all today is time. Americans are time-impoverished. In a study by Kurt Salmon Associates, a New York retail consulting firm, 60 percent of those queried said they had less time for leisure, and 44 percent confessed that given the choice they'd rather have more free time than more money.[1]

Time Is (Even Better than) Money

We live in an era of more and more material wealth and less and less time. Americans have now surpassed the Japanese as the nation clocking in the most hours in a workweek. This change that has been gathering momentum for a while now is a fundamental shift in the fabric of our culture, and there are no references from the past to give perspective. While past generations may have been busy, there is obviously no comparison with our hyperdigitalized world today, where not only are we ourselves so busy but everything around us is moving at an incredibly fast pace. In this Information Age we are constantly barraged with data and pressured to make important decisions and choices in a split second. What this means on the whole is that people are now keenly aware of the need to relax as well as the need to kick up their heels and really enjoy the free time they do have.

Instead of acquiring more material goods, people want to spend money to create quality time for themselves.

In this atmosphere, services are winning over products. Instead of acquiring more material goods, people want to spend money to create quality time for themselves and spend it with friends and family. Two polls, one conducted by Britt Beemer, founder of America's Research Group, and one conducted by the

National Retail Federation and Deloitte & Touche, found that Americans are largely redirecting their gift spending to presents that enhance family life and personal well-being, such as vacations, massages, and golf lessons, at the expense of "gifts that come in a box."[2] Any brand that can either save consumers time or enhance the quality of an experience of time spent will do well in the future. On the one hand, people will be spending more and more on time savers, such as financial advisors, personal trainers, housecleaners, dog-walkers, and party planners. On the other hand, hotels, spas, casinos, restaurants, theaters, and other leisure-related businesses will do very well. Of course the Internet will be hugely popular as a time-saving device as well as for its entertainment value.

Baby Boomers are a big part of this trend. They are now at the stage in their lives where they have acquired most of the goods that they need and they are looking for quality-of-life solutions and services. Nearing fifty, they are ready to enjoy more of the income they have worked so hard for through the years to spend on leisure and recreational activities. As the number of Americans aged forty-five to fifty-four rises by 34 percent through 2005, we will see an enormous boom in services spending. But this trend is certainly not specific to the Baby Boomer generation. In our era of hypertime stress, people of all ages are looking for relaxation, entertainment, education, and adventure.

We see this trend in the enormous boom of products and services related to anything that helps people to unwind and check out from their hectic pace for a while. The average hotel today often has a full-service spa, as opposed to just a health club. Resorts abound, such as Canyon Ranch that offers, in addition to all of the usual spa amenities, treatments and workshops that emphasize the mind/body connection. Urban spas such as Bliss (just purchased by LVMH and on the expansion trail), which offer the quick escape from the stresses of city life that have always been available to the wealthy, are now proliferating on a mass scale. And, of course, this is also what is behind the explosion in the home spa–treatment category with aromatherapy, bath, massage, and facial products.

This trend is also the reason for the flourishing travel business, theme parks, and restaurants, luxury cruises designed to be multigenerational (so that busy families who rarely find that quality time together can reconnect), and mega–mall/entertainment complexes. For many product and service categories it will not be difficult to fulfill the needs that the time deprivation trend is creating. For other, more traditional categories, the answer will be in their ability to innovate. Innovation in consumer products and appliances, for example, will be key for growth in these categories since people are focusing their spending on services. The Sonys of the world must create new products that either save us time or wow us so much with their entertainment, aesthetic, or novelty value that we cannot resist purchasing them, despite the fact that they may not be necessary in our lives crowded with goods.

Retailers will also need to innovate, to better show their appreciation for the time customers spend in their stores in some very practical ways. Megastores are a great example. On a weekend, shopping with family or friends in these enormous stores can be a fun experience, but these stores are often extremely difficult to navigate if you are in a hurry and need to find specific items quickly. How many of these stores are already losing this kind of "quick buy" business to Internet companies like Kozmo.com? This problem could also be solved with computerized guides strategically placed throughout the store, equipped with product search capabilities, detailed store maps, price scanners, and more in-depth question/answer software. Any larger store, including more upscale clothing retailers, could use this kind of technology in addition to (but never ever replacing) helpful store employees. Department stores should also consider developing technology that would allow consumers to take a handheld store navigator along with them throughout the store. The device could be interactive, answering specific questions, and so on. These large stores have no idea how many customers are leaving the store in frustration after not being able to find the item (or sometimes even the department!) they came in search of. And who knows how many consumers dare not even enter a dauntingly large mega- or department store when they are pressed for time. I also can't begin to count the times I have abandoned an item I had every intention of purchasing at the sight of a long cashier line. One large grocery store that I know of in Connecticut has implemented a self-service check-out line with a scanner and credit card swipe machine to solve this problem. Another angle on the time-stress phenomenon is to lull shoppers into a more relaxed state, through either entertainment or an added-value experience, such as offering free in-store foot massages! There are many, many other approaches to the time dilemma for retailers to explore.

In the food sector, we see innovations based on saving time for consumers who don't even want to take the time to boil water, such as Lipton's Cold Brew, an iced-tea bag developed to infuse in cold tap water in just five minutes. Kraft Foods is marketing Handi-Snacks for adults, which include various elements of a snack-type meal in one ready-to-go package. Campbell Soup now has

Soup to Go lunch packs that combine microwavable soups with other ready-made elements of a meal. To accommodate our on-the-run lifestyle, we now see even chips and dip packaged together. Kelloggs has a new line of Eggo Toaster Muffins that are portable, with no messy syrup. Chef America's Hot Pocket frozen sandwiches are advertised as "Real food for a busy life."

While time-saving devices and solutions are certainly a viable approach for brands to take, the opposite approach of coaxing consumers to indulge in spending time with the brand will also continue to work. One of the reasons that Martha Stewart is so popular is that she evokes an old-fashioned sensibility of taking the time to nurture things. She gives simple quick solutions and approaches to beautifying one's environment, which are essentially modern because they do recognize the need for economy of time. But overall, Martha Stewart can be seen as almost a sort of rebellion from our rushed, prefab way of life that has us ordering Christmas trees sight unseen from the Internet. Martha Stewart shows us how we can also luxuriate in taking the time to put our own individual touches on creating a personal, intimate home environment.

On the Internet, of course, many sites must be designed for speed of access to information and quick, easy purchases, but other sites succeed so well in capturing our attention and imagination that, invariably, we spend far longer than we'd planed surfing the site (probably when we should have been doing something else!) and walk away with a great brand impression or purchase. I am thinking of inventive, entertaining rich-media sites, such as the Altoids' "Too

Hot" Web site (*www.toohot.com*). I believe that brands that appeal to the senses in a creative way and envelope the consumer in a rich story will always be able to successfully convince people that the pleasure of the brand experience is worth their valuable time, no matter how squeezed that time may be!

Whether a brand positioning is about saving time or convincing consumers to spend time with the brand, it is most important to be constantly aware of just how precious that time is for consumers. From an Emotional Branding standpoint, this means accentuating the positive. Because people are experiencing so much stress in their daily lives, it is much less effective to emphasize the difficulties at hand. Much better to talk about the lack of time through humor and demonstrate that your brand has a wonderful solution. Or take people entirely away from their stresses with soothing brand imagery.

The Zenification of America: The Search for Meaning Is On!

In 1989, when the Dalai Lama spoke in New York City's Central Park, he addressed a crowd of about five thousand Americans. In 1999, when the Dalai Lama returned to speak in Central Park, he was greeted by a gathering numbering close to forty thousand.[3] According to recent statistics, seven out of ten Americans say they are religious and consider spirituality to be an important part of their lives.[4] Seventy-one percent of Americans say they "never doubt the existence of God" (up from 11 percent in 1987), 72 percent of Americans believe in heavenly beings, while 79 percent believe in miracles.[5] Sixty-nine percent of Americans now say that they are more interested in spiritual matters than they were five years ago, and there is an 80 percent increase in people participating in non-church spiritual groups.[6] There are now five thousand New Age bookstores in the United States.[7] Spiritual retreats have become a commonplace vacation alternative, and "spiritual travel," travel that involves seeking some form of enlightenment in faraway places such as Asia, is one of the fastest-growing segments of the travel and tourism industry, according to the World Travel and Tourism Council.[8] Richard Gere, an American icon, speaks often in the press about his practice of Buddhism and friendship with the Dalai Lama. From the media, we know that Madonna and Roseanne, among a long list of other celebrities, are studying the Kabala.[9] Actually, it is extremely rare that we do not hear about a celebrity's spiritual journey.

People are no longer embarrassed to speak about their spiritual affinities and private soul searching; it is now in vogue. It is so in vogue, in fact, that it is almost passé. America has mainstreamed spirituality. Just turn on the TV any evening. You will have a choice of watching *Angel, Charmed, The Others, Sabrina the Teenage Witch, Roswell, Touched by an Angel, Buffy the Vampire Slayer, The X-Files*, or if it is daytime, the tone and subject matter of Oprah along with her daily special segment, "Remembering your Spirit," as well as her spirituality-infused magazine, *O*, will certainly attest to this trend!

The trend is one of openness and exploration. While traditional church-based religion has also seen a resurgence in membership, personal spirituality has largely surpassed formalized, practical religion. It seems that people are seeking direct experience as opposed to dogma and the freedom to take meaning where they find it, from a mixture of traditions. Buddhism has become one of the most popular spiritual traditions in this mixture. In the past few years, the number of English-language Buddhist teaching centers has jumped from 429 to 1,062.[10] Baby Boomers first embraced Buddhism as a way of protesting war and expanding the limitations of the "American as apple pie" culture of their youth. Gens X and Y are now showing a decided predilection for Eastern mysticism. These younger generations have been one of the driving forces to bring Buddhism back to the forefront, giving birth to the popular phrase "Tibet Chic," with hip endorsements like the Buddhist-influenced music of the band the Beastie Boys.

People are no longer embarrassed to speak about their spiritual affinities and private soul searching.

This trend has much to do with the time-deprivation trend as it relates to stress and a fast pace of life. Eighty percent of all Americans are seeking to simplify their lives, and 78 percent want to reduce stress. Three million Americans are actively seeking tranquility (and improved health) by practicing yoga and Eastern martial arts such as tai chi.

Overstressed people everywhere today are clearly looking to soothe their senses and regain their balance. "Consciousness is not a state of doing, but a state of being," says Veronique Vienne, the author of *The Art of Doing Nothing*,[11] a wonderful book about finding beauty and peace in our everyday lives. People love this book because it recognizes our inherent need to get in touch with our deeper selves in the simplest ways; to lie on a beach and listen to the magical sound of the waves as they carve the sand around our feet, for example. Many corporations are now beginning to seriously consider the advantages of this perspective and the importance it has for their employees.

Some companies, such as Acacia Life Insurance in Maryland, are actually building "Quiet" or "Meditation" rooms or zones for employees to take a break. To help spur creativity, the Austin-based advertising firm GSD&M has built a Zen garden and labyrinth where no cell phones or computers are allowed. As Veronique Vienne says, "Some of our best thinking happens when our mind is on sabbatical." She illustrates this point by mentioning Isaac Newton who figured out the law of gravity while sitting under a tree, and Albert Einstein pondering the riddle of the universe with a cat on his lap. Companies such as Spirit Employed offer workshops, training, individual and team consultation to help corporations bring a dimension of spiritual insight into the workplace. One of our clients, a large Japanese company, regularly invites Buddhist monks to come and speak to employees about Zen principles and how they can be used to help management.

Consumers are, of course, bringing this newfound awareness of spiritual matters to bear in the marketplace. According to the Book Industry Study Group, in 1997 consumer expenditures in "inspirational" category were $268 million, up from $74 million in 1992 with a five-year annual compound growth rate of 31 percent![12] In 1998 consumers spent $27 billion on alternative medicine, according to a Harvard University study, and spending on holistic medical care such as acupuncture, chiropractors, and psychologists is up 36 percent in the past five years.[13]

In fashion imagery, Eastern mysticism abounds. The skin care, health, and beauty industries have also caught on to this trend and done extremely well incorporating the concept of products that also provide health benefits into the

idea of products that reflect spirituality. Examples are plentiful. Aveda, the plant-based, ecofriendly cosmetics company, was of course one of the very first to pioneer in this area, with chakra products. Many others have now followed suit. The Tony&Tina cosmetics brand has had immense success with their line of color therapy products designed to stimulate the body's chakra zones. Shiseido has a fragrance called "Relaxing Fragrance," designed to calm, and their lower-end company 5S is based on the "fundamental and mythical significance of 5." The brand philosophy delineates its products according to the area of one's emotional life that needs attention, such as self-worth. Sally Hansen's line of nail and body-art jewels has names such as Mystic, Meditate, Harmony, and so on.

Other manufacturers and retailers would be wise, I think, to pay attention to this particular trend in their approach to product and retail design as well as advertising. Brands as identity reflectors need to somehow recognize the need people have for deeper spiritual meaning in their lives. From an Emotional Branding standpoint, this means approaching this need with respect, as an open-ended dialogue. Whether a brand approaches this trend in an overt or a more subtle manner, it is important to exercise caution, not to offend people's sensibilities in this touchy area. This means that brands should not take themselves too seriously. The real objective is to simply show consumers that you are aware and responsive to the growing importance of this dimension of their lives. It is about recognizing who your consumers are and that their personal aspirations extend far beyond the world of commercialism.

People are most definitely looking for brands with more promise than simply "no more ring around the collar!"

Nostalgia: A Convergence of Eras

Retro-chic, cheesy, futuristic, sentimental, individualistic, kitsch, glam, geek . . . Nostalgia/retro trends are all around us today. The VW beetle, the round headlights in the latest Mercedes, the retro look of the new Jaguar, the success of Nick at Nite and TV Land, the fifties-style of the Old Navy stores, the revival of Johnny Rockets hamburger restaurants, Walt Disney's Celebration, Florida–a real forties-style community–Hollywood's espousal of retro-chic glamour (witness Winona Ryder in a vintage gown twice as old as herself at the year 2000 Oscars), and a veritable daily deluge of images and songs from the fifties, sixties, and seventies in advertising (such as Gap's "swing" and *West Side Story* ads) . . . these are just a few of many examples! The nostalgia/retro trend has definitely taken off and doesn't seem to be slowing down anytime soon. As we move

This trend is partly about our need to be reassured and grounded as we move forward into a super fast-paced and seemingly uncertain future.

into a new millennium, people are digging into the past for nuggets of what was good to take along with them into the next century, often personalizing and blending these cultural cues into a modern or even futuristic sensibility. This trend is partly about soothing anxiety; a need to be reassured and grounded as we move forward into a super fast-paced and seemingly uncertain future. It is also equally about a sense of excitement and empowerment; being at a vantage point in time when we are able to choose from the best of all eras. It is part of a global attitude of being able to have it all; having the freedom to cherry pick and personalize things from all times, which means there's so much more cool stuff available!

This is an important but difficult trend to utilize in branding programs. The nostalgia/retro trend so evident in our pop culture is complex because Baby Boomers and younger Gen X and Y generations are all buying into it, but each for different reasons. In other words: a mix of current generations are pulling elements that resonate emotionally for them from a mix of previous generations (forties, fifties, sixties, seventies, and now even the eighties)! Baby Boomers are increasingly becoming nostalgic for cultural elements of the fifties and sixties, the decades of their youth, as they move into their fifties, and Gen X and Y are entranced by a mixture of past eras they did not get to experience firsthand, often flavoring their retro tastes with a dash of ironic irreverence.

Nostalgia began to take hold as a new phenomenon in the seventies, as a reaction to the tumultuous sixties when the fallout from modern society was beginning to be very apparent in the form of the Vietnam War, warnings of pollution, rising statistics of violence, Watergate, great confusion in terms of gender roles, and the dissolution of the classic family structure (rising divorce rates). People were looking for the comfort of the simpler, more carefree times portrayed in the then hit shows *Happy Days* and *Grease.*

By the time we reached the safe distance of the eighties era, Baby Boomers, fully morphed from hippies into yuppies, began to feel nostalgic for the sixties, and the music, images, and fashions of the sixties became rampant in pop culture and in branding programs.

For the past decade Gen X and Y have added their twist to the nostalgia/retro trend. A big part of their approach to the past is to use elements from different eras to accentuate their individualism as a reaction against a cookie-cutter culture of look-alike stores and products.

They are looking to rediscover elements of an America they never knew. John Flanagan of Thermostat, a Connecticut-based marketing research firm that specializes in Generation X, says, "They are attracted to authenticity, to ties with the past, to the real deal. In a nutshell, that's why retro works."[14] As Gen Xers get older, watch for more nostalgia surrounding the eighties. Most of all, with the younger generations, it is a message of hope that they are looking for as they sift through the past.

In my opinion, the best branding programs using retro/nostalgia borrow from the past, but infuse that past in an innovative manner with the present. This means a fresh, eclectic look at recycling the past.

The highly popular original Kellogs' "Mikey likes it" Life cereal commercial ran from 1972 to 1984 and featured two little boys who give their younger brother a bowl of Life cereal, sure that he won't like it because "he hates everything."[15] The remake, launched in early 2000, shows three young adults, two men and one woman, at the breakfast table together and follows the original script word for word. The fact that the commercial follows the dialogue of the original commercial exactly with a drastic change of characters says it all. Nothing and everything has changed for Mikey!

The American icon Maxwell House has resurrected its old tag line "Good to the last drop," and applied it to themes that are about getting the best out of one's life on a day-to-day basis, in tune with the current sensibility of spiritualism.

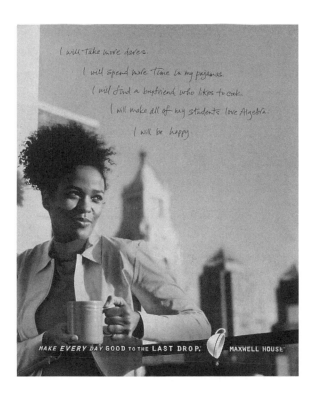

Converse's seventies-style ad that introduced the Dr. J model to younger consumers combined Peter Max–style psychedelic artwork and Stevie Wonder's song "Higher Ground" (a hit in the seventies that was also remade by the Red Hot Chili Peppers in the late eighties, making it more relevant to the demographic) with footage of the NBA star. This was an excellent use of eclectic retro/nostalgic themes from several different decades for Gen Y.

Bacardi rum's Web site (*www.bacardi.com*) has a retro look that emphasizes its Cuban heritage of 137 years with black-and-white streaming videos of sexy, glamorous, palm-treed Havana in its heyday and a gallery collection of their stylish advertisements from the inception of the brand.

Ford's new Thunderbird, which harkens back to the 1957 T-Bird, will hit the market in late 2000, this time with a 290-horsepower engine.

Altoids funky, unmistakable retro-cool ad campaign with campy black-and-white fifties-style photos consistently framed by a background of the Altoids signature mint green is arresting, fun, and gives added dimension to the brand with a "curiously strong" personality!

In 1994 Coca-Cola's sales grew by double digits in some markets when it introduced a plastic version of its contour bottle, in the popular big-gulp sizes of our times.[16]

But many brands that could refresh their current images by calling on their past, for some reason are not doing so. Betty Crocker and Dove spring to mind immediately as examples of brands that could better leverage their identities for their retro/nostalgia potential. Betty Crocker redesigns the ideal image of the "Betty Crocker woman" every decade or so to convey a more current look, as well as updating the overall visuals of its packaging. However, Betty Crocker seems to me to be trying too hard to modernize its image without taking into account the latent possibilities in the brand for a new/old feel, which would be truly modern. Dove soap also has, through the years, taken great pains to prove to us that there are continuing generations of "Dove women," but why not trade more on its heritage with a retro-glamorous touch?

On the whole, I would say that the fragrance-and-beauty industry is also largely overlooking the leveraging of its knowledge of emotions to create products around concepts that are at once futuristic and bring back recipes of the past. Clinique's fragrance "Happy," which evokes the fifties, is a new product example in this category that works.

Almost any brand that has a branded relationship with consumers that spans more than a decade or so, or has an interesting story to tell from a historical

perspective, can take advantage of this trend to revitalize the brand, because in our time-compressed age, retro is fast becoming "only a short while ago."

Both new and old identities should think of ways to serve this emotional longing that consumers have to experience our past alongside our present.

Cause Marketing: Stand for Something Bigger!

The trend of cause marketing has hit and hit big. The list of companies that are smartly supporting causes that accurately reflect their consumer's concerns is long: The Body Shop, Reebok, Avon, Wal-Mart, Ben & Jerry, Target, Kmart, Starbucks, Liz Claiborne, Timberland, Levi's, IKEA, and Sears, just to name a few! A 1999 Cone/Roper national survey of consumer attitudes toward cause marketing confirms that these efforts pay off: 83 percent of Americans have a more positive image of companies that support a cause they care about, nearly two-thirds say that when price and quality are equal, they would likely switch brands or retailers to those involved with a cause, and 68 percent say they would happily pay more for a product associated with a good cause. In addition, the survey found that nine in ten workers at companies with cause programs said they are proud of their company's values, versus just 56 percent at firms not committed to a cause.[17] Jed Pearsall, a marketing consultant, sums it all up quite well in an article in the *Wall Street Journal* by saying, "People are telling us they're tired of having advertising in their face. They want it to do something for them. Marketing will become a field that solves people's problems."[18] This is perfectly in sync with

Get to know who your consumers really are, what really matters to them, and show them that you feel the same way. the premise of Emotional Branding; it has everything to do with getting to know who your consumers really are, what really matters to them, and showing them that you feel the same way. The effectiveness of these programs can no longer be questioned; done the right way, they can bolster a brand's equity and provide an open conduit forum through which the consumer/brand relationship will deepen. But what exactly is the "right way" to approach cause marketing?

Here are a few of the very best examples of cause marketing programs that work: (Many of these companies do much more in many other areas in addition to the particular effort I am choosing to mention here)

LIZ CLAIBORNE
Since 1991 Liz Claiborne has sponsored the Liz Claiborne Foundation, an endowed program supervising donations to causes of concern to women and their families, such as domestic violence and relationship abuse.

This award-winning program, which is comprised of billboards, TV announcements, posters, brochures, workshops, and partnerships with local retailers is very compatible with the Liz Claiborne image of a brand that caters to real, everyday women.

WAL-MART
Wal-Mart's funding for major programs aiding children, education, family issues, and local communities resulted in it being named in 1999 by consumers as the nation's most socially responsible company in America.

The fact that these programs are designed for local communities and almost all of them are managed locally by the stores in those communities, means that Wal-Mart is able to integrate into and actually become a tangible part of the communities it serves.

REEBOK
Since 1988 Reebok has sponsored an annual human-rights awards program, which honors young human-rights activists worldwide who protest, often at risk to themselves, acts of cruelty and violence. This program has recognized fifty-six people under the age of thirty with $50,000 grants to the cause of their choice, along with a network of support through other activists and agencies that can help further their causes.

On Reebok's Web site, CEO Paul Fireman claims that the statement of an inner-city child he met at a summer camp–"If you don't stand for something, you'll fall for anything"–expresses perfectly the ideology of the company. Reebok certainly backs this claim through its support of a plethora of cause marketing that centers on human rights and quality of life issues for the very people to whom it is marketing its products.

AVON

Since 1993 Avon has been very active in fighting breast cancer through the Avon Breast Cancer Crusade, which raises funds for support services for breast cancer patients, educational seminars, and medical research. Funds are raised both through the sale of Avon Pink Ribbon products and through a series of fund-raising walks. The Avon Breast Cancer Crusade is one of thirty Avon-sponsored programs.

The programs Avon funds for women's health are perfectly synonymous with the company's brand positioning as: "the company for women." The fact that these programs work on a grassroots level, involving the Avon consumers themselves on a direct, participatory level, is consistent with the Avon heritage as a door-to-door, word-of-mouth brand that creates a community of women.

HOME DEPOT

Home Depot funds a wide range of employee volunteer community-service programs that mostly focus on housing, such as partnerships with Habitat for Humanity to build affordable housing, and Christmas in April to rehabilitate housing for the elderly and disabled, as well as disaster relief programs to help people rebuild their homes after a natural disaster strikes.

This is, of course, a perfect angle for Home Depot in the cause marketing arena. It is doing what it does best for others, and an added benefit is that the construction done is a great advertisement for Home Depot, and its employees further familiarize themselves with the company's products while volunteering.

SEARS

Sears has been working in partnership with the Dress for Success organization that helps low-income women looking for work to acquire professional clothing. In 1999, in addition to contributing $10,000 to Dress for Success, Sears chose twelve women from the program to work with fashion editors recruited by Sears in picking out two free outfits each from the Sears stores.

This program is very well tailored to Sears because it serves to reinforce Sears's image as a friendly American place to shop, while bolstering, through the addition of the fashion editors, the idea of Sears as being a store that carries contemporary, hip fashions for younger women.

STARBUCKS

The Starbucks Foundation focuses on literacy initiatives; giving monetary support, building celebrity-driven community programs, and organizing grants to nationwide and local community literacy programs.

Starbucks, in partnership with the organization Care, also supports efforts to provide assistance to coffee-growing countries of the world.

Both of these programs are terrific for Starbucks. The programs in support of literacy conjure the longtime connection between drinking coffee and reading; cafés as literary outposts. The effort to give something back to the often third-world countries where their product is harvested shows a recognition of the need for respect for human conditions at the product's source and a perspective of global diversity.

The best cause-marketing programs integrate a social cause or issue into the brand's very persona. From the point of view of building a strong emotional brand strategy, it would be an interesting test to see if we could determine the name of the brand if we were given only the description of the causes supported. In many of the examples cited above the answer is yes. However, in some cases, it seems that the honorable and very well-intentioned efforts of a company are not serving to also reinforce the brand equity.

The cause marketing in effect for Lee Jeans, for example, seems scattered. While it is certainly very laudable that Lee maintains an employee committee to review requests and determine contributions, there seems to be no cohesive brand strategy behind the programs it supports, ranging from causes aimed at helping children, the elderly, and health causes. In other cases the causes supported are too singular and are not folded into a larger mix of programs that would give an overall concise sense to consumers about the brand statement, enabling them to associate it with a particular cause.

As with any other marketing endeavor, it never hurts to take an innovative, unusual approach to cause marketing. This can also serve to make addressing serious, often intimidating or overwhelming issues more inviting for consumers.

A couple of examples of cause branding with a creative flair are:

THE BODY SHOP

The longtime activist company (and true trailblazer in the cause marketing arena!) has through the years found many inventive and powerful ways to not only support causes that are important to its consumers, but also to take the initiative itself in sensitizing the community to and involving it in human rights and environmental and political issues it feels strongly about. The Body Shop's "Make Your Mark" campaign is a great example.

This campaign collected thumbprints of people around the world at sponsored store and public events which were used to created artistic portraits of human-rights victims and activists and serve as a petition for the causes connected to these people. In 1998 it collected approximately three million thumbprints!

JOE BOXER

Joe Boxer sponsored a GM Chevy Ventura cab custom designed by Nick Graham, CEO of Joe Boxer. The cab, which sported the Joe Boxer logo and was loaded with lots of fun, wacky detailing, cruised the streets of New York for one year. All of the proceeds went to a breast cancer awareness program called Concept: Cure.

Also from Joe Boxer: A Think-Pink in-store campaign to boost breast cancer awareness with a collection of "Think Pink" bras, panties, T-shirts, and so on.

An important result of this trend is that in supporting causes important to consumers, these companies are raising the bar for the expectations of social responsibility on the part of corporations. This means that corporations that are caught in the act of negligence or disregard in terms of social or environmental issues are largely being taken to task by consumers. In this age of consumer empowerment, it would be wise to pay heed to this as a real possibility. Faith Popcorn has identified a trend on her Web site called "Vigilante Consumer" that is all about consumers taking matters into their own hands with protests and boycotts when brands disappoint them. Using Nike and Kathie Lee Gifford as examples, she talks about how consumers really do care about the truth of what's behind the brand. The Internet makes consumer outrage all the more powerful, and Internet activism is on the rise.

Web sites such as ShopForChange.com attempt to carry environmentally and socially responsible products, donate 5 percent of every purchase to progressive nonprofit groups like Rainforest Action Network and Human Rights Watch, and inform you by e-mail of political updates and progressive events. After episodes of picketing, protests, and pressure from environmental groups for marketing products made of wood from endangered forests,[19] Home Depot announced in August 1999 that it would begin giving preference to vendors that provide wood harvested responsibly. Home Depot has also recently made its first commercial touting an environmental theme, staring two giant pandas and showing the volunteer efforts of Home Depot employees to build a habitat for the animals in their new home at the Atlanta Zoo. Apparently, Home Depot is now wisely attempting to expand its effort at being a socially responsible corporation beyond its work in the housing causes to include the environmental concerns of its consumers. Given the fact that in a poll conducted by Environmental Research Associates in 1999, 87 percent of adults say that they are "concerned" about the condition of the environment in the United States and 44 percent say they are "very concerned," almost 50 percent of consumers look for environmental labeling on products, *and* the upcoming Gen Y group is highly sensitized to environmental issues;[20] they are wise to do so!

Mass Customization: Be Something for Someone, not Everything to Everyone

In reality, mass customization, the widespread use of computers and manufacturing techniques to make customized products available at little cost to everyone, is much more than just a trend. It is, in fact, the way we will be doing business in the future! Already in 1995 Bill Gates was indicating the future when he said: "Once you know exactly what you want, you'll be able to get it just that way. Computers will enable the kinds of goods that are mass-produced to be custom-made for particular customers."[21]

Dell Computers was at the forefront of this movement, proving to the rest of us that complex manufactured products could be made to order. At Dell, consumers can order the exact computer they want from a staggering sixteen million possibilities over the phone or by Internet. Dell only assembles computers that have already been ordered, building its computers from modular components that are always readily available using a sophisticated logistics software that takes the information gathered from customers and steers it to the parts of the Dell organization that need it, and then shipping them directly to the consumer's home or business. This means that there is little to no waste in the manufacturing process.

In the past year mass customization has taken off like wildfire and will only continue and become more and more refined in the future. Today we already see a great number of excellent examples of mass customization working well in the marketplace. At little extra cost, we can buy a pair of Levi's to custom fit our body's measurements (Levi's Original Spin jeans), pills or vitamins with the precise combination of ingredients we want, CD compilations of the exact music tracks we choose, cosmetics mixed to match our skin tone and type with a name and packaging we have designed ourselves (Reflect.com for mass, and Lab21.com for high-end), international news edited and compiled to suit our specific interests (NewsEdge.com), textbooks whose chapters are expressly chosen by our professors, a loan structured within several minutes online according to our financial profile, a completely original pair of shoes from Milan (Digitoe.com) or a tailored suit made exactly to our body's measurements, the finest perfumes designed to our personal specifications (Ashford.com), a doll for our child that matches their aspirational ideal in terms of combination of skin, hair and eye color, name, and so on (Barbie.com), or a Ford Explorer custom-ordered from Ford's Web site with 2.5 million combinations available[22] . . . the list, quite simply, goes on and on and on!

There are new technological breakthroughs allowing for further refinement of mass customization of products. Lab21.com, the new upscale cosmetics Internet start-up, is a case in point. Lab21.com will use a sophisticated proprietary software program and patent-pending technology that enables a manufacturing process without heat so that products can be made fresh, to spec, in a matter of minutes. There are even recent advances in biotechnology that through the ongoing process of cracking the DNA code now allow doctors to individualize drugs.[23] Joseph Pine, author of the book, *Mass Customization*, said that, "Anything you can digitalize, you can customize," and so far he appears to be right.[24]

What is behind this huge trend, apart from the economic progress of our society along with drastic improvement in manufacturing technologies and the Internet, is the fact that people feel a certain lack of individuality in the world and they want to explore the possibility of creating a world of objects and experiences that are uniquely their own. As this trend picks up speed, it will go beyond even the individualized psychographics approach of one-to-one marketing (which is certainly a good place to start). It will eventually really and truly put the consumers in the "brand driver's seat." One potential interesting result of this trend could be that as customization goes mass, the more old-fashioned, personal-touch luxury concept may well expand into other retail venues as a point of difference. A truly human touch could become a highly coveted element of a retail experience in an environment where everything is personalized by impersonal computers! Imagine, having a real live person as a shopper's assistant in certain stores to guide you through the store, hand-pick purchases for you, set you up to be fitted by a fashion consultant for a custom designed outfit, arrange a make-over, and so on! Many people would love to receive this kind of personalized attention as a part of an indulgent shopping experience! Certainly this trend will influence much of the retail landscape. In New York City there has been a recent cropping up of a more old-fashioned formula of small independent boutiques offering custom wares, such as the 3 Custom Color Specialists lipstick specialists who blend lipsticks to match swatches of fabric, or the Filth Mart, which transforms one-of-a-kind old rock T-shirts into trendy, rhinestone-studded fashion-statement wear. This list goes on to include trendy jewelers, hat makers, shirt and suit tailors, perfumers, and so on. Without being necessarily exclusive or stuffy, these retailers are all commanding–and getting–top dollar for their unique products.

It will eventually really and truly put the consumers in the "brand driver's seat."

There are of course many, many questions about how this important business trend will affect branding. Only one thing is for certain; it most definitely will strongly influence branding strategies as we know them today. And every company, no matter what product/service consumer category, will be affected by mass customization. In a general sense we can say that the evolution of mass customization will mean that brand identities will need to be much more flexible with a much wider scope in order to encompass the varying meanings attributed to the brand by different, individual consumers. Amazon.com is many things to many people; for some it is about books, for others antiques or CDs, for some the brand experience is about functionality and speed, and for still others it is about the pleasure of browsing and researching the world of books. Only a brand that spans a wide scope of activity can provide this many niche experiences for consumers. And this niche experience is what consumers will be expecting from their brands. Brands that are too static or narrowly defined will lose out in this environment!

Conclusion

Although this book is meant to share my own branding experiences, and could be interpreted as a sure way to reach the "promised brand," it also supports the theory that branding is not for everyone. Unfortunately, branding has become such a buzzword that it has transcended its own meaning. Almost overnight, everyone and everything wanted to be a brand, a branded environment, a branded experience, or a branded institution. It now seems we can't buy, enjoy, or do anything that's not branded; countries, states, and cities and even people are presented to us as branded entities. Sometimes I am even tempted to look at my cats as branded animals! For a fun, irreverent look at just how far-gone our love affair with branding is, call up the *www.enormicom.com* Web site. I promise you a good laugh!

Captains of industry now believe that branding is the only road to success, and so public relations, corporate identity, advertising, consult-

Branding is about cultural relevance and emotional connection, not hype!

ing, promotion, financial, Web, and research firms have all become brand specialists overnight. Is everyone mad? Or is this the only savvy way to approach the world of business today? Is it only "brand smoke"? In a conversation with Nick Graham of Joe Boxer, he and I pondered the current branding mania. We discussed how the Swedish clothing store H&M, which opened in New York at the beginning of 2000, is having one of the most successful entries of any store in this country. Is H&M a brand or is it simply a popular store with low prices? And why do "brand darlings" like Nike and Tommy Hilfiger lose their branding edge? Why are brands like Guess?, Gucci, and Apple able to make turnarounds? *According to Nick Graham, effective branding is about cultural relevance and emotional connection, not hype!*

The cause for this speculative "brandmania" is that most corporations confuse awareness and emotional connection. How much a product is known does not make it relevant to a market, nor esteemed or preferred by consumers. Kmart is a well-known brand but Wall-mart has an emotional aura; Compaq is a major player in the computer industry but Apple strikes a chord with users; Folgers is a great coffee brand, but we love Starbucks!

Branding is a people to people business, not a factory to people business. A brand needs to have human qualities and emotional values—it needs to have a personality, expressing corporate culture through imagery that engages people. If you can make consumers desire a partnership with your brand, you have created an emotional connection that spells long-term success.

I hope that this book has demonstrated to you the power of this emotional connection, and given you new insight and inspiration for ways of creating, re-creating, and sustaining this connection through the Emotional Branding process. Being a truly emotionalized brand means constantly reevaluating the strengths and weaknesses of one's brand. I would like to leave you with three last thoughts that are essential to managing a successful, emotionalized brand:

- FIRST: *Brands have life cycles.* Popular brands today are not necessarily the winners of tomorrow. The future of a brand is defined by its relevance at any given time and by how well it can protect the values that made it great.
- SECOND: *Brands are elected every day* based on their emotional relevance with the public and its commitment to quality. The biggest enemy of branding is overexposure. Consumers will quickly tire of the "buzz" and begin searching for something new.
- THIRD: *Real brands are about meaning and truth.* Brands can have a credible emotional connection with customers, a connection that is sincere and felt. A good example is Hermès; people remain on waiting lists for years for its products. Hermès is a brand because the company and its products are refined and unique, supported by a vision with integrity and craftsmanship.

The biggest misconception about branding is that it does not need to evolve. Even this book is a work in progress, in the truest meaning of that phrase. We all have a perennial need to search out magic formulas, but it is actually much more interesting to look for the evolving dynamics of the market, that fascinating brand/market interplay. To get people interested in a long-term relationship, keep your ear to the ground and always be ready for any market changes. Change is good, but predicting change is better—the answer is within people's hearts.

notes

Acknowledgments

1. Bernd Schmitt and Alex Simonson, *Marketing Aesthetics: The Strategic Management of Brands, Identity and Image* (New York: The Free Press, 1997).

Introduction

1. Herbert Muschamp, "Seductive Objects with a Sly Sting," *New York Times*, 2 July 1999.
2. Thomas Perzinger Jr., "So Long, Supply and Demand," *Wall Street Journal*, 1 January 2000.
3. Sarah Larenaudie, *W Magazine*, 9 January 2000.
4. Poll of 10,830 people nationwide conducted by the Reputation Institute and Harris Interactive in August 1999. Ronald Alsop, "The Best Corporate Reputations in America," *Wall Street Journal*, 23 September 1999.
5. "Now, Coke Is No Longer 'It'," *Business Week*, 28 February 2000.
6. Daniel Goleman, *Working with Emotional Intelligence* (USA and Canada: Bantam Books 1998).
7. John Huey and Geoffrey Colvin, "The Jack and Herb Show," *Fortune*, 11 January 1999.
8. Andy Law, *How St. Luke's Became the Ad Agency to End All Ad Agencies* (London: John Wiley & Sons 1999).
9. Ronald Alsop, "The Best Corporate Reputations in America."
10. Ibid.
11. Ron Lieber, "Startups: the 'inside' stories," *Fast Company*, March 2000.
12. Geoff Cook, "Hey, I Just Work Here," *Wired*, March 2000.
13. Ibid.
14. Jason Fry, "What's in Store," *Wall Street Journal*, 1 January 2000.
15. Bernd Schmitt, *Experiential Marketing* (New York: The Free Press, 1999).
16. Fairchild Publications Furniture Conference, 1998.
17. Howard Schultz, *Pour Your Heart into It; How Starbucks Built a Company One Cup at a Time* (New York: Hyperion, 1999).
18. Alex Williams, "Super Fly," *New York Magazine*, 31 January 2000.

Chapter 1

1. Glen Thrush, "When I'm 64," *American Demographic*, January 1999.
2. "Boomers Plot Exit Strategies: A Generation Checks Out New Ways of Checking Out," *USA Today*, 15 May 1999.
3. Lev Grossman, "Generation Gap," *Time Out Magazine*, 20 January 2000.
4. Kemper Scudder cited by Robert Scally, "Gen X grows up," *Discount Store News*, 25 October 1999.
5. Elena Romero "Urban Outfitters Successfully Caters to the 'Newly Homeless'," *DNR*, 28 December 1998.
6. Jane Levere, "BBDO New York Breaks Down Why, When, Where and How Young Adults Get Information," *New York Times*, 9 December 1999.
7. Rebecca Quick, "Is Ever-So-Hip Abercrombie & Fitch Losing Its Edge With Teens?" *Wall Street Journal*, 22 February 1999.
8. "What Is the Big Help?" section of Nickelodeon's Web site: *www.nick.com*, 14 March 2000.
9. Melanie Wells, "Teens and Online Shopping Don't Click," *USA Today*, 7 September 1999.
10. David S. Murphy, "Delia's Next Big Step," *Fortune*, 15 February 1999.

Chapter 2

1. Felicia Griffin, "African-Americans Gaining Market Power," *Business Journal Serving Greater Milwaukee*, 28 January 1999.
2. Graham Stedman, "Marketing to African-Americans," *ANA/The Advertiser*, December 1997.
3. *New York Times Magazine*, 7 May 2000.
4. Graham Stedman, "Marketing to African-Americans."
5. Hilary S. King, "How Cosmetic Companies Reach Their Target Market–Women of Color," *Drug and Cosmetic Industry*, October 1998.
6. Eugene Morris, "The Difference in Black and White," *American Demographics*, January 1993.
7. Felicia Griffin, "African-Americans Gaining Market Power."
8. Graham Stedman, "Marketing to African-

Americans."
9. Ibid.
10. Geoffrey Brewer, "Spike Speaks," *Incentive*, February 1993.
11. U.S. Census Bureau online: *www.census .gov*, April 20, 2000.
12. Excellent information on this subject is available from Strategy Research Corporation, "Population & Demography," *U.S. Hispanic Market Survey* (1998).
13. Ibid.
14. "The State of the Hispanic Economy," *Hispanic Business*, April 1999.
15. Christy Haubegger, "The Legacy of Generation Ñ," *Newsweek*, 12 July 1999.
16. Strategy Research Corporation, *US Hispanic Market Survey* (1998).
17. Helene Stapinski, "Generation Latino,' *American Demographics*, July 1999.
18. "Minority Phone Users Make Different Demands," *Wall Street Journal*, 7 April 1999.
19. "Asian-Americans Fastest Growing Minority Group," *Retail Ad World*, October 1999.
20. Wei-Tai Kwok and Vicky M. Wong, "Tapping into the Asian-American market," *The DMA Insider*, Winter 2000.
21. Stuart Elliott, "Ads Speak to Asian-Americans," *New York Times*, 6 March 2000.
22. Becky Ebenkamp, "Ancient Chinese Secrets?," *Brandweek*, 8 November 1999.
23. Jonathan Boorstein, "New York Times Targets Chinese-American Market," *Direct*, August 1999.

Chapter 3
1. Karen Epper Hoffman, "Internet as Gender-Equalizer?" *Internet World*, 9 November 1998.
2. Jonathan Silver, "Never Underestimate the Buying Power of Women," *Washington Business Journal*, 15 June 1998.
3. Gerry Meyers, "Selling (a Man's World)," *American Demographics*, April 1996.
4. Beth Fuchs Brenner, "Plugging into Women," *Brandweek*, 15 March 1999.
5. Thyra Porter, "Ace Is the Place (for Women)," *HFN*, 12 July 1999.
6. Betsy Spethmann, "Speaking to the Sisterhood," *PROMO Magazine*, October 1998.
7. Gerry Meyers, "Selling (a Man's World)."
8. Micheline Maynard, "Windstar's Designing Women," *USA Today*, 19 July 1999.

9. Christopher Farrell, "Women in the Workplace: Is Parity Finally in Sight?" *Business Week*, 9 August 1999.
10. Michelle Conlin and Wendy Zellner, "The Glass Ceiling: The CEO Still Wears Wingtips," *Businessweek Online*, 22 November 1999.
11. Bureau of the Census and National Foundation for Women Business Owners.
12. Leslie Kaufman, "The Dot-Com World Opens New Opportunities for Women to Lead," *New York Times*, 9 March 2000.
13. Jennifer Shu, "SAS Institute: An Employer that Redefines 'Family-Friendly'," *www .womenconnect.com*, 9 March 2000.
14. Stephanie Armour, "Corporate Women Perform Balancing Act," *USA Today*, 9 December 1997.
15. Michael Wolff, "Waiting to Exhale," *New York Magazine*, 14 February 2000.
16. Ibid.
17. Lisa H. Guss, "Targeting Women," *Supermarket Business*, May 1999.
18. Mark Dolliver, "Balancing Act: All About Our Mothers," *Adweek*, 13 March 2000.
19. Judith Langer, "Focus on Women: 3 Decades of Qualitative Research," *Marketing News*, 14 September 1998.
20. Diane Harris, "Why Can't a Man Invest More Like a Woman?" *Investor Magazine*, February 2000.
21. "A Man's Place," *New York Times Magazine*, 16 May 1999.
22. Lisa H. Guss, "Targeting Women," *Supermarket Business*, May 1998.
23. Kathleen Sampey, "This Is Not Your Mother's P&G," *Adweek*, 13 March 2000.
24. Hershel Sarbin, "Claiming Ownership," *Folio*, 15 September 1999.
25. Rob Eder, "Twenty-somethings Get Serious," *Drug Store News*, 25 October 1999.
26. Judith Langer, "Focus on Women: 3 Decades of Qualitative Research."
27. Mary Lou Quinlan, "Women: We've Come a Long Way, Maybe," *Advertising Age*, 22 February 1999.
28. Anne Jarrell, "Models, Definitely Gray, Give Aging a Sexy New Look," *New York Times*, 28 November 1999.
29. Mary Lou Quinlan, "Women: We've Come a Long Way, Maybe."
30. Ginia Bellafante, "Feminism: It's All About Me!" *Time*, 28 June 1998.

31. "Twentysomething Women Declare Themselves Primary Purchasers," *Quirks,* May 1997.
32. Wayne Friedman, "Barbie is Working Harder," *Advertising Age,* 6 March 2000.
33. Scott M. Roy, "Marketing to WWWomen," *Digitrends,* Winter 2000.
34. Ibid.

Chapter 4

1. Karen S. Peterson, "Homosexuality No Longer Phases Most Teenagers," *USA Today, http://www.usatoday.com/usatonline/20000301/1981906s.htm,* 3 March 2000.
2. Ronald Alsop, "Are Gay People More Affluent Than Others?" *Wall Street Journal,* 30 December 1999.
3. Mark Dolliver, "Out of the Closet," *Brandweek,* 23 August 1999.
4. Richard A. Oppel Jr., "Exxon to Stop Giving Benefits to Partners of Gay Workers," *New York Times,* 7 December 1999.
5. Michael Wilke, "Ads Targeting Gays Rely on Real Results, Not Intuition," *Advertising Age,* 22 June 1998.
6. Ibid.
7. Ronald Alsop, "Cracking the Gay Market Code," *Wall Street Journal,* 29 June 1999.
8. Ronald Alsop, "Web Site Sets Gay-Themed Ads for Big, National Publications," *Wall Street Journal Interactive Edition: www.wsj.com,* 17 January 2000.
9. Grant Lukenbill, *Untold Millions: Marketing to Gay and Lesbian Consumers* (New York: Heyworth, 1998).
10. Laura Koss-Feder, *Marketing News,* 25 May 1998.
11. Ronald Alsop, "Web Site Sets Gay-Themed Ads For Big, National Publications," *Wall Street Journal Interactive.*

Introduction to Section II

1. Morris B. Holbrook and Elizabeth C. Hirschman, "The Experiential Aspects of Consumption: Consumer Fantasies, Feelings, and Fun," *Journal of Consumer Research,* Volume 9, 132–140 (September 1981).
2. Michael Tuan Pham, "Representativeness, Relevance, and the Use of Feelings in Decision Making," *Journal of Consumer Research,* Volume 25 (September 1998).

3. Morris B. Holbrook and Elizabeth C. Hirschman, "The Experiential Aspects of Consumption: Consumer Fantasies, Feelings, and Fun," 313.
4. Gerald J. Gorn, "The Effects of Music in Advertising on Choice Behavior: A Classical Conditioning Approach," *Journal of Marketing,* Volume 46, 94–101 (Winter 1982)

Chapter 5

1. Gerald J. Gorn, "The Effects of Music in Advertising on Choice Behavior: A Classical Conditioning Approach," *Journal of Marketing,* Volume 46, 94–101 (Winter 1982)
2. Jane Bainbridge, "Scenting Opportunities," *Marketing Magazine,* 19 February 1998.
3. Ibid.

Chapter 6

1. Lesa Sawahata, ed., *Color Harmony Workbook* (Massachusetts: Rockport Publishers, 1999).
2. Laura Ries and Al Ries, *The 22 Immutable Laws of Branding: How to Build a Product or Service into a World-Class Brand* (New York: Harper Collins, 1998).
3. Mr. Talley's statement was culled from: *www.pantone.com/allaboutcolor/guru2000.htm.*
4. We spoke with Pat Brillo by telephone in February 2000.
5. Lesa Sunabata, ed., *Color Harmony Workbook.*

Chapter 7

1. Robert Spector and Patrick D. McCarthy, *The Nordstrom Way,* 145 (New York: John Wiley & Sons Inc., 1995).
2. Ibid.
3. Ron Lieber, "Super Market," *Fast Company,* April 1999.
4. Ibid.
5. Paco Underhill, *Why We Buy* (New York: Simon & Schuster, 1999).
6. Paul Rozin, "The Importance of Social Factors in Understanding the Acquisition of Food Habits," *Taste, Experience & Feeding: Development and Learning,* Elizabeth D. Capaldi and Terry L. Powley, Ed. (Washington, D.C.: American Psychological Association, 1993).

Chapter 8

1. Phyllis Berman and Katherine Bruce, "Makeover at the Makeup Counter," *Forbes*, 19 April 1999.
2. Paco Underhill, *Why We Buy: The Science of Shopping* (New York: Simon & Schuster, 1999).
3. Ibid.

Chapter 9

1. Allaine Cervonka, "A Sense of Place: The Role of Odor in People's Attachment to Place," *The Aroma-Chology Review*, Volume 5, Number 1 (1996). Also see Rachel S. Herz, "The Relationship Between Odor and Emotion in Memory," *The Aroma-Chology Review*, Volume 5, Number 2 (1996).
2. Susan Fournier, "Consumers and Their Brands: Developing Relationship Theory in Consumer Research," *Journal of Consumer Research*, Volume 24 (March 1998).
3. We interviewed Gail Vance Civille by telephone in March 2000.
4. "Decorating with Fragrances," *Happi*, August 1999; *The Color Cosmetics Market*, *http://www.happi.com/special/sep991.htm*.
5. Reuters, "Aroma Sofas Come Up Roses in Latest British Home Trend," *Indian Express Newspapers*, *http://expressmedia.com/fe/daily/19990125/0255215.html*, 25 January 1999.
6. Linda Dyett, "Something in the Air," *House Beautiful*, October 1996.
7. Susan C. Knasko, "Congruent and Incongruent Odors: Their Effect on Human Approach Behavior," *Compendium of Olfactory Research* (USA: Kendall Hunt Publishing Company,1995)
8. Robert A. Baron, "Of Cookies, Coffee, and Kindness: Pleasant Odors and the Tendency to Help Strangers in a Shopping Mall," *Aroma-Chology Review*, Volume 6, Number 1 (1998).
9. Atmospherics, a company that specializes in in-store scents, implements these devices, among others.
10. "Dollars and Scents," *Success Magazine Online*, *http://www.successmagazine.com/issues/dec97/hottopps.html*, April 2000.
11. Ibid.
12. Allaine Cervonka, "A Sense of Place: The Role of Odor in People's Attachment to Place," *The Aroma-Chology Review*, Volume 5, Number 1 (1996).

Section II Conclusion

1. See *www.felissimo.com*.
2. James Fallon, "Urban Renewal," *W*, April 2000.
3. Ibid.
4. Ibid.

Chapter 10

1. Catherine McDermott, *20th Century Design* (Woodstock, New York: The Overlook Press, 2000).
2. Veronique Vienne, *The Art of Doing Nothing* (New York: Clarkson Potter, 1998). I interviewed Veronique Vienne by telephone on 23 April 2000.
3. Frank Gibney Jr. and Belinda Luscombe, "The Redesigning of America," *Time*, 20 March 2000.
4. Ibid.
5. Bob Garfield, "VW: Best of All Media," *Advertising Age*, 31 May 1999.
6. *Wallpaper*, May 2000.

Chapter 11

1. Malcom Brown and Barnaby Marshall, "Where Does David Carson Want to Go Today?" *Shift*, *www.shift.com*, April 1999.
2. We interviewed Mattew Kirschenbaum by e-mail in April 2000.
3. Mattew G. Kirschenbaum, "The Other End of Print: David Carson, Graphic Design and the Aesthetics of Media," Media in Transition Conference at MIT, 8 October 1999.
4. Ed Razek's current title at The Limited is president & chief marketing officer for Limited brands and creative services.
5. *Red Herring*, January 2000.

Chapter 12

1. Becky Ebenkamp, "Good Wal-Hunting," *Brandweek*, 20 March 2000.
2. Shelly Branch, "How Target Got Hot," *Fortune*, 24 May 1999.
3. *www.rei.com*, 12 April 2000.
4. Rosemary Feitelberg, "Conversation Spurs Commerce in Active," *Women's Wear Daily*, 10 February 2000.
5. We interviewed Barry Steiner by telephone in May 2000.

Chapter 13

1. Hillary Chura and Amanda Beeler, "Absolut Bolsters Outdoor Budget," *Advertising Age,* 17 July 2000.
2. These vehicles are owned and operated by Manhattan Rickshaw Co. (*www.manhattanrickshaw.com*).
3. Jonathan Bond and Richard Kirshenbaum, *Under the Radar: Talking to Today's Cynical Consumer,* (USA: John Wiley & Sons, 1998), 96.
4. Ibid.
5. Becky Ebenkamp, "A Briefs History," *Brandweek,* 23 November 1998.
6. T. L. Stanley, "Bringing Out the Faithful," *Brandweek,* 27 March 2000.
7. Ibid.

Chapter 14

1. Ken Banta, "Message in the Bottle," *Metropolis,* June 1999.
2. Ibid.

Chapter 15

1. Peter Leach, "The Blue Period," *Critical Mass,* Fall 1999.
2. Benetton gets only 5 percent of its 2 billion annual sales in the United States. Silvia Sansoni, "Capital Offense: Benetton Ads Act as Live Bait," *Forbes,* 19 October 1998.
3. Greg Farrell, "Mercedes Ads Tickle Buyers' Funny Bones," *USA Today,* 6 December 1999.
4. "Internet Ads: Why They Work—and Don't," *Research Business Report,* October 1999.
5. Elisabeth Dalbey, "Measuring Online Branding Impact," *Digitrends,* Winter 2000.
6. Marianne Foley, "Advertising Online: Some Questions We Should Be Asking," *Digitrends,* Winter 2000.
7. Kathryn Kranhold, "Banner Ads Are Driving Web Purchases," *Wall Street Journal,* 24 November 1999.
8. *E-Marketer online* (*www.emarketer.com*), 31 March 2000.
9. Research shows that the average recall of Internet ads has dropped between 1998 and 1999. Marianne Foley, "Advertising Online: Some Questions We Should Be Asking."
10. IBM's banner ads won 2 Gold Clios and 3 CyberLions at the Cannes Ad Festival in 1999.
11. Elisabeth Dalbey, "Measuring Online Branding Impact."
12. "PepsiCo and Yahoo! in Marketing Deal," *New York Times,* 23 March 2000.
13. Greg Farrell, "Company Transforms Your Cursor Into a Tiny Ad," *USA Today,* 2 March 1999.
14. Kathryn Kranhold, "Humor Is Used to Slow Down Web Surfers," *Wall Street Journal,* 17 August 1999.
15. Andy Marx, "Dissatisfaction with Banner Ads Is on the Rise," *Internet World,* 28 June 1999.
16. Neal Leavitt, "GM Drives Response with an Engaging Ad," *Digitrends,* Winter 2000.
17. Ibid.
18. Barbara Lippert, "Double Play: Hilfiger Exploits On and Offline Media," *Adweek,* 20 March 2000.

Chapter 16

1. Joanna Pearlstein, "The Online Beauty Business Doesn't Look So Pretty," *Red Herring,* January 2000.
2. Philip Evans and Thomas S. Wurster, *Blown to Bits: How the New Economics of Information Transforms Strategy* (Massachusetts: Harvard Business School, 1999).
3. Leslie Kaufman, "Playing Catch Up at the Online Mall," *New York Times,* 21 February 1999.
4. Joseph B. White, "The Company We'll Keep," *Wall Street Journal,* 1 January 2000.
5. Ed Razek told me this during a phone conversation.
6. I interviewed Bernard Frelat by telephone 10 May 2000.

Chapter 18

1. Lauren R. Rublin, "Too, Too Much!" *Barron's,* 9 March 1998.
2. Ibid.
3. Charlie Hess, "Women Lead Way in Profound but Quiet Revolution," *Advertising Age,* 24 January 2000.
4. Richard Cimino and Don Lattin, "Choosing My Religion," *American Demographics,* April 1999.
5. Ibid.
6. "Spirit Employed: Hire a New Employee—Your Spirit!" *PR Newswire,* 15 October 1998.
7. Becky Ebenkamp, "Celestial Season,"

Brandweek, 16 November 1998.

8. Shirley Brady, "Spiritual Journeying: Om Away from Om," *Time,* 6 July 1998.

9. David Van Biema, "Pop Goes the Kabbalah," *Time,* 24 November 1997.

10. Jeanne McDowell, "Buddhism in America," *Time,* 13 October 1997.

11. Veronique Vienne, *The Art of Doing Nothing* (New York: Clarkson Potter, 1998).

12. Richard Cimino and Don Lattin, "Choosing My Religion," *American Demographics,* April 1999.

13. Ibid.

14. Heather Chaplin, "Gen X in Search of a Drink," *American Demographics,* February 1999.

15. Stuart Elliott, "Even as an Adult, Mikey Still Likes Life," *New York Times,* 10 January 2000.

16. Keith Naughton and Bill Vlasic, "The Nostalgia Boom," *Business Week,* 23 March 1998.

17. Dick Silverman, "Every Going Concern Should Get Its Concerns Going," *DNR,* 21 July 1999.

18. Jonathan Kaufman, "Marketing in the Future Will Be Everywhere—Including Your Head," *Wall Street Journal,* 1 January 2000.

19. Brent Israelsen, "Environmental Groups Picket S.L. Home Depot," *Salt Lake Tribune,* 15 October 1998; Allan Dowd, "Green Groups, Firms in Talks on Canada Rainforests," *Reuters,* 16 March 2000.

20. Lisa E. Phillips, "Green Attitude," *American Demographics,* April 1999.

21. Bill Gates, *The Road Ahead* (New York: Viking, 1995), 188.

22. *The Right Stuff: America's Move to Mass Customization,* National Center for Policy Analysis—Idea House: Policy Report No. 225 (June 1999).

23. Ibid.

24. Joseph Pine, *Mass Customization: The New Frontier in Business Competition* (Boston: Harvard Business School Press, 1993).

index

Books from Allworth Press

Citizen Brand: 10 Commandments for Transforming Brands in a Consumer Democracy *by Marc Gobé* (hardcover, 5¾ × 8¾, 288 pages, $24.95)

Design Issues: How Graphic Design Informs Society
edited by DK Holland (paperback, 6¾ × 9⅞, 272 pages, $21.95)

Looking Closer 4: Critical Writings on Graphic Design
edited by Michael Bierut, William Drenttel, and Steven Heller
(paperback, 6¾ × 9⅞, 304 pages, 21.95)

Graphic Design Reader
by Steven Heller (paperback, 5½ × 8½, 320 pages, 19.95)

The Education of a Design Entrepreneur
edited by Steven Heller (paperback, 6¾ × 9⅞, 288 pages, $21.95)

Graphic Design History
edited by Steven Heller and Georgette Ballance (paperback, 6¾ × 9⅞, 352 pages, $21.95)

Design Literacy: Understanding Graphic Design
by Steven Heller and Karen Pomeroy (paperback, 6¾ × 9⅞, 288 pages, $19.95)

Graphic Design and Reading: Explorations of an Uneasy Relationship
edited by Gunnar Swanson (paperback, 6¾ × 9⅞, 240 pages, $19.95)

AIGA Professional Practices in Graphic Design
edited by Tad Crawford (paperback, 6¾ × 9⅞, 320 pages, $24.95)

Business and Legal Forms for Graphic Designers
by Tad Crawford and Eva Doman Bruck
(paperback, 8½ × 11, 240 pages, includes CD-ROM, $24.95)

What Money Really Means
by Thomas M. Kostigen (paperback, 6 × 9, 240 pages, $19.95)

The Advertising Law Guide: A Friendly Guide for Everyone in Advertising
by Lee Wilson (paperback, 6 × 9, 208 pages, $19.95)

The Trademark Guide: A Friendly Guide for Protecting and Profiting from Trademarks *by Lee Wilson* (paperback, 6 × 9, 192 pages, $18.95)

Turn Your Idea or Invention into Millions
by Don Kracke (paperback, 6 × 9, 224 pages, $18.95)

The Entrepreneurial Age: Awakening the Spirit of Enterprise in People, Communities, and Countries
by Larry C. Farrell (hardcover, 6¾ × 9⅞, 352 pages, $24.95)